HARVARD
BUSINESS
Press

Best wishes

Peter
Skarzynski

INNOVATION
TO THE CORE

PETER SKARZYNSKI

ROWAN GIBSON

INNOVATION

A BLUEPRINT FOR TRANSFORMING
THE WAY YOUR COMPANY INNOVATES

TO THE CORE

HARVARD BUSINESS PRESS
BOSTON, MASSACHUSETTS

Printed in the United States of America

12 11 10 09 08   5 4 3 2

Skarzynski, Peter.
  Innovation to the core : a blueprint for transforming the way your company innovates / Peter Skarzynski, Rowan Gibson.
      p. cm.
  Includes bibliographical references and index.
  ISBN-13: 978-1-4221-0251-0
  1. Organizational effectiveness. 2. Organizational change. 3. Leadership. I. Gibson, Rowan. II. Title.
  HD58.9.S556 2008
  658.4'063—dc22

                                                                              2007036566

The paper used in this publication meets the requirements of the American National Standard for Permanence of Paper for Publications and Documents in Libraries and Archives Z39.48-1992.

To our children, all potential innovators in the future:
Greta, Henry, Jake, James, Luke, Mack, Meghan, Sophie

And to leaders and team members around the world who are
already working hard to translate innovation rhetoric into reality.

It is best to do things systematically.

—Hesiod, 700 BCE

CONTENTS

Acknowledgments   xiii
Introduction by Gary Hamel   xvii

PART ONE: TURNING RHETORIC INTO REALITY

1   The New Innovation Challenge   **3**

Making Innovation Happen   4
The New Innovation Leaders   7
More Buzzword Than Core Competence   11
Toward a Systemic Understanding   13
Innovation to the Core   16

2   Creating the Preconditions for Innovation   **21**

Creating Bandwidth   22
Maximizing Diversity   28
Connection and Conversation   36
Is That All There Is to It?   43
Innovation Challenges and Leadership Imperatives   43

3   Building a Foundation of Novel Strategic Insights   **45**

The Four "Lenses" of Innovation   46
Challenging Orthodoxies   47
Harnessing Discontinuities   55
Leveraging Competencies and Assets   61
Understanding Unarticulated Needs   69
Organizing the Discovery Process   76
Drawing on Collective Wisdom   77
Selecting and Using "Discovery Insights"   78
Innovation Challenges and Leadership Imperatives   80

PART TWO: ENLARGING AND ENHANCING THE INNOVATION PIPELINE

4   **Producing a Torrent of New Opportunities**   85
     Involve Many Minds   87
     Sow Enough Seeds   95
     Widen the Front End   97
     Increase the Combinations   100
     Ideate Around Specific Themes   104
     Innovation Challenges and Leadership Imperatives   106

5   **Innovating Across the Business Model**   109
     What Is Business Model Innovation?   111
     Two Distinctly Different Objectives   114
     Thinking Holistically   115
     Asking New Questions   117
     Stretching Your Business Model   120
     The Acid Test   121
     Innovation Challenges and Leadership Imperatives   121

PART THREE: EVALUATING AND ALIGNING NEW GROWTH OPPORTUNITIES

6   **Asking the Right Questions at the Right Time**   125
     Evaluating Ideas   125
     The Limits to Incrementalism   127
     Radical Innovation Defined   128
     Radical Doesn't Have to Mean Risky   131
     Will It Have *Impact*?   132
     Innovation Challenges and Leadership Imperatives   134

7   **Constructing an Innovation Architecture**   137
     Focusing the Innovation Process   138
     Shaping Your Innovation Portfolio   140
     Screening and Sequencing Ideas   147
     A Shared Point of View   148
     More Than a Mission, a Vision, or a Plan   150

Strategy from the Bottom Up   151

Proprietary—but Not Confidential   153

Creating and Testing a Trial Architecture   155

A Blueprint for Building the Future   156

Innovation Challenges and Leadership Imperatives   157

PART FOUR: MAXIMIZING THE RETURN ON INNOVATION

8   **Managing and Multiplying Resources**   161

Barriers in the Budgeting Process   162

Incubators and Skunk Works   163

A Marketplace for Ideas, Capital, and Talent   164

Creating a Portfolio of Projects   170

Reallocating Talent   171

Toward the Hybrid Organization   172

Multiplying the Available Resources   173

Innovation Challenges and Leadership Imperatives   177

9   **Pacing and Derisking Innovation Investments**   179

Know the Race You Run   180

Understanding Marathons   181

Understanding Sprints   184

Becoming a "Smart Mover"   185

Avoiding Risk   186

Maximizing Learning over Investment   189

Learn Faster, Learn Cheaper, Learn Better   193

Managing a Portfolio of Experiments   194

Sharing Risk with Partners   196

Innovation Challenges and Leadership Imperatives   197

PART FIVE: DRIVING INNOVATION TO THE CORE

10   **Dynamically Balancing Supply and Demand**   201

Driving Innovation *Supply*   202

Driving Innovation *Demand*   208

Creating the Right Pressure Points   212

Aspirations Beyond the Numbers   215

Measuring Innovation Performance   216

A Comprehensive Matrix of Metrics   218

The "Innovation Scorecard"   223

Fine-Tuning the Balance   225

Innovation Challenges and Leadership Imperatives   227

11   Building a Systemic Innovation Capability   **229**

Leadership and Organization   230

People and Skills   238

Processes and Tools   242

Culture and Values   245

Making the Cultural Transition   250

Innovation Challenges and Leadership Imperatives   253

12   Making Innovation Sustainable   **255**

Identifying Innovation Impediments   257

"Management Process Makeover"   258

The Ultimate Challenge   262

Balancing Innovation and Efficiency   263

Tensions *Within* Innovation   266

Your Own Innovation Journey   268

Innovation Challenges and Leadership Imperatives   270

Notes   *271*

Bibliography   *277*

Index   *279*

About the Authors   *295*

ACKNOWLEDGMENTS

This book has been many years in the making, and it draws on the collective wisdom and experience of many minds. To all of them we are deeply grateful.

First and foremost, we owe a huge debt to our colleague and friend Gary Hamel. From the initial conception of *Innovation to the Core*, right through to the final revisions of the manuscript, Gary has worked with us tirelessly to make this book a practical and useful guide for executives who are leading innovation in organizations around the world. Over a period of almost three years, we had the honor of spending considerable time with one of the world's leading thinkers on business strategy—in meetings at the London Business School; in long, productive days at Gary's home in California; and in countless telephone conversations. Gary encouraged us not only to consider the principles of innovation strategy and management that he has put forth over the last one and a half decades but also to look broad and far at other successful practices, tools, and approaches. We cannot overstate the contribution he has made to this book.

We would also like to acknowledge the many authors of books and articles on innovation that have influenced our thinking over the years—we hope we have included most, if not all, of them in our bibliography. Three names deserve special mention: Clayton Christensen for his work on disruptive innovation, Henry Chesbrough for clearly defining the paradigm of open innovation, and Stefan Thomke for his research and writing on experimentation as an essential part of innovation.

We are grateful to the entire team at Strategos for their patient and enthusiastic support in the development of this book—especially where we forced our way into their already busy agendas. The practical insights our colleagues passed on to us from their firsthand experience with clients, along with the substantial assistance they gave us with research and editing, have been invaluable to this project. In particular, we extend our deep appreciation to George Chen, Dave Crosswhite, Pedro do Carmo Costa, Jennifer Dominiquini, Pierre Loewe, Naveed Moosa, and Amy Muller.

Our clients, too, have played a crucial role in shaping our thinking, and we thank them for demonstrating that the principles we present in this book really can help corporations build an enduring enterprise capability for innovation. Nancy Snyder, corporate vice president at Whirlpool, has earned special acknowledgment for her pioneering work as an innovation process champion inside a large, global organization, as well as for her book *Strategic Innovation* (coauthored with Deborah Duarte), which we consider to be a key reference work in the field of innovation management. Nancy also graciously took time out to review our manuscript and to offer suggested improvements, for which we are very grateful. In addition, we thank Sean Lindy of Whirlpool, as well as Fernando Flischfisch, innovation director at CEMEX, for clarifying important data used in our references to their respective companies throughout the book.

We have had the enormous privilege of working with one of the best publishing teams in the world at Harvard Business School Press. Our senior editor, Jeff Kehoe, guided us masterfully through the writing process with wise and discerning advice that helped us to continually strengthen and refine the manuscript. We would also like to thank Todd Berman, Mark Bloomfield, Julie Devoll, Stephani Finks (for her great cover design!), Sarah Green, Daisy Hutton, Sarah Mann, Carolyn Monaco, Zeenat Potia, and Jen Waring (who so deftly handled the production of the book), as well as the anonymous peer reviewers who suggested detailed, insightful changes to improve our work.

Our administrative assistants—Miriam Gribnau, Kathy Leslie, and Grace Reim—have been a tower of strength behind the scenes, juggling our impossible agendas and helping us to cope with the myriad of calls and correspondence that such a project inevitably generates. They played a crucial role in helping us making this book happen.

Rowan would especially like to express his gratitude to Peter Barratt-Jones, a close business colleague and dear friend for over twenty years, along with John Naisbitt, the world's greatest futurist (and, Rowan would argue, the world's greatest mentor). Their generosity of spirit and unflagging belief provided Rowan with a powerful tailwind. He would also like to thank the team at RethinkingGroup: Gerard Buitendijk (now at Buro De Hoge), Hans Schoenmaker, Sabine Swinkels, Jan van Buul, Rik van de Schoot, and Digna Yuen, as well as his longtime IT adviser and Web designer, Mark Hoevenaars, for their willing and unselfish support at all times.

Peter's personal thanks go out to dozens of client leadership teams with whom he has worked—for tenaciously deploying innovation as a capability within their organizations. He would also like to thank Dan Simpson for his thoughtful reading of early manuscripts, Wayne Clark for his insights on managing both the supply *and* the demand side of innovation, and Amy Muller for her detailed research and insights into innovation metrics. Special thanks, too, to Strategos Founder Linda Yates for her early efforts, focusing Strategos on helping clients to build and deploy an innovation capability for achieving sustainable growth.

We reserve the last and most important word of thanks for our wives—Anke Gibson and Caren Skarzynski—along with our dear children, who are the underlying reason for everything we do. We owe them our deepest gratitude for their unending support.

INTRODUCTION

In 1995 I, along with a band of young colleagues, founded a new company, *Strategos*. Our goal was not to build just another consulting company—*that* was simply a means to an end. Instead, we wanted to test a hypothesis: that with effort and persistence, large, bureaucratic organizations could become as good at game-changing innovation as they were at disciplined execution. My partners and I were not naive. We knew that it might take us a decade or more to develop the materials, tools, metrics, processes, and IT systems that would allow our clients to embed the DNA of innovation deep within their management systems and organizational cultures. We knew we would struggle to find corporate partners who were willing to venture out beyond the boundaries of best practice and tackle the challenge of making innovation an everywhere, all-the-time capability. We knew we would have to address deep questions: why, for example, can some prescient folks spot new and unconventional opportunities while so many others seem unable to see beyond the status quo? On the other hand, we knew we were not alone in our quest. We would be able to learn much from the many managers and scholars who were equally committed to unleashing the power of human imagination at work.

As we set out, we looked to the work of W. Edwards Deming and the apostles of Total Quality Management (TQM) for inspiration. Prior to their pioneering work, the responsibility for quality was narrowly focused in most companies, the preserve of highly trained quality inspectors. These individuals were paid to weed out defective products at the end of the production line. Hence, if you had visited a typical manufacturing company in the decades before TQM, you would have found that quality was not rigorously measured, not designed into products from the get-go, not built into manufacturing systems and protocols, not a significant factor in management compensation, and, most definitely, not the responsibility of "ordinary" line employees. While in some companies, such as Patek Philippe and Hermès, skilled artisans carried the burden of delivering outstanding quality, in most other companies quality depended on the work of those in the quality *department*. Yet by the end of the twentieth century, quality had become a broadly distributed capability in many of the world's leading companies. Today, progressive organizations often field a veritable army of Six Sigma black belts who have been trained to wield the weapons of statistical process analysis and continuous improvement first deployed by Deming and his peers.

If it was possible to make something as ethereal and elusive as quality a broad-based capability, why, we wondered, couldn't we do the same thing for innovation? Like quality in years past, innovation was, in our experience, too often viewed as the work of specialists, the "creative types" who are paid to innovate and sit in R&D or new-product development. Or of innovation "artisans"—those rare souls who, despite having no formal innovation role, occasionally succeed in pushing a truly radical idea through the conservative, ass-covering ranks of middle management and out into the marketplace. These "intrapreneurs" were iconoclastic and courageous and, in most companies, exceedingly rare.

If, as we believe, innovation is the only way to deliver peer-beating results over the long term, then it is impossible to be satisfied with a management model in which creative thinking is sequestered in innovation ghettos or is the occasional, heroic act of those with the patience of Job and the courage of Richard the Lionheart. Innovation is too important to be a function, or a department, or a one-time initiative, or an exceptional act. And it will only become more critical in the years to come.

In a world of ever-accelerating change, innovation is the only insurance against irrelevance. In an environment of steadily decreasing friction and crumbling entry barriers, innovation is the only antidote to margin-crushing competition. And in a global economy where knowledge advantages dissipate ever more rapidly, innovation is the only brake on commoditization.

Yet, as Skarzynski and Gibson will argue in the pages that follow, there's hardly one company in a hundred that has succeeded in making innovation a wall-to-wall, top-to-bottom capability. I don't believe this failing reflects a lack of commitment from the top as much as it reflects the lack, thus far, of a clear road map for making innovation everyone's job. Let me go back to my quality analogy. If in 1970 you had asked the chairman of General Motors if he was interested in improving the quality of GM's products, the answer probably would have been "yes." Higher quality brings lower warranty costs and happier customers. Unfortunately, though, thirty-odd years ago, GM's top management team had no practical idea of how to achieve a step-function change in quality. While GM's competitors in Japan were already making great strides in institutionalizing quality, most of these efforts were invisible to Detroit's auto executives. GM's boss might have *wanted* to take the quality high ground, but he simply didn't know how to do it.

I think many executives are in a similar quandary about innovation today. Where does one actually *start* in making innovation a systemic capability? How does one sequence the capability-building process? What are the things you have to get right first, if later efforts are going to pay off? How do you identify and neutralize the deadly, and often hidden, toxins that destroy innovation? How do you firmly implant the innovation gene in a company that has spent a decade focused on efficiency and short-term operational performance? How do you turn "ordinary" employees into extraordinary innovators? How do you enlarge the scope of innovation so that it encompasses entire business models as well as individual products and services? How do you manage the tension between the need to "let a thousand flowers bloom" and the need to focus scarce resources? How do you create the slack and freedom that are essential for innovation, without folks going off the rails? How do you pursue game-changing ideas without taking outsize risks? How, as an executive, do you manage, measure, and lead innovation? How, in short, do you drive innovation to the core?

These are some of the questions my colleagues have wrestled with over the past dozen years. And the book you now hold in your hands is a distillation of what they have learned. In these pages you will find practical examples, tools, and methods for bringing innovation to the core of your business, organization, and culture.

—Gary Hamel
Woodside, California
November 2007

PART ONE

TURNING RHETORIC INTO REALITY

CHAPTER 1

The New Innovation Challenge

IMAGINE IF EVERY PERSON in your firm came to work every day believing their ideas could influence the destiny of the company.

Imagine if every corner of your organization was pulsing—at all times—with radical, rule-breaking concepts for new products, services, strategies, and businesses, providing you with a continual flow of innovations with which to delight your customers, confound your competitors, and richly reward your shareholders.

Imagine you could go online 24/7 and get a comprehensive, real-time window on your company's global innovation activities—a dashboard that showed you how many ideas were being produced, which parts of the world they were coming from, how fast they were progressing through the pipeline, when they were going to be commercialized, and what their future financial value was expected to be.

Imagine if every single one of your employees, at every level and in every location, had been trained in the principles, skills, and tools of innovation—greatly enhancing their ability to discover new insights, spot unexploited opportunities, and generate novel business ideas.

Imagine, too, that your company had a worldwide innovation infrastructure where those people could quickly find the cash, the talent, and the management support they needed to turn their ideas into market success stories.

Simply put, imagine if the notion of building and sustaining a deep, corporate-wide capability for innovation were not just a vague aspiration but a daily reality inside your own organization.

Now stop imagining. At some of the world's leading companies—GE, P&G, IBM, Whirlpool, Royal Dutch/Shell, CEMEX, Best Buy, W. L. Gore, and others—much of the above is already happening.

In this book, you will learn how to dramatically improve your organization's own capacity for innovation by mobilizing and monetizing the imagination of your employees, customers, and business partners—every day, everywhere. On the pages that follow, we will share the tools, techniques, and methodologies we have used successfully for well over a decade to help companies turn innovation into a core competence and thereby outperform industry rivals.

MAKING INNOVATION HAPPEN

Innovation. From the boardroom to the business press, everyone is talking about it. Most senior executives would tell you that they get the message. In any survey of management priorities these days, innovation is almost always one of the top two or three items on the corporate agenda.[1]

But making innovation a priority is not the same thing as making it happen. All too often, innovation becomes nothing more than a buzzword or a bumper sticker—the management theme du jour—that receives a lot of reverential rhetoric in company meetings, corporate ad campaigns, and annual reports.

The difficult challenge for most organizations is how to turn all that rhetoric into hard-nosed, revenue-growing reality—not just by making incremental tweaks to existing products or services, or by pursuing a "once in a blue moon" blockbuster, but by producing a constant stream of breakthrough innovations that compound over time to build a formidable competitive advantage.

Very few firms have managed to pull this off. In the vast majority of cases, pouring money and effort into innovation has produced remarkably little in terms of new wealth. After conducting studies of the world's one thousand biggest spenders on R&D, for example, consulting firm Booz Allen Hamilton concluded both in 2005 and 2006 that there is "no discernible statistical relationship between R&D spending levels and nearly all measures of business success, including sales growth, gross profit, operating profit, enterprise profit, market capitalization or total shareholder return."[2] To illustrate the point, guess which U.S. firm has spent more money on R&D than any other company in the world during the last twenty-five years? The answer is General Motors.[3]

Sure, business history is replete with examples of successful innovation. Over the years, many a company has been able to take the lead in an industry—or invent an entirely new one—by leveraging a disruptive technology, a radical new product idea, a truly novel service concept, or a game-changing business model. But in case after case, those companies eventually ceded their leadership position to a competitor—often a newcomer—that later seized on a superior idea. Not many organizations have so far managed to build *a deep, enduring capability for innovation*—one that consistently drives profitable revenue growth and that enables the company to maintain a competitive advantage over the longer term.

Not yet, that is. Right now, the list of major companies that are working methodically on the innovation management challenge is growing rapidly, and the progress of a few pioneering firms provides hope and inspiration for the rest of the business community. These leading-edge players are demonstrating that large industrial organizations really can tackle the challenge of innovation successfully in a broad-based and highly systemic way.

Consider the well-documented efforts of GE and P&G—two of the biggest and best-known companies on earth—to drive innovation to the core of their respective organizations.

GE: From Cost Cutter to Innovation Powerhouse

Since taking over the reins from Jack Welch in 2001, Jeff Immelt, GE's chairman and CEO, has launched nothing less than a cultural revolution at the company, pushing its strategic focus beyond continuous improvement and bottom-line results toward the creation of bold, imaginative ideas. His aim has been to "grow the boundaries" of the company, this time organically rather than through acquisitions—by taking GE into new lines of business, new geographic areas, and new customer segments. Immelt knows this is the only way his company can continue to meet its grueling financial targets. Currently, he is under pressure to achieve an incredible 8 percent of organic growth each year. For a company of GE's magnitude, this represents around $15 billion of new revenue annually—equivalent to adding a new business the size of Nike.[4] To this end, Immelt has worked hard to make innovation a deep, systemic capability all across the company—an "engine" that will drive and sustain new revenue growth.

P&G: From "Not Invented Here" to Open Innovation

Similarly, when Alan G. Lafley became chairman of P&G in 2000, he made it clear that he wanted innovation "across the spectrum"—in how the company invents, markets, manufactures, and distributes its products.[5] The reason is simple. Like Jeff Immelt at GE, Lafley is on the hook to deliver relentless levels of profitable growth each year—around $7 billion of new revenue annually—and he needs to find imaginative new ways to fuel it. One of his major initiatives at the Cincinnati-based consumer goods giant has been to break down the walls that used to separate product categories, business units, sectors, and brands, thus allowing innovation to flow freely across the entire organization. More importantly, in 2001 Lafley threw open P&G's doors to innovators who are not on the company's payroll, setting a goal for his organization to source at least 50 percent of its innovations from outside the company (up from roughly 10 percent at the time). Thanks to a new organizational model called Connect and Develop, the company has since been able to bring hundreds of new products to the market that had their genesis, in whole or in part, outside P&G.

Clearly, when Immelt and Lafley talk about the innovation imperative, it's not merely rhetoric—it's something that is deeply transforming their organizations. And the precedent these companies are setting is not going unnoticed. Geoff Colvin writes in *Fortune* magazine, "Immelt and Lafley are going down a road everyone in business will have to travel. Watch and learn."[6]

THE NEW INNOVATION LEADERS

Some companies—like Apple, or Google, or W. L. Gore—seem to have been *born* innovative. But what if your organization is not one of them? What if your firm is a whole lot better at disciplined execution than it is at wealth-generating innovation? If so, there's only so much you can learn from innovation's "usual suspects." Instead, you need to learn from companies, perhaps like your own, that have transformed themselves from innovation laggards into innovation leaders.

Consider two unlikely innovation champions. One is Whirlpool, the global leader in domestic appliances, and the other is a Mexican firm called CEMEX, one of the world's leading producers of building materials (including, for example, cement, ready-mix concrete, and aggregates). These two companies, among others, are demonstrating that it's perfectly possible to turn "old-line" industrial organizations into catalysts for continuous, break-the-rules innovation.

Whirlpool: Thinking Outside the "White Box"

When Whirlpool's former CEO Dave Whitwam set out to define his company's global innovation strategy back in 1999, the exact words he used were "Innovation from Everyone and Everywhere." This was a huge aspiration, considering that at the time Whirlpool had 68,000 employees in 170 countries, as well as 50 manufacturing and technology research centers around the globe. But today, Whirlpool has become a best-practice model for the embedment of innovation as a capability across a large, global enterprise.

Instilling innovation as a core competence at Whirlpool took a massive, broad-based effort over several years, involving major changes to leader accountability and development, cultural values, resource allocation, knowledge management, rewards and recognition systems, traditional hierarchies, measurement and reporting systems, and a whole host of other management practices and policies.

Here are just a few examples of these changes:

- The appointment of vice presidents of innovation at both the global and the regional level

- The creation of large, cross-functional "innovation teams" in each region employed solely in the search for breakthrough ideas

- The introduction of a companywide training program aimed at developing and distributing the mind-set and skills of innovation

- The appointment of more than six hundred part-time "innovation mentors" and twenty-five full-time "innovation consultants," who act as highly skilled advisers to new project development teams around the world

- The creation of "innovation boards" in each region and each major business unit, made up of senior staff who meet monthly not just to review ideas and projects, set goals, and allocate resources, but to oversee the continuing innovation capability-building process

- The organization of big communication events called Innovation Days where innovation teams showcase their ideas to other Whirlpool people, the media, and even Wall Street analysts. Sometimes these events are also held in suburban shopping malls as a way of collecting feedback and additional ideas from potential users

- The creation of a comprehensive set of metrics to continually measure the company's innovation performance as well as its progress in embedding innovation as a core competence

- The establishment of a sophisticated IT infrastructure called Innovation E-Space, which integrates all of Whirlpool's people into the innovation effort and allows them to track progress on innovation activities across the corporation

The key objective to all of this has been to help every single employee at Whirlpool think outside the traditional "white box" of home appliances, and imagine exciting, customer-relevant solutions that create new wealth for the company. The outcome has been a stream of breakthrough ideas for products and businesses that have come from all over the Whirlpool organization—ideas that deliver value to consumers in ways never before seen either at the company or in the industry.

This has produced a steep upturn in the company's annual revenues from innovative new products—rising from $78 million in 2003 to $1.6 billion in 2006 (a figure over twenty times higher).[7] Today, Whirlpool has well over five hundred projects in its innovation pipeline, representing expected future revenues of $3.5 billion. And the company's innovation juggernaut shows no signs of slowing down. As current CEO Jeff Fettig told *BusinessWeek*, "If we keep innovating we'll keep growing."[8]

Not surprisingly, Whirlpool's overall revenues and profits are now at all-time highs and growing at a brisk rate—this in a stagnating industry where many of Whirlpool's global rivals are struggling.

CEMEX: Remixing the Cement Business

One of the fastest-growing and most profitable companies in the world in the last few years has been a global building materials firm from Mexico called CEMEX. *BusinessWeek* lists CEMEX among "a new class of formidable competitors" from emerging markets that is rapidly rising up to challenge corporate America. Today, the company is number three in the world cement market.[9]

Cement may not seem like an industry that inspires revolutionary thinking or that attracts the creative, curious, and contrarian type. Yet CEMEX's ability to reinvent both its industry and itself serves as an example to any company aspiring to make innovation work.

Back in the early 1990s, CEMEX's CEO, Lorenzo Zambrano, decided that the key to building a better future for his company was innovation. He resolved to push CEMEX beyond its tradition-bound roots by investing in the problem-solving skills of rank-and-file employees. This vision has spawned a corporate-wide innovation capability that has helped the company achieve sales and profit growth over the last decade of more than 20 percent on average, and raise its operating margins by the same percentage, making them nearly twice as high as its two global rivals—France's Lafarge and Switzerland's Holcim. It has also helped CEMEX become one of the most highly regarded employers in Mexico.

Here are some of the components of CEMEX's innovation system:

- A dedicated innovation group, led by the innovation director, with full-time employees responsible for millions of dollars in annual budget

- Multifunctional teams, each consisting of ten to twelve members from across the company, whose mandate it is to generate new ideas and breakout proposals around major platforms or themes

- An innovation board that is set up to screen and fund these proposals, with initial funding ranging between a few hundred thousand dollars and several million dollars

- Hundreds of trained and highly visible "innovation champions" in every part of the organization, who are there to guide and mentor any employee who comes up with an idea

- Virtual, online "ping-pong" competitions—held regularly and judged by one of the company's innovation experts—in which people "bat" exciting ideas back and forth across the organization, improving them as they go

- A dedicated IT platform that expedites the spread of new ideas across CEMEX, featuring an online idea bank designed to make it easy for employees to share their ideas, big or small

- Annual Innovation Days, devoted to recognizing and celebrating the work of innovators, which feature "Oscars" for the best implemented ideas

At CEMEX, nobody has a monopoly on new ideas. Innovation is a collective act that springs from a collaborative approach to solving business problems. By tapping into as many minds and as many different talents as possible, and by getting people to swap ideas, innovate together, and feel jointly responsible for success, CEMEX has been able to invent a variety of novel approaches to its business that nobody in the industry had ever thought of before. The innovation process has produced hundreds of opportunities in all aspects of the company's business model, including new products and services, improvements in the manufacture and distribution of cement, and ideas for radically streamlining the company's operations, such as logistics. Some of these ideas have delivered hundreds of millions of dollars in operations savings, sometimes in just a few months.

What the examples of Whirlpool and CEMEX teach us is that, with a serious, broad-based effort and with the right set of design rules, innovation can become a systemic capability inside any organization—as ubiquitous as Six Sigma, cycle time, rapid customer service, or any of the other complex processes that companies have been honing over the last thirty years. These companies are proving that you can indeed turn innovation from an ethereal, hit-and-miss thing into a deep core competence, something that becomes part of a company's bloodstream.

Why is it, then, that in most organizations today—even those where organic growth and innovation are supposed to be top strategic priorities—we still find nothing that even remotely resembles a systematic, corporate-wide approach to innovation?

MORE BUZZWORD THAN CORE COMPETENCE

Pick up the average annual report. Open it at the "CEO's letter to the stakeholders" and look for the word *innovation*. Usually, you will find it in the first few lines: "We thrive on innovation," "We're committed to growth through innovation," "We have an unwavering commitment to innovation," and so on. But try this little experiment: visit that company and talk to some of its midlevel employees. Ask them a few questions like these:

- Could you describe your company's corporate innovation system?

- Do you believe that top management regards every employee in your company as an innovator, potentially capable of shaping corporate direction?

- Have you personally been trained as a business innovator?

- How important is innovation in your own performance metrics and in your compensation?

- How difficult would it be for you to get small amounts of experimental capital to test a new idea?

- Would you know where to go in your organization to find coaches and mentors who could help you push an idea forward?

- In what ways do your company's management processes—strategic planning, capital budgeting, and so on—support your work as an innovator?

Ask people these kinds of questions, and you will usually be met with a blank stare. It's quite obvious that, in most companies, innovation is still more buzzword than core competence. But why is this?

We certainly wouldn't put it down to a lack of sincerity on the part of senior executives. Most corporate leaders understand quite well that there is only one way to drive the kind of aggressive top-line growth that investors demand from them year after year—and that is not through tired old management practices like cost cutting, restructuring, buying back shares, or mergers and acquisitions. They realize that in the longer term, if they want to stand any chance of growing faster than the industry average or the overall economy, they have no alternative but to innovate in their products, their business models, and, indeed, their management systems.

They also know that, with today's intense competition and rapidly changing market dynamics, strategy life cycles are getting shorter. Most senior managers recognize, therefore, that what they really need is not just another incremental efficiency program, but some fundamentally new strategic thinking—that radical innovation is the only option they have left for creating new wealth.

The reason for the large and yawning gap between rhetoric and reality concerning innovation is that most organizations have not yet developed a clear model—reflected in management practice—of what innovation actually looks like as a highly distributed, "all the time, everywhere" capability.

TOWARD A SYSTEMIC UNDERSTANDING

For an analogy, think back to the quality movement of the 1970s. When the first Western executives went over to look at Japanese companies a few decades ago, they initially failed to recognize that quality was a deep, systemic capability in those organizations. Most of them came back with a very superficial understanding.

"Quality is not very difficult" was the typical response; "it's about quality circles. These people meet on Friday afternoons; they sit around for a few hours talking about how to improve quality and . . . presto! Quality goes up. So let's have quality circles." Many Western companies did just that. And they found that it made no difference to their quality whatsoever.

At that stage of the game, many organizations said, "Okay. We tried that . . . it didn't work," and they quietly closed down their quality initiatives. It took several years before they had the courage to make another attempt.

Eventually, when those companies went back and studied what the Japanese were really doing, they realized that quality was a much deeper discipline than they had originally imagined. This time their response was "Gosh, they're training people. They're training *thousands* of people. They're giving them tools to use. They're completely changing the metrics. They're empowering ordinary workers. They're giving shop-floor employees the authority to stop a million-dollar production line." That was when Western companies began to grasp that quality could be an intrinsic and ubiquitous capability rather than a specialized function—that it could actually be embedded and institutionalized in an organization's core DNA.

In other words, the initial failure with many quality initiatives did not reflect any lack of conviction or seriousness on the part of top management. What it reflected was a lack of knowledge about the processes, the tools, and the mechanisms that were critical for making quality happen. Those executives simply didn't understand how to make quality *systemic*.

The bleeding edge for companies is no longer quality; it's innovation. But right now, innovation is still more or less where quality was in the late 1960s. The problem today, as it was back then, is not top management complacency or hypocrisy. It is the fact that making innovation work inside a large organization is a much more complex and multifaceted challenge than most people imagine. It simply cannot be solved with some Band-Aid or silver bullet.

We might compare it to a Russian *matryoshka* doll. From the outside, the doll appears simple and straightforward. But, as we all know, there's much more to it than first meets the eye. When we open it up, we discover that it's actually made up of many nested layers, one inside the other, and that it takes every one of those layers to make the doll complete. So, too, when we move beyond a superficial understanding of innovation—when we begin to dig down—we find that it is a deep, systemic challenge that involves considerable effort across a whole range of interdependent dimensions. As with quality, innovation requires new training, new tools, new IT systems, new metrics, new values, new management processes, and so on, and all of these mechanisms must be tightly integrated—or "nested" together—for the system to function effectively.

Many senior executives may never have even considered innovation in these terms. They might think of innovation as breakthrough technology, or cool product design, or individual creativity. Or they may know it as a specialized unit called "R&D," or "new product development," or "corporate venturing." But they have probably never contemplated the idea of recalibrating all their core management systems and processes to make innovation an everyday "part of the system"—something that becomes reflexive and natural to everyone.

Up to now, the management literature on innovation has not been a big help in this regard. Much of it has focused on playing creative thinking games, or improving brainstorming techniques. Other books and articles have made a more serious contribution to helping companies understand innovation as an organizational process, but so far, none of them seem to have had a deep enough impact on management think-ing. According to innovation strategist Larry Keeley, "The field has ad-vanced to about the same state as medicine when leeches, liniments and mystery potions were the sophisticated treatments of the day."[10]

No wonder innovation has gone through a crisis of credibility in many organizations, just as the quality movement did in its early years. In the absence of any reliable guide, companies have often wasted con-siderable time and money on innovation initiatives that were doomed from the outset. In most cases, these efforts have delivered little in the way of new wealth-creating products, services, strategies, and business models. A global study in 2007, for example, involving almost twenty-five hundred senior executives in fifty-eight countries, revealed that more than half of all executives surveyed were still dissatisfied with the financial returns on their company's innovation investments.[11]

That's why, for decades, innovation has been something of a side-show in many firms—nice to have, and nice to talk about, but not doing very much to contribute to growing the business. Like those long-departed auto executives who underestimated the complexity of the quality challenge, many companies have simply concluded, "We tried innovation. It didn't work."

The central tenet of this book, however, is that innovation—when systemically applied—*does* work. We argue that it is entirely possible to boost your company's innovation performance in a dramatic and endur-ing way, but it can only be done if you are prepared to make innovation a systemic enterprise capability. Nobody can hope to achieve anything by throwing a light switch and saying, "Okay, from Monday morning we're all going to be a lot more innovative." Anyone who seriously wants to influence the values and dynamics of a large-scale, distributed human system is going to have to roll up their sleeves and get ready for some really hard work.

Despite the gargantuan nature of the challenge, building a deep, sys-temic capability for innovation is now the inescapable imperative for every company—as important to an organization's success and survival as the quality movement was in its day. Granted, in the short run, there may be some substitutes for innovation—some quick ways to prop up a company's share price and earnings over the next few quarters. But in the medium to long term, there are absolutely *none*. In today's innovation-based economy, where organic growth and strategic renewal are the new business mantras, either companies learn to drive innovation to the core or they risk becoming footnotes in the history books.

INNOVATION TO THE CORE

Making such a profound cultural change requires time, money, and commitment. In our experience, it can take an organization three to five years to build the kinds of skills, tools, management processes, metrics, values, and IT systems that are required to support ongoing, across-the-board innovation. But as James Andrew and Harold Sirkin, senior partners at The Boston Consulting Group, argue in their book, *Payback*, managing and mastering innovation as a disciplined business activity can help an organization reap dramatic financial rewards.[12]

Of course, it can't be done piecemeal—an innovation reward program here, a corporate venture fund there, or a few days of brainstorming somewhere else isn't enough. But the message is that *it can be done*. If companies like GE, P&G, Whirlpool, and CEMEX have taken on this challenge—and are already achieving extraordinary results—your company can do the same.

Again, the quality movement sets an encouraging precedent. Look how adept today's organizations have become at systematically manufacturing world-class products. Who would have thought that what once seemed so daunting could become almost run-of-the-mill business practice? In the years to come, we see no reason why corporate *innovation* systems shouldn't become just as efficient—and just as commonplace—as corporate quality systems.

Already, the "innovation movement" is gathering momentum. The challenge of building a systemic innovation capability has become the focus of increasing attention in both business and academic circles around the world. Companies everywhere are asking themselves exactly what they need to do to drive innovation to the core—to make innovation an "all the time, everywhere" reality inside their organizations.

That's why we felt it was time to write this book. Having spent more than ten years helping companies tackle the innovation challenge ourselves (learning firsthand about what works and what doesn't), we believe we can now begin to talk in a practical way about how your own company can embed innovation as a systemic enterprise capability—using an approach suited to your organization.

We are not by any means claiming to have cracked the code on innovation; there is still very much to be learned. But what we do have is a considerable body of knowledge and frontline experience, along with many practical tools and techniques that we believe can be very useful to your own organization. This book is an attempt to share as much of that as possible with you. Its purpose is to give you and your company a sense of what it takes to create the organizational conditions within which radical innovation can continually flourish. Our hope is that it will not only make a convincing case for innovation embedment, but also help set the agenda for making innovation a way of life inside more and more organizations.

For too long, innovation has been viewed as a random, often serendipitous, act. In this book, we describe the basic principles, techniques, and methods common across all successful innovators and innovative companies. Whether you are an executive leading innovation from the top or a frontline innovator with a passion for addressing unmet customer needs, you can learn to apply these basic principles and techniques to spur profitable growth through winning innovations.

Perhaps you picked up this book because you are looking for a way to increase the quantity and quality of new ideas entering your innovation pipeline. Maybe it was because you want to know how to build a portfolio of strategic growth opportunities or how to derisk a bold idea. It might be because you'd like guidance on how to organize effectively for innovation or how to overcome one or more of the challenges innovators commonly face. Possibly it was because you and others in your firm have already recognized the need to deeply and profoundly change your company's approach to innovation. Whatever your motivation for reading this book, we invite you to read on and find helpful answers on all of these issues.

Here is what awaits you on the pages ahead:

In the first part of the book, we will examine three critical preconditions for making innovation happen inside your company. We will also show you how to systematically build a foundation of novel strategic insights that can serve as the raw material for game-changing innovation.

In part 2, we will provide you with a set of design rules for enlarging and enhancing your company's innovation pipeline. We will share market-proven methodologies for dramatically improving your firm's ideation efforts and for innovating across every aspect of the business model.

In part 3, we will look in detail at how to evaluate the potential of new growth opportunities by asking the right questions at the right time. Next, we will describe how your company can construct an innovation architecture that will enable you to frame those opportunities in the context of your corporate strategy.

Part 4 is where you will find useful guidelines on how to manage and multiply your organization's resources for innovation—both financial and intellectual—as well as on how to pace and derisk your innovation investments.

Finally, in part 5, we will provide some pragmatic advice on measuring and fine-tuning innovation performance. We will outline the four key organizational components that need to come together to institutionalize innovation as an enterprise capability, offering some practical guidance to help you make organizing decisions. We will also share what we and others have found to be critical if you want to make innovation sustainable in your company.

In writing this book, we have endeavored to make the content as hands-on as possible. To this end, we cite a rich variety of cases from the real world, illustrating how companies—maybe similar to yours—have met and overcome the same innovation challenges you might be facing. We also incorporate practical elements, wherever possible, to assist you in turning innovation from rhetoric into reality. These include focused sets of diagnostic questions, as well as a recurring feature at the end of each chapter called "Innovation Challenges and Leadership Imperatives." These elements are intended to help you assess your own situation, jump-start your organization's innovation engines, and facilitate progress on actually making innovation a core competence.

So, if you are up for the challenge of building a deep innovation capability inside your own company, let's waste no time. The following chapters will show you how to get started.

CHAPTER 2

Creating the Preconditions
for Innovation

WHERE DOES INNOVATION actually come from? How do you generate an idea that is so radical—so compelling—that it fundamentally alters customer expectations, or reinvents the cost structure in your industry, or redefines the basis for competition in a way that devalues the skills and assets of your rivals?

Even after all these years, the innovation process that either consciously or subconsciously leads to such breakthroughs is little understood. To be sure, we have lots of ways to evaluate an idea or a business strategy once it's already there. We can use a whole set of criteria to assess whether it's worth investing in or not—for example, we can ask whether it is likely to deliver above-average profits, or create a sustainable competitive advantage, or satisfy customers in new ways. But these measures, useful as they are, will only help us determine whether an innovative idea is likely to go somewhere; they won't tell us where it came from in the first place.

While most corporate leaders view the innovation imperative with urgency, many companies are having a difficult struggle creating and fostering the cultural and constitutional conditions that serve as catalysts for breakthrough innovation. When asked where quality comes from, executives at these companies can usually talk at length about training, tools, metrics, values, IT, and management processes—they know how the Total Quality Management system works. Yet when they are asked where *innovation* comes from, their answers remain a lot less confident. There is still a sense that innovation is something ethereal and elusive—the twenty-first century equivalent of El Dorado or the Holy Grail.

This should strike us as more than a little odd in an era when practically every other business process has been honed to a fine art. Can you imagine any other major capability in a large company—supply chain management, customer service, quality—being ascribed to a mysterious mix of happenstance, individual brilliance, and the occasional bolt of lightning?

In this chapter, we will begin to demystify the innovation process by identifying three critical preconditions for making breakthroughs happen:

1. Creating time and space in people's lives for reflection, ideation, and experimentation

2. Maximizing the diversity of thinking that innovation requires

3. Fostering connection and conversation—the "combinational chemistry" that serves as a breeding ground for breakthrough ideas

These three preconditions form a vital part of the answer to where innovation comes from. They are the starting point for making your organizational culture more conducive to innovation.

CREATING BANDWIDTH

When we asked more than five hundred senior and midlevel managers in large U.S. companies to identify the biggest barriers to innovation in their respective organizations, one of the most common responses was "lack of time." In an age when business worships at the altar of operational efficiency, every company has a mandate to work harder and faster, or lose out to someone who will. Over the last few decades, organizations have been pulling the reins tighter and tighter, giving most of today's companies very little room for playing around with creative ideas, exploring new possibilities, and running lots of experiments.

It's also a world where our attention is fragmented into tiny shards—where we are constantly distracted by e-mails, instant messages, mobile phone calls, faxes, meetings, express deliveries, and so forth. This places severe limits on our ability to think, reflect, and innovate in a focused manner. Therefore, one of the fundamental challenges for leadership is how to create space for innovation in people's lives—how to give them the extra bandwidth and scope they need for this kind of thinking. Building a culture where employees have time to imagine and experiment and develop their own ideas is the first commandment of innovation.

Whirlpool, the global appliances manufacturer, has approached this challenge in a very systematic way. On the first step of the company's journey to embed innovation as a core competence, seventy-five people were selected from three geographic regions around the world to learn about and apply an innovation process that would later be scaled across the company. They worked together to develop a rich foundation of strategic market insights that could inspire radical new thinking and new growth fueled by innovation. They learned how to efficiently generate hundreds of ideas, how to apply discipline and judgment to the process of selecting the most important ones, how to shape these growth opportunities into compelling business plans, and how to take their plans to market to capture financial value for the company.

These people, who were taken out of their normal everyday jobs for nine months, were not "spare" employees who nobody wanted. According to Nancy Snyder, Whirlpool's corporate vice president of innovation at the time, "They included some of the top talent in the organization, pulled from their operational roles at a time when the business needed them."[1] It was the first time Whirlpool had ever dedicated seventy-five people full time to a key strategic initiative, and this in itself was a signal about how important the initiative was to the company.

At the time, a lot of objections were raised internally about how the organization could spare so much bandwidth. But top management realized that in order to build a critical mass of skilled innovators, as well as a foundation of truly novel strategic insights, it would need to commit a lot of bandwidth to the innovation challenge right at the beginning. Just as in any other large company, there were many things working against innovation within Whirlpool, and many other priorities to think about. Without this big initial push, top management would never have been able to move the whole organization in the direction of innovation.

After nine months as members of Whirlpool's innovation teams, roughly one-third of the original seventy-five people returned to their previous work to spread the innovation "religion" among the ranks. Another third became full-time innovation consultants, responsible for teaching others their newfound innovation skills. The final third were assigned to lead the new innovation projects that the initiative had spawned, some of which have since become very successful ventures. One ex-participant is Tom Arent, who was in the innovation group that came up with the original idea for Gladiator GarageWorks, a modular system of storage units and accessories for organizing the garage. Now Arent is general manager of this highly profitable business, managed as a new and growing brand within Whirlpool.

Today, thousands of people across the Whirlpool organization, at one time or another, have taken part in the same basic program as those first seventy-five employees.

In the early days of its companywide innovation initiative, Whirlpool also set up innovation boards, comprised of senior leaders within three regions: North America, Latin America, and Europe. These were given the responsibility of steering innovation activities at the regional business level. Every month, innovation board members had to set aside a minimum of a half day to a full day to meet and discuss the company's progress on embedding innovation as a core competence, and to review ongoing innovation projects. Nancy Snyder says, "The meetings carved out innovation from the normal workday and became the only place where innovation took center stage away from the day-to-day demands of the business."[2] Thus, the innovation boards became an important tool for focusing top management time and attention on innovation. Today, Whirlpool's executives schedule regular innovation board meetings, and these have become firmly ingrained in the corporate culture.

As part of the strategic innovation initiative, senior executives were asked to carve out time—both for themselves and their work units—to advance innovation projects and to support the ongoing process of innovation embedment. Not only were these leaders expected to systematically foster "Innovation from Everyone and Everywhere," they were also made *accountable* for helping would-be innovators find time during regular work hours to pursue their ideas. No specific percentage of discretionary time was required to be allocated for innovation, but in practice it came down to about 10 to 15 percent.[3]

By creating this extra bandwidth for people to work on new ideas, Whirlpool's leaders have been able to unleash the imagination of employees across the organization and create a slew of new innovation opportunities. Often, the process begins quite informally, with employees spending just a small portion of their time kicking an idea around in its early stages. Later, if the idea receives seed funding, managers will make sure that team members get more time away from their normal responsibilities to move the project forward. In the end, if it really starts to take off, these employees could find themselves assigned to the project, potentially on a full-time basis.

CEMEX, the Mexican building materials firm, takes a similarly systematic approach. The company creates multifunctional "innovation platform teams" (with ten to twelve rotating members from all across the company) to explore innovative solutions around major platforms or themes—for example, how to sell "solutions" to contractors and not just building materials. The people invited to join these teams are first intensively trained as business innovators. Then they devote at least one day a week over three or four months to their innovation challenge, generating new ideas and breakout proposals in these major opportunity arenas. Their goal is to develop eight to ten strategy "experiments" focused on the designated platform theme. At the end of the ten- to twelve-week assignment, each team is replaced by a new team, and the process starts all over again.

Other companies, too, have gone a long way toward putting innovation on everyone's agenda by allowing their employees to schedule discretionary time for creative thinking. 3M has its famous "15 percent rule," which allows employees to spend 15 to 20 percent of their time working on their own personal projects using the company's resources. And at W. L. Gore, another innovation powerhouse, every employee can set aside 10 percent of his or her time to "dabble" with new applications for the company's unique materials.

Dave Myers, for example, was working at one of Gore's medical-product plants in Flagstaff, Arizona, where he was helping to invent new kinds of plastic heart implants. What did he do with the 10 percent of his time that he was supposed to spend dreaming up new ideas? Myers tinkered with the gears on his mountain bike, eventually coating the gear cables with plastic to make them shift more smoothly. These experiments led to the development of Gore's popular Ride-On bike cables. After this success, Myers wondered what would happen to guitar strings if he coated them with a similar plastic. The result was Elixir—now the best-selling brand of acoustic guitar strings, with a 35 percent market share, in a field that had previously seen no significant innovation for decades.

Google's method for creating bandwidth is the "70/20/10" formula: employees allocate 70 percent of their time to the company's main business, 20 percent of their time to new strategic projects (like Google News, Google Earth, Google Book Search, Google Checkout, and Google Apps), and a 10 percent slice of their time to "pet" projects—basically, whatever interests them. The latter have a good chance of landing on the "Top 100 Pet Projects" list, kept by founders Larry Page and Sergey Brin, which has been the launchpad for many of the company's current services.

If you took an honest look at your own organization, would you say you are giving your people the time and space they need to exercise their innovation muscles?

Ask Yourself

- Does my company have a legitimate and acknowledged mechanism through which employees can dedicate a certain percentage of discretionary time to innovative projects?

- Are leaders at every level accountable for helping employees take advantage of this mechanism?

- Does top management reserve time for regular meetings where the sole purpose is to discuss the company's growth and innovation efforts, reflect on new strategic insights and ideas, track ongoing innovation projects, set priorities, and allocate resources?

- Do we have a significant number of people in this organization—outside of R&D and new product development—who officially work on a full- or part-time basis on growth and innovation activities?

- Does my company have formal programs, perhaps companywide, for teaching people the principles, skills, and tools of innovation in the same way it has taught Six Sigma?

- Would a large percentage of our employees say that innovation is part of their job?

- Is innovation on my own agenda? Have I set aside significant time and space over the past six months for pursuing innovation activities and for helping my company/business unit/team improve its innovation capability?

- Have I actually dedicated a specific percentage of my managerial time to mentoring innovators?

If your answers to many or all of these questions were negative, it may be that your company needs to think seriously about freeing up more time, energy, and brainpower across the organization to devote to innovation and growth.

MAXIMIZING DIVERSITY

A lot of discussion is going on in corporate circles these days about ethnic, racial, and gender diversity. If it's not a big deal in your own company or geographic region yet, chances are it soon will be.

Compliance with government legislation and political correctness are not the only issues driving this new push for diversity. It's also very much about the globalization of business. It's about the need to understand and leverage the rapidly changing demographics of customers, markets, and employees around the world. Luke Visconti, partner and cofounder of *DiversityInc* magazine, says, "If you want to compete globally, you have to understand that 80% of the globe isn't white and 50% isn't male."[4]

That's a big reason why a string of global companies—from PepsiCo to P&G to GE—have made it a strategic priority to diversify and globalize their leadership teams. Some of the biggest American firms, for example, are now doing well over half of their business outside the United States, so it makes sense for at least half of the people on their top leadership teams to be non-Americans. Walk into any meeting about product development or marketing in one of these organizations, and you're likely to find a lot more female faces, a lot more skin colors, and a lot more nations represented in the room than you ever used to. The hope is that these people can help the company build bridges to all the segments, subsegments, and niches in an increasingly global customer base, and thereby give the organization a competitive advantage.

However, what is really crucial in the composition of innovation teams is not just the ability to connect various genders, races, cultures, and ethnicities; it's the ability to connect people with different skill sets, capabilities, and perspectives. When we work with companies to assemble teams for building innovation insights and new opportunities, we have a selection mechanism that ensures we get a group of individuals whose *thinking* is as diverse as possible. Below is a list of the actual criteria we use in practice. We specifically look for the following diversity characteristics:

- People who are *di*vergent thinkers, and people who are *con*vergent thinkers

- People who are more analytical, and people who are more creative

- People who are close to the head office, and people who work farther away

- People who are younger, and people who are older

- People with a lot of experience, and people with a lot of imagination

- People who understand technology, and people who understand people

- People from inside the firm, and people from outside the firm

In most companies, you will rarely find any teams that reflect this kind of diversity, particularly at a leadership level. Let's face it: if you draw a typical organizational pyramid with senior management at the top, the question is, Where in that pyramid do you usually find the least diversity when it comes to thinking about the company's future, the industry, the competition, and the customers? It would be at the top. Yet, ironically, where in that pyramid do we place almost all the responsibility for strategic innovation? It's invariably with the same set of managers (see figure 2-1).

FIGURE 2-1

Hierarchy versus diversity

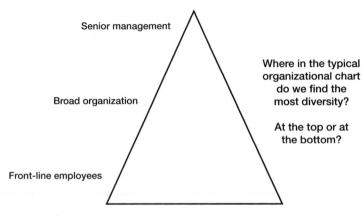

Source: Adapted from Gary Hamel.

That's one of the reasons why the ideas coming out of many organizations are as dull as dishwater—all the power for inventing the company's future is concentrated in the hands of a tiny, homogeneous elite. Often it's the very group of people that is least likely in the organization to come up with radical new thinking and rule-breaking innovations. This is one of the huge dilemmas that troubles large companies.

The Need for New Voices

New voices are essential for new thinking. When managers sit down to think about strategy and innovation, too often the people who get involved in the process are the old guard, not the vanguard. What companies need is more vanguard in the mix. Of course, corporate leaders still have a great deal to contribute. We are not by any means trying to denigrate their role. Instead, we are arguing that in today's complex and rapidly changing business environment, senior executives need to recognize how much they can learn from all the other people around them. In particular, they need to start giving a disproportionate share of voice to three constituencies that are typically underrepresented:

Young people: Or at least people with a youthful perspective. These are the folks who are living closest to the future.

Newcomers to the company: Preferably those who have worked in other industries, because more often than not, industries get reinvented by outsiders, not by veterans.

People from the geographic periphery of the organization: It's just a fact that creativity and entrepreneurial thinking increase proportionately the farther you move away from corporate headquarters.

So far, these three constituencies have mostly been disenfranchised from the strategy-making and innovation process. We believe that, henceforth, they should be overrepresented.

This is no doubt going to require a degree of humility on the part of top management, because it essentially means that senior executives will have to give up the old, elitist view about who is responsible for the destiny and direction of the organization, and start involving many new and different voices in the process of charting the company's future.

Best Buy's Brad Anderson is one CEO who understands this principle. Judge for yourself as you read how he describes a particular innovation opportunity:

> I believe that some of our best ideas have come from the people who are furthest removed from the CEO's office—those line-level employees who interact with our customers each and every day. We've got a wonderful team of eccentric people working in our Manhattan store on 44th Street and Fifth Avenue. Now, there's a large Brazilian community near the store, and the manager said, "Hey, we don't do anything to cater to them." So he hired folks who spoke the language in the store. They wound up discovering that there are cruise ships of Brazilians that come to New York City, so they contacted the travel company and found that the store was a desirable stop for them. So all of a sudden we have buses of tour groups pulling up on Sundays. If we waited for someone in Minnesota to come up with that idea, we'd still be waiting.[5]

Diversity Fuels Innovation

Still need convincing? Okay, why not try the following experiment. Get two sets of innovation teams together.

The first set of teams should be exclusively made up of seasoned senior executives, along with some of your most loyal, longtime customers and suppliers. These are people who know each other so well they can probably finish each other's sentences.

The second set of teams should contain a handful of the above, but also a few young people, one or two new recruits from different companies or industries, some people from your most far-flung subsidiaries, plus some of your coolest customers and most cutting-edge suppliers. Try to load the teams with people from widely different backgrounds, hierarchical levels, disciplines, and functions. Don't be afraid to add some nonconformists, some frustrated activists, and some people who are perhaps a little weird and eccentric. You might also want to invite some smart individuals from external companies or pioneering universities that you're interested in collaborating with. And don't forget to get a good mix of both men and women. Finally, try to ensure that 50 percent of those you invite have never been members of an innovation team before.

Now give each set of teams—the "old guard" group and the "vanguard" group—the same innovation challenge. Which one of those two sets of teams do you think has the best chance of producing the most refreshing, most radical, most rule-breaking ideas?

The notion that diverse teams of problem solvers are likely to outperform homogeneous teams is not just conjecture. Allow Scott Page, author of *The Difference: How the Power of Diversity Creates Better Groups, Firms, Schools, and Societies*, to relate the results of his experiments at the California Institute of Technology: "Diverse groups of problem solvers . . . consistently outperformed groups of the best and the brightest. If I formed two groups, one random (and therefore diverse) and one consisting of the best individual performers, the first group almost always did better."[6]

His conclusion: "Innovation . . . depends as much on collective difference as on aggregate ability." The reason this is so, explains Page, is that different individuals look at a given problem from different perspectives—and they try to solve it in different ways. Logically, the more diverse the perspectives and the approaches to problem solving (called *heuristics*) in a group, the more new thinking is brought to a problem. Thus, the less likely it is that the group will get stuck at conventional solutions. Diverse teams literally have a better chance of thinking differently, and therefore, of coming up with fresh, new answers.

Whirlpool's experience seems to confirm this. When the company was starting out on the journey to build a deep innovation capability, it made sure that its core innovation teams were populated with employees from every different level of the hierarchy, from shop floor to senior management. They mixed all kinds of different functions, some of them more customer focused, others more operations focused. They chose team members who were different in terms of experience; some were fresh to the company and even to the industry, some were dyed-in-the-wool Whirlpool people. They also made sure the team composition was mixed in terms of gender, ways of thinking, disposition, cultural background, nationality, and demographics. In short, Whirlpool created the most diverse groups of people ever assembled in the organization's history. They understood that it's the differences that create the value—that diversity fuels innovation. This made the company's innovation teams very fertile ground within which an abundant crop of new insights and ideas could flourish.

Corporate HR people also need to keep this principle in mind when formulating their recruitment strategies. Robert Sutton, Stanford University professor and author of *Weird Ideas That Work: 11½ Practices for Promoting, Managing, and Sustaining Innovation*, warns against bringing in legions of clones. His advice to companies is to hire some people "who are different" and "who make you feel uncomfortable." And he adds, "Don't force them to become 'homogenized' or be fired."[7]

Hiring people who are "different" doesn't just mean people who are different in terms of gender, race, culture, or ethnicity; it also means people who can *think different*, to borrow Apple's famous slogan.

Bringing the Outside In

Bringing a wealth of new and different voices into the innovation process includes looking outside the boundaries of your own organization. On some deep level, even the most diverse team of employees will still share the same organizational DNA. There's a moment when all that thinking going on inside the company can get a little stale and incestuous. That's why it's good to mix up the intellectual gene pool by bringing in voices from outside the organization—as well as from outside the industry—and seeding them into the innovation process.

In recent years, GE's CEO, Jeff Immelt, has made a big effort to do just this, observing that it stimulates new, nonlinear thinking and helps the company avoid an overly internal focus. As a benchmark for open innovation, Immelt used P&G, where innovation teams have long been augmented with people from all kinds of different companies and industries and where consultants like IDEO are regularly called in to help the company's innovators look at challenges with "fresh eyes from the outside."[8] P&G's much-publicized Connect and Develop program taps into a global network of external scientists, laboratories, suppliers, individual inventors, venture capitalists, and other organizations, in the search for new breakthrough ideas. Both GE and P&G understand that their companies' next killer innovation may have its origin outside the organization. That's why they are doing their best to blur the boundaries of their companies, making them porous enough to allow more and more insights and ideas to seep in from the outside and become integrated into their own innovation activities.

At Steelcase, the global office furniture giant, employees on the company's innovation teams might find themselves sitting next to an IT specialist from IBM, an architect from Foster + Partners, a designer from IDEO, a scientist from MIT, and a whole collection of other non-Steelcase/non-office furniture people like ergonomists, anthropologists, environmentalists, futurists, and management experts. This approach not only leads to more successful product innovations for the office world, it also has an interesting second-order effect. The discoveries that come out of these diverse project teams are often seeded back into other industries. For example, the insights and patented technologies that Steelcase generated for an innovative office chair called Leap were later able to help leading automotive supplier Johnson Controls Inc. (JCI) develop a revolutionary new seating product for cars. By looking for inspiration outside their own companies—and outside their own industries—both Steelcase and JCI have reaped the benefits.

"Mixing Is the New Norm"

Clearly, if you want to generate breakthrough thinking and game-changing innovation, your chances of getting it from a homogeneous group of behind-the-times senior executives are nil. Instead, you need to create a potent mix of diversity, energy, youth, and hustle.

Think about the world's most progressive, most trendsetting cities—hotbeds of coolness like New York, London, Los Angeles, and San Francisco. What do we find there? We find a rich mélange of different ethnic groups, age groups, skin colors, cultures, perspectives, experiences, and values. We find incredible diversity.

The same goes for Silicon Valley. In an article titled, "Diversity Powers Innovation," Scott Page, whom we quoted a few pages earlier, remarks, "Silicon Valley's breadth of bright engineers from different academic disciplines and from almost every corner of the globe out-innovates other technology hot spots with equal brainpower but less diversity."[9]

Indeed, think about America—arguably the most innovative nation on earth. What is America if not the ultimate melting pot, a giant "mash-up" of immigrants from everywhere on earth?

In his book, *The Global Me*, Gregg Zachary writes, "Diversity defines the health and wealth of nations in a new century . . . Mixing is the new norm . . . Mixing trumps isolation. It spawns creativity, nourishes the human spirit, spurs economic growth, and empowers nations."[10] Mixing different people, ideas, assets, and competencies has spurred new thinking and driven progress throughout history—in every civilization and in every field of human endeavor. Why shouldn't it do the same thing for your company's innovation initiatives?

Ask Yourself

- Are the innovation teams in my company noticeably more diverse in their composition than they were a year ago?

- Are we paying as much attention to "diversity of thinking" as we are to diversity of gender, race, culture, or ethnicity?

- Is my company increasing the ratio of imagination over experience in the groups that are pursuing product and strategy innovation?

- Have we put a selection process in place to ensure that young people, newcomers, and people from the edges of the organization are overrepresented in our innovation teams?

- Are we doing enough to mix up the intellectual gene pool by bringing in voices from outside the organization and outside our industry?

CONNECTION AND CONVERSATION

One of the great myths of innovation—and one that still defines the way many organizations operate—is that breakthrough ideas are produced solely by intuitive individuals or by small creative teams working in isolation. It's a myth that has long been popularized by mainstream business books and magazines, in which we usually find a single "great mind"—quite often the CEO—who is portrayed as the innovation hero: somebody who is sitting alone, staring off into space, waiting for that "eureka" moment. This view of innovation is not only erroneous, it also does us a great disservice because it creates a false understanding about the innovation process.

The reality is that whether we think of Thomas Edison, Ted Turner, Jeff Bezos, or Steve Jobs, those leaders came to important new insights because they embedded themselves in a vibrant web of connection and conversation. Their big ideas were built by interacting and networking with a rich and diverse community of people; they were not exclusively the products of their own intellectual brilliance.

In essence, innovation is about "combinational chemistry"—it's about taking ideas, half-baked notions, competencies, concepts, and assets that already sit out there and *recombining* them in ways that allow you to do interesting new things or invent entirely novel products and services. Unpack any successful innovation, and you're likely to find that it's a recombinant mix of previously existing ideas and domains. What's new in most cases is the mix itself.

As Andrew Hargadon points out in his book *How Breakthroughs Happen: The Surprising Truth About How Companies Innovate*, many of history's most famous innovations had their genesis this way.[11] Henry Ford's revolutionary assembly line, for example, was inspired by the "disassembly line" for butchering hogs that Ford had seen at Philip Armour's Chicago meatpacking company, as well as by manufacturing techniques that were already being used at the time to build Singer sewing machines or to automate canned food production at Campbell's and H. J. Heinz.

When *Star Wars* first appeared on the screen in the 1970s, George Lucas candidly admitted that it was a cocktail of plots and scenes recycled from old sci-fi stories, pirate movies, westerns, biblical epics, and war films like *The Battle of Britain*. What made it special was the powerful and unexpected concoction of these genres—a formula that has since gone on to generate an estimated $20 billion in revenue.

Another example is eBay. For many decades, we had classified advertising in newspapers. We had flea markets. We had garage sales in the United States and car boot sales in Britain. We had auctions. And then we had the Web. But it took Pierre Omidyar to see the opportunity for putting all of that together in a global, peer-to-peer, Web-based auction platform. Today, eBay has a market value in excess of $50 billion.

Or think about Apple's winning combination of iTunes and iPod. Before there was an iTunes Music Store, there was Napster. And before we had the iPod, we had flash memory, MP3 decoders, digital-to-analog converters, lithium batteries, and basically everything else inside the device. None of the essential components of the iPod are unique; they can almost be bought off the shelf. What made iPod such a winner was the way Apple combined all of those elements, infused the whole thing with classic Apple attributes—user-friendliness, cool design, and iconic branding—and then linked it to the iTunes business model.

In other words, the essence of innovation is "creative collision." Radical innovations are spawned by the interplay of different ideas and domains that don't usually belong together. And the only way to create that interplay is through connectivity and conversation. Quite simply, the more connections a company makes between individuals and their ideas, the greater the number of possibilities for combinational chemistry. Creating this rich tapestry of connection, conversation, and interaction is central to a company's ability to innovate.

David Hill, at San Francisco–based Power Decisions Group, says, "Great ideas rarely have single parents. They tend to take shape through a series of genuinely spontaneous free associations among groups of uninhibited people."[12] The issue for large companies therefore is, How do we create this level of free association and conversation on a corporate-wide scale? How do we increase the level of connection and conversation going on between business units, divisions, product groups, departments, research labs, geographies, and so forth—and outside the company with customers, suppliers, dealers, strategic partners, universities, and other constituencies?

Making Serendipity Happen

Many companies would say they value serendipity as a driver of innovation. But if serendipity, by definition, is about making fortunate discoveries by accident, then how on earth can we consciously make it happen? Golf legend Gary Player hinted at the answer when he said, "The more I practice, the luckier I get." Since serendipity springs largely from the constant juxtaposition of new voices, fresh perspectives, and contrarian views, logic tells us that the more we foster connection and conversation inside an organization—and with the world outside—the greater the odds that serendipity will happen.

If we think about the social systems or institutional structures that have proven to be most conducive to innovation—universities, cities, industry clusters like Silicon Valley, or, most recently, the Web itself— what creates the vibrancy and serendipity is the matrix of ever-changing human connection and conversation. However, in a large organization, over time, the conversational patterns tend to become etched in stone. There are fixed reporting lines, committee groups, task forces, and so forth. Companies end up having the same people talking to the same people, year after year, so they lose that conversational richness. In many ways, the organizational chart actually inhibits rather than increases the chances of making random, serendipitous connections.

Companies not only need to include new voices in the innovation and strategy-making process, they also need to *connect* those voices in new ways. Here are four ways to think about maximizing connections so as to dramatically improve the odds of serendipity happening:

1. Rethink the organization chart

2. Create an open market for ideas

3. Utilize the net to harness imagination

4. Make more time for face time

We will examine each of these issues in more detail in later chapters of this book, but for now let us briefly introduce them, along with some diagnostic questions to gauge your company's progress along these parameters.

Rethinking the Organization Chart

For decades, organization charts have reflected the outdated notion that it is impossible or even dangerous to innovate in a company's core business. This has forced innovation to live in a disconnected "silo" (e.g., R&D, new product development, Skunk Works, incubators) where it neither involves nor infects the rest of the organization. Making innovation a pervasive and corporate-wide capability calls for new structures that actively foster cross-boundary interaction and that distribute the responsibility and expertise for innovation throughout the company.

Ask Yourself

- Do we have a management infrastructure for innovation that spreads the responsibility through every level of the organization and involves everyone in the company? Or does our organization structure continue to make innovation the exclusive responsibility of specific departments or groups?

- Which steps has my company taken in the last year to maximize cross-boundary interaction and encourage previously unconnected groups to trade ideas and competencies?

- What are we doing to facilitate direct, person-to-person communication across the organization rather than up and down traditional chains of command?

Creating an Open Market for Ideas

In many companies, new ideas are in short supply—stifled by a corporate climate that cuts off intellectual oxygen, discourages change, and demands conformity. The "immune system" in such organizations tends to attack new ideas like foreign organisms that are threatening the host. The antidote: companies that want to get serious about innovation need to break the monopoly that closes off the executive suite from new ideas percolating in other corners of the company. To encourage innovation, they need to create a culture where anyone—from anywhere in the organization—can voice an idea and, if it's an interesting one, obtain fast, easy access to capital and talent for pushing that idea forward.

Ask Yourself

- Is my company building an "innovation democracy" where ideas really can come from anyone and anywhere, both inside and outside the company?

- Have we changed our management systems and processes to create an open market for ideas, based on the understanding that there are potential innovators everywhere in the company?

- Does our management truly believe, deep down, that "ordinary" employees can be a source of extraordinary innovation?

- What have we done to communicate—both in word and in deed—that everyone at our company is expected to innovate?

- If a person or a group comes up with an idea, how easy or difficult is it for them to get access to funding and top management support?

- What have we done in the last twelve months to engage the imagination, know-how, and resources of people outside our organization?

Utilizing the Net to Harness Imagination

Usually, corporate IT infrastructures end up being rather sterile tools that do nothing more than propagate simple, explicit knowledge. They usually don't play much of a useful role in facilitating the kind of cross-boundary interaction that creates *new* knowledge. Companies must learn to use IT as a global operating system for innovation, engaging tens of thousands of people throughout the organization—and millions of people beyond it—in a global, twenty-four-hour, innovation-focused dialogue. They must learn to utilize the Web not just to tap the insights, expertise, creativity, and passion of countless minds, but also to harness the combinational possibilities of all those minds networked together and interacting with one another.

Ask Yourself

- Has my company created any new forums for cross-corporate, innovation-focused dialogue/conversation in the past twenty-four months?

- Are we using our IT infrastructures to distribute the responsibility for generating new ideas throughout the organization and beyond its walls?

- Does our corporate intranet provoke innovation by inspiring people with new insights and perspectives? Does it teach people how to stretch their thinking, and show them how to initiate an innovation project?

- Could we describe our intranet as an electronic marketplace that brings ideas, capital, and talent together?

- Are the people in our company connected with a rich community of internal/external experts who can quickly help them solve innovation challenges?

- Are we making proper use of Web-based opportunities for testing new ideas in the market and gauging direct customer feedback?

- Are we using our IT infrastructure to help "unstick" opportunities and rekindle projects that seem to be going nowhere?

Making More Time for Face Time

How many opportunities do your employees usually get to interact deeply with people who work outside their own business unit, or product category, or geography—or outside your industry? Companies that want to foster innovation should think about organizing regular opportunities for large, diverse groups of people to meet face-to-face, share insights, and generate ideas together in an experiential setting. These kinds of events not only help to harness the imagination of many constituencies that are usually disenfranchised from the innovation process, but also create an appetite and an enthusiasm for innovation that can be highly infectious.

Ask Yourself

- Within the past twelve months, has every employee in my division had the opportunity to participate in some organized innovation process?
- How often does my company/division/business unit organize large, face-to-face events for knowledge sharing and collaborative ideation?
- When was the last time we invited hundreds or even thousands of our people to participate in a "live" conversation on innovation and future strategy?

In industry after industry—from computers to consumer goods to toys—all kinds of companies are waking up to the power of "connection and conversation" for driving new thinking and innovation. They are increasingly bringing people together from different backgrounds and disciplines so they can share insights and think collectively about specific challenges and opportunities. What they are coming to realize is that everyone has the potential to be an innovator—to play a role in the creation of radical ideas and exciting new solutions that could potentially influence the destiny of the company. They are learning to view their organization (and the world outside it) as a reservoir of skills, assets, experiences, disciplines, and perspectives—all of which can be combined and recombined to invent hitherto undreamed-of business innovations.

IS THAT ALL THERE IS TO IT?

Creating bandwidth. Maximizing diversity. Connection and conversation. These are critical preconditions for spurring innovation. But is that all there is to enhancing a company's innovation capability? Is the challenge merely to give employees 15 percent of their time to spend on pet projects, invite a rich mixture of different people to join the innovation effort, and ensure that a lot of interaction and collaboration is going on, both internally and externally? Not if a company really wants to get serious about building a high-performance innovation system.

The truth is, you can bring diverse people together, you can give them time and space, you can have them connect and converse, and hope that they produce some new ideas, but if those people are starting with the same old data, the same old orthodoxies and the same old perspectives, you will never get anything very radical coming out of the other end. Asking people to innovate in a breakthrough way without first building a foundation of novel strategic insights is mostly a waste of time. As our colleague Gary Hamel often puts it, "You end up grinding the same old grist through the same old mill and will inevitably get the same old bread."[13]

The fact is that in order to discover new and unexploited opportunities of any real value, people need to stretch their thinking beyond the conventional. They need to develop fresh perspectives. They need to dig deep to discover insights that others have overlooked or ignored. They need to learn how to look at the world, at their industry, at their customers, and at their company through a very different set of "lenses."

In chapter 3, we present four particular kinds of "perceptual lenses" that, in our experience, are critical to finding opportunities for breakthrough innovation.

INNOVATION CHALLENGES AND LEADERSHIP IMPERATIVES

Innovation challenge: Has your organization reached the stage at which many or all of your colleagues believe that innovation is part of their job?

Leadership Imperatives

- Ensure that all managers—or at least those under your direction—have an explicit, measurable innovation goal as part of their annual performance.

- Put mechanisms in place to provide time for employees to innovate. Hold managers accountable for helping employees find time during their normal work hours for innovation.

- Create an organizational infrastructure that spreads innovation responsibility through every level and every department (more on this in chapter 11).

- Make innovation training a priority. Create the programs to teach everyone the skills and tools of innovation. Recruit the veterans from these programs as teachers and mentors for new innovators.

Innovation challenge: Are you taking full advantage of the diverse talents of your internal organization—and the broader markets in which you compete?

Leadership Imperatives

- When you are organizing a formal or ad hoc innovation effort, consciously staff the team with a genetically diverse group of people—different backgrounds, organizational levels, and work experiences.

- Provide mechanisms, both virtual and face-to-face, to solicit ideas from anywhere, both inside and outside the company.

- Deploy simple IT-based tools and platforms, making it easier to broaden your pool of potential innovators.

- Create or extend a network of external innovators—relevant to your key strategic challenges.

CHAPTER 3

Building a Foundation of Novel Strategic Insights

S TEVE JOBS. RICHARD BRANSON. Bill Gates. James Dyson. Michael Dell. Brilliant innovators and entrepreneurs all. These are individuals for whom, it seems, innovation and wealth creation came naturally, almost "reflexively," as Gary Hamel would put it.[1] The conventional view is that innovation is the exclusive province of creative geniuses and business leaders like these—people who are somehow "wired" differently from the rest of us, making them capable of innovating in ways that mere mortals, or ordinary companies—cannot possibly hope to match.

Clearly, intuition and creative ingenuity—as well as happenstance—may unquestionably be part of the innovation equation. But what if we could unpack the discovery process much more precisely by getting inside the mind of the innovator? What if we could open up that mysterious "black box" and take a good look at how it works? What if we could find out how radical innovators come up with their breakthrough ideas; how they spot those big, strategic opportunities that are invisible to others; how they seem to have an intuitive feel for the way in which the world will be (or should be) different, whereas others do not? Most importantly, what if we could actually reverse engineer this process—allowing us to turn the enigmatic into the systematic?

This chapter reveals the answers to these questions. It describes how organizations—not just highly gifted individuals—may become perpetual innovators by learning how to discover novel insights that others have missed.

THE FOUR "LENSES" OF INNOVATION

If one looks deeply at hundreds of examples of business innovation, an interesting pattern begins to emerge. Specifically, what we find is that, time and again, innovation came not from some inherent, individual brilliance but from looking at the world from *a fresh perspective*—if you will, through a different set of "lenses." It came from an alternative way of seeing things: a particular angle of view that enabled the innovators to look through the familiar and spot the unseen. In fact, four essential perspectives—four "perceptual lenses"—seem to dominate most successful innovation stories and often characterize the entrepreneurs or companies behind them.

In case after case, we find that the innovators came to their insights by:

1. *Challenging orthodoxies:* Questioning deeply held dogmas inside companies and inside industries about what drives success

2. *Harnessing discontinuities:* Spotting unnoticed patterns of trends that could substantially change the rules of the game

3. *Leveraging competencies and strategic assets:* Thinking of a company as a portfolio of skills and assets rather than as a provider of products or services for specific markets

4. *Understanding unarticulated needs:* Learning to live inside the customer's skin, empathizing with unarticulated feelings and identifying unmet needs

Here's the big news: building an innovation capability has less to do with increasing personal creativity—long the accepted wisdom—and more to do with assembling the right sorts of insights (from the four lenses listed above) to provoke a business breakthrough.

In this chapter, we will look in more detail at the four discovery lenses and describe how innovators have used them to uncover new insights and opportunities. We will also describe hands-on tools and techniques—for each lens—that can be used by your company's own innovation teams to generate powerful strategic insights. By powerful, we mean insights with the potential to open up *significant* new opportunities for innovation. Toward the end of this chapter, we provide some specific criteria for evaluating the quality of prospective insights.

CHALLENGING ORTHODOXIES

The first thing one discovers about radical innovators is that they are, almost by definition, contrarians. They are people who take some piece of conventional thinking—that everybody in the industry has accepted as absolute gospel—and turn it completely on its head.

For example, the people at IKEA asked, "Why does home furniture have to be delivered custom-made and fully assembled? Why can't we create standardized products that customers can pick up and assemble themselves?" The people at Dell asked, "Why do computer companies need a huge network of dealers to sell their PCs? And why do they manage their own inventory when they could let their suppliers do it?" The people at Charles Schwab asked, "Why do equities have to be traded through high-commissioned brokers? Why can't it simply be done online?" And the folks at Southwest Airlines asked a series of contrarian questions that were not only about dramatically lowering the

Orthodoxies:

Deeply held and broadly shared conventions about what drives success within a company or an industry price of flying, but about dramatically changing the airline industry's traditional business model. For example:

- Why does an airline need a "hub and spokes" route system? What if we could run point-to-point flights instead, keeping the airplane in the air for longer and passing on the efficiencies to the customer?

- Why do airlines need a complicated and ever-changing fare structure, with a choice between business class and economy class? Why can't we just offer one-class seating and make the whole thing simple and straightforward?

- Why does an airline need a fleet of different aircraft? What if we could run an airline with just one type of plane?

- Why is stealing other airlines' passengers the only way to compete in the airline industry? What if we could attract people who are currently taking the bus or train, or driving?

Innovators are people who are willing to challenge industry orthodoxies that are so big, so uncontestable, and so deeply embedded that they have become beyond discussion—orthodoxies that blind industry incumbents to the possibility of any other business model. Time and again, the strategy innovations that radically change customer expectations, or competitive rules, or industry structures, come from questioning beliefs that everyone else has taken for granted.

Orthodoxies are about mind-sets—how we have conditioned ourselves to perceive, to filter, to respond. They tend to become embedded in the way a company or industry does business, forming the dominant logic about the "right" way to compete, price, organize, market, and develop products and services. Orthodoxies are not by definition "bad" or necessarily *wrong*. In fact, they are often essential for creating a common understanding across a dispersed organization, allowing teams to work together smoothly and efficiently. The problem starts when their usefulness has eroded and they start to stifle rather than foster progress. Orthodoxies are potentially limiting if a company can't see beyond or around them. If left unchallenged, they may blind the organization to new opportunities for creating wealth. In too many cases, success turns "one way" of doing business into "*the* way," at least in the minds of senior executives—and this opens up opportunities for innovative challengers.

Don't Follow the Leader

Let's imagine that your company competes in an industry that has a strong, deeply entrenched leader. What would be your strategy for attacking and undermining the leader's position? For example, how would you go up against a giant like Microsoft in the software business? Not by trying to compete head-to-head—we all know what happened to Netscape, Lotus Notes, IBM's rival operating system OS/2, and a whole list of other hopefuls. The only way to undermine Microsoft's powerful position is by challenging the company's *orthodoxies*—as Google and Linux have managed to do.

For years, Microsoft has organized and managed itself around a particular orthodoxy about how to develop and sell software—that is, create very complex programs with millions of lines of code and then deliver them to the customer in shrink-wrapped boxes under license. This business model is obviously not *wrong*—after all, Microsoft has used it to dominate the software industry for several decades, creating tremendous wealth for shareholders. Well done, indeed. But the evolution of the software industry did not stop with the creation of Microsoft's legacy business model. Consider, for example, how Google has challenged one of Microsoft's fundamental orthodoxies by making software that is delivered through Web-based services rather than in packages you pick up in a computer store.

Historically, Microsoft has tried to make all of its software programs work together in a tightly integrated way, with the Windows operating system as the glue that holds everything together. What this creates is an impossibly large knot of interoperating programs, which is why it took Microsoft's massive army of programmers about half a decade to build Vista—the latest version of Windows. In fact, after years of delays and colossal development budgets, Microsoft still had to omit some of Vista's promised features (unfortunately, the most revolutionary ones) to get it out the door at all. Since all of Microsoft's software has to be interdependent and backward-compatible, successive upgrades present ever more complex programming problems as product groups struggle to mesh their software strategies together. Google, on the other hand, has overturned this "integrated software" paradigm by making each of its services independently accessible via your browser. This has taken a huge amount of complexity out of the software development process.

Then there are the updates. If you're a Windows user and you want to use the latest version of a particular program, you continually have to buy software updates from Microsoft—which is a huge revenue source for the company. By contrast, any update to a Google Web-based service is available to users instantly, as soon as they power up their browser.

Microsoft's core business model is essentially based on selling software. Google, on the other hand, makes its money through a self-reinforcing network of connections: advertisers who pay for space and click-throughs, and users who enjoy the simplicity of Google searches. Further, Google's free search software captures valuable attention that advertisers are willing to pay big money for. Today, Google's programs—like the Google Toolbar for Web and PC search—are installed as standard on Dell computers, and there is even talk of a Google browser. This is a direct threat to the margins Microsoft earns from Windows and from its Office productivity suite, one reason why the company has been investing billions of dollars to make the shift into online advertising. In an attempt to steal ad revenues from Google, CEO Steve Ballmer says he aims to make digital advertising account for 25 percent of Microsoft's business within a few years.[2]

Another big challenge to Microsoft's orthodoxies is Linux. Whereas Microsoft develops software in-house with legions of paid employees, Linux is an open-source platform based on a global network of impassioned volunteers. And instead of selling software under a proprietary license that doesn't allow users to change any of the source code, Linux has created a "general public license" that allows any user to change the source code as long as those changes are made available to the broader community of users.

For many years, Microsoft's orthodoxy regarding software development was that "software needed to be built like cathedrals, carefully crafted by individual wizards or small bands of mages working in splendid isolation." But, according to Eric Raymond, author of *The Cathedral & the Bazaar*, "Linux is subversive, resembling a bazaar of different agendas and approaches."[3]

Between them, Google and Linux have slaughtered a whole herd of sacred cows about what drives success in the software industry—which, paradoxically, is exactly what has helped them become so popular.

Doing the Opposite

Look at other industries, and the pattern is often the same. The companies that are radically reinventing customer expectations and creating most of the new wealth are invariably the industry *challengers*—those willing to question deeply held dogmas and to be contrarian.

Consider the food industry, for example, where innovative companies like Whole Foods Market, Odwalla, VitaWater, and Fresh Express have chosen to go in exactly the opposite direction to the big global food companies. Instead of "convenience and value," their strategy is "nutrition and authenticity"—they charge a premium for fresh, natural food that's sourced locally, and they let consumers "discover" them rather than promote themselves as global brands. They are companies that have had the courage to turn industry orthodoxies upside down. No wonder some of them have since been snapped up by the very firms they challenged—Coca-Cola now owns Odwalla and VitaWater, and Chiquita owns Fresh Express.

Exploring and challenging orthodoxies—overturning conventional beliefs about what drives success in your company and your industry—is a key way to surface opportunities for profitable innovation and growth. It's a lens that allows you to discover possibilities for new industry rules, new structures, new offerings, and new competitive space.

Getting Started

Are you ready to be a corporate rebel? If you want to start using the first lens of innovation—challenging orthodoxies—your assignment will be to question the deeply held dogmas in your company and your industry, to spot the absurdities that no one else has spotted, and to ask the stupid questions that no one else has asked.

The goal of this exercise is to lead a brave rebellion against the stranglehold of conventional thinking—to identify and challenge any industry practice that is justified by nothing more than precedent, and to discard the mental models that prevent people in your organization from imagining the kind of unorthodox strategies that outperform industry averages.

Identifying Orthodoxies

Now that we have defined what orthodoxies are, how do we actually go about identifying them? The following four approaches are ways that we use to help companies think about where and how to look for orthodoxies. We have found them very useful as a starting platform—for both groups and individuals—when trying to think about where orthodoxies might exist in a company or an industry.

1. *Surfacing the dogmas:* Identifying common assumptions (such as "Price is the key variable" or "This particular customer group is the key segment") as well as convergent industry strategies (business models that are basically indistinguishable in terms of value proposition, supply chain, product configuration, pricing, marketing strategy, and so on).

    Ask yourself why these commonalities exist. Are they due to some fundamental law of economics? Or are most industry players simply hostage to the same deeply entrenched beliefs? Think about what would happen if you reversed these common assumptions and industry strategies. Could you imagine alternative ways of doing things? If so, what new opportunities would present themselves? How would customers benefit?

2. *Finding the absurdities:* Looking for things that companies or industries do almost habitually every day that are "absurd" when seen through the eyes of customers.

Step back and think about the annoyances, frustrations, and inconveniences that are unwittingly being foisted on your customers for the sake of the company's own convenience.

In most industries, there are a lot of these "absurdities"— some of them are rather small, but even the little things present opportunities for innovation. Take the hotel industry. Why do the hangers in hotel closets have that stupid little ring system to prevent you from stealing them? Why not just charge guests for the hangers they take—and have the person who checks the minibar also look in the closet? That way, hotels could even turn the closet into a profit center! Or why is it that even if you check in to a hotel at midnight, you still have to check out the next day by noon? Why can't you just pay for the room for twenty-four hours, the same way you would rent a car from, say, Hertz or Avis?

The point of this exercise is to learn how to recognize these nonsensical things and to look for solutions. The fact that most absurdities are "hidden" to industry insiders reflects the fact that many of these people are not thinking creatively about how to make life easier for their customers. They are not thinking about how to reinvent their business model from the customers backward—in every respect.

3. *Going to extremes:* Taking widely accepted industry norms and asking what would happen if we pushed them to a ridiculous limit.

Innovators who create sustainable disruptions tend to be those who go to extremes. Take Amazon.com. Back in the early 1990s, you could go to a big, bricks-and-mortar bookstore like Barnes & Noble or Borders and expect to get access to about 250,000 titles, which still sounds like a lot of books. But when Jeff Bezos set out to create his online business, he wasn't thinking in terms of offering 275,000 to 300,000 titles—or 10 to 20 percent more books than traditional bookstores. His concept was to give Amazon's customers access to about 2.5 *million* titles. Now that's going to extremes.

Unfortunately, most of us never think about taking things to these seemingly ridiculous extremes—we just accept them as they are. We continue to operate in a narrowly bounded space of possibility because we don't explore the outer limits of what is possible.

As an intellectual exercise, try looking at any common performance parameter like, say, price, efficiency, or speed of services, and then ask yourself what would happen if you *dramatically* improved it. Consider how you might change that parameter not by x or $1x$, but by $10x$, or $50x$, or $100x$. If you did that, how would customers benefit?

4. *Searching for the* and: Looking for situations where the customer faces a trade-off, and thinking about how to resolve it.

   Quite often, customers are told that they can *either* have this *or* have that—but they can't have both. What if you found a way to give customers both things at the same time? Think about diet soda, low-calorie foods, decaffeinated coffee, alcohol-free beer, and so forth. All of these products allowed consumers to avoid making comprises and trade-offs that, given an alternative, they would otherwise not make.

   There are many more examples. Toyota reinvented the rules in the car industry by offering both low cost *and* high quality in an automobile. In the United States, Costco has done something similar in retail, by offering low cost *and* great, high-end products. Companies like Zara and H&M (and, these days, even Target) sell highly fashionable clothing at relatively inexpensive prices. And Southwest Airlines showed us that we could have a low-priced air ticket *and* extremely high quality, *and* more convenience, *and* a whole lot more fun.

   What would happen if you turned an *either/or* into an *and*? For example, search for situations where the customer is getting a benefit on the one hand but simultaneously losing out somewhere else, and try to take the negative out of the equation. Ask yourself how you could turn a win-lose situation into a win-win.

This exercise teaches you that whenever you hear the word *or*, it's an invitation to innovate.

HARNESSING DISCONTINUITIES

Radical innovators are not forecasters or scenario planners. They are not people who are trying to predict the future or imagine how the world might be ten years from now. Instead, they tend to be people who are aware—on some deep level—of things that are already fundamentally changing, and who understand the revolutionary portent in those things, in ways that others do not. They intuitively grasp, as renowned futurist John Naisbitt puts it, that "the future is embedded in the present."[4]

Revolutionary strategies often harness some deep, systemic change force. For example, it might be digitization (Google News), or globalization (the international expansion of MTV over the past several decades), or the rise of extreme sports (the invention of a new super-high-flying pogo stick). The goal is to surf one of these "tides of history"—to exploit some trend that is gathering force and speed around the world.

So, what exactly is a "discontinuity"? It is not a single trend, invention, or technology. Rather, it's a *convergence* or *pattern* of trends; a confluence of several, apparently unrelated developments in, for example, technology, demographics, lifestyle, regulation, geopolitics, and so forth, that together create the potential for dramatic industry change. It's these deep discontinuities—these *clusters of trends*, as opposed to individual trends—that have the power to substantially change the competitive rules, or

Discontinuity

A pattern of trends that has the potential to dramatically change competitive rules or industry structures, opening up substantial new opportunities the structure of an industry. They are often the launching pad for radical innovation.

We usually phrase discontinuities as "from-to" statements to reflect the seismic shift they point to in consumer needs, or lifestyles, or industry climates, and so forth.

Can You Find the Bigger Story?

Let's take an example. Here are four seemingly unrelated trends that likely are common to every developed country today:

- People are working longer hours than they used to.

- The number of single-parent families is steadily increasing.

- People are getting married later in life.

- People are spending more and more time online.

Ask Yourself

- Where is the intersection between these trends? When you put them together, what is the bigger story that emerges?

The bigger story here is increasing *social isolation*. People used to meet somebody at college and get married quite young. Now they tend to delay getting married, choosing instead to pursue a career that puts them under a lot of pressure to work longer and longer hours. That means they have less time for hanging out and dating.

What we end up with is a lot of single people, some of whom are also parents, who are incredibly busy and who are coming home from work exhausted. They have very little time for themselves, and when they get an hour or two to spare, they increasingly tend to spend it online—sitting by themselves in front of a computer screen. In other words, we have more and more young adults with less and less "social time" and fewer and fewer opportunities to explore relationships. That's what Robert Putnam's book *Bowling Alone: The Collapse and Revival of American Community* is all about.[5]

So if social isolation is the theme that emerges from the interaction of these trends, what sorts of opportunities does that create? One of the huge opportunities is Web-based social networking.

Take the popular community site Craigslist. Founder Craig Newmark created a marketplace that brings together people who have mutual interests. Let's say you've decided that this weekend you want to go cycling in the Santa Cruz Mountains or wine tasting in Napa Valley. You could go online to www.craigslist.com and ask whether anybody out there wants to join you. That's basically how it started in the 1990s, and since then, Craigslist has grown into a hugely successful service in the United States, offering everything from local events to classified advertising, forums for jobs and housing, and the AdultFriendFinder, an online dating service. All these things are designed to match people's interests and activities so they can find ways to connect with one another.

It's also no surprise that online dating itself is now one of the most profitable businesses on the Web. Look at the millions of unique visitors per month to Web sites like Match.com, FriendFinder.com, eHarmony .com, Lavalife.com, AmericanSingles.com, Plentyoffish.com, Matchmaker .com, and Yahoo! Personals. Clearly, social isolation has opened up a very big opportunity for "love online." As a discontinuity, this might be phrased as "from love at first sight to love at first byte." Business built on Web-enabled social networking is what future thinker Peter Schwartz would describe as "an inevitable surprise."[6] You could see it coming—if you had the lens.

This example shows the importance of understanding and harnessing discontinuities—the intersection points between various individual trends—that have the power to create dramatic change or disruption. Looking at the world through this lens can open up significant opportunities for industry revolution.

Getting Started

Ready to start using the second lens of innovation—harnessing discontinuities? If so, forget about grand corporate visions of the future. Instead, focus on identifying changes in the external environment that competitors have either underestimated or ignored, and then try to understand how the momentum of these changes can be influenced or amplified to shape the future.

Your goal is to recognize patterns of change (at the intersections of technological change, sociodemographic change, political change, economic change, lifestyle change, etc.) that could drastically alter the current rules of competition and potentially create new opportunities—if you act on them before others do.

Identifying Discontinuities

Here are some general guidelines you may want to use when searching for discontinuities.

The first thing to remember is that everyone has access to the same information about what is changing in the world. How, then, can you construct proprietary insights out of publicly available data? The way you do that is by:

1. Looking where your competitors are not

2. Amplifying weak signals to anticipate their second- and third-order consequences

3. Trying to understand trends in their historical context

4. Looking for interactions between trends

Let us consider each of these approaches.

1. Looking where your competitors are not

Ask yourself, Where is the bleeding edge? Where is the fringe? Where could we go to get some firsthand experience of technological changes, lifestyle changes, sociodemographic changes, and so forth? Where could we go to get those inspiring bursts of insight that trigger innovative new ideas?

You won't get these kinds of insights from business magazines, or market research, or trend forecasters, or management consultants, or from a colleague's warmed-over report. These are all channels through which reality gets filtered to us, which makes it very difficult for us to see the deeper meaning. You also won't develop these kinds of insights by staring out the window and trying to think creatively. The only way to get them is by personally experiencing new and inspiring things in out-of-the-ordinary places. That's when the learning goes from intellectual to visceral, and people start to say, "Okay, this is real. This is going to happen. We need to get in front of this thing." It's very hard to ignore something once you have experienced it for yourself.

For example, mobile phone giant Nokia began to take note, back in the early 1990s, of the emergence of a global youth culture. Instead of simply reading about it in trend reports, the company decided to send a group of engineers out into the field to observe it "firsthand" in some of the world's trendiest youth hot spots: Venice Beach in California, King's Road in London, and the club scene in Tokyo's Roppongi district. As a result, those engineers came back to Finland with new insights that helped Nokia reinvent the whole concept of the cell phone, rapidly pushing the company to the cutting edge of the industry.

Another example is Best Buy, the largest consumer electronics retailer in the United States. To learn more about the future, the company decided to look in some unusual places where they had never looked before. One of those places was South Korea, where on every corner you find what is called a *Baang*—somewhere people go to play video games socially, which is a very popular pastime in Korea. Visiting those *Baangs* helped to inspire Best Buy with innovative new strategies aimed at tech-savvy youngsters and early adopters—people who like to keep up with the bleeding edge of gaming and electronics. Strategies like these are vital if Best Buy wants to stay ahead of rival retailers like Circuit City or even Wal-Mart and Target.

In the case of both Nokia and Best Buy, it was not about discovering things that were invisible to competitors—all of these insights were "hidden in plain sight," so to speak.[7] The issue was that they were looking in places where they would never even *meet* their competitors—places where change was happening first.

2. Amplifying weak signals

Time and time again, what starts out as some seemingly insignificant development will eventually turn into a major discontinuity—one that threatens old business models and opens up opportunities for exciting new ones. However, instead of amplifying these "weak signals" and asking where they might lead, companies usually discount them. Their reasoning tends to be, "Right now, it's just this little, tiny thing, so why should we bother about it?"

What you need to do is take these incipient trends—these things that are changing in perhaps a very minor way at first—and exaggerate them, projecting them out into the future. Play an imaginary game of "scale-up," asking yourself what would happen if a particular trend grew and became more important. What kind of difference would it make? What are the second- or third-order consequences of this trend? Who would be affected by these consequences?

The point is that, to some extent, a lot of developments are inevitable. They are clearly going to come. But the time to start figuring out where they are leading is at their nascent stage, not when they are already upon you and beginning to undermine your business.

3. Understanding the context

When you spot a trend, or even just the beginnings of a trend, how can you tell whether it's important or unimportant? How do you know whether it's just a ripple in the ocean or the first sign of an oncoming tsunami? One thing you can do is step back, look at that trend in its historical context, and ask yourself, Is this just a random event, or is it a tide of history? In other words, is this trend something superficial and isolated, or is it actually part of a development that has far greater magnitude and much broader implications?

4. Finding the interactions

One of the problems we all face today is information overload. There are simply too many things happening—too many different pieces of information—and we can't see the connections between them.

Once you have built a comprehensive library of trends from many different categories—facts and data, if you will—your key analytical task is to imagine how these trends might interact and reinforce each other. What you need to figure out is whether certain trends fit together in some way.

To do this, look for the intersections—the interactions *between* all the isolated facts and trends—and see whether you can spot the emerging patterns, as well as the opportunities those patterns may create. Ask yourself, When this group of trends or that group of trends is put together, what is the bigger story that emerges? Does this set of trends point toward an inevitability?

As an example, look at the following set of trends:

- Experienced older workers looking to reskill and renew

- Interest in alternative medicines, naturalistic or holistic

- Search for spirituality, balance, or quality of life

- Shift to information or knowledge economy

- Cheaper or better communication

- Ability and desire to look younger or stay young due to medical advances

- Fewer births (people are having fewer children in developed countries)

- Aging but increasingly active population

- Declining savings rates

Ask yourself, What is the overarching theme here? One possible theme is that future senior citizens will redefine the senior citizen lifestyle. We could express this theme in a succinct and catchy statement like "from aging with grace to aging with energy."

LEVERAGING COMPETENCIES AND ASSETS

Radical innovators tend to view their companies not as business units or organization charts, but as portfolios of competencies and strategic

Core competence:

A unique (or rare) bundle of skills, knowledge, and experience that delivers a valued customer benefit and competitive differentiation

---

assets. Usually, it's difficult to see things like skills, processes, technologies, assets, and values as distinct, stand-alone entities because they are completely embedded in a company's current business model. But radical innovators have the ability to decouple particular skills and assets from the existing business and then leverage them in their own right to generate growth opportunities.

Take Disney. Most people would have looked at the company's theme parks as just a business unit, and that would have been that. Not the folks at Disney. They were able to see that those theme parks actually made the company the world's largest producer of what they call "three-dimensional entertainment." They realized they had a unique set of skills and capabilities in set building, costume design, storytelling, and performing arts. So what if they could take that core competence in live, lavish entertainment and actually separate it from the theme parks? Where else could they apply it? What if they used it in a new and different context, in combination with some of the company's strategic assets—like the stories and characters from Disney's popular movies as well as the Disney brand itself? What, for example, if they took that core competence to Broadway or to London's West End and turned a Disney movie into a stage musical? Enter *Beauty and the Beast, The Lion King, Aida*, and so on—some of the most successful theater productions of all time. Disney Theatrical Productions, which was only

Strategic asset:

A corporate possession that is difficult to imitate, develop, or acquire and that provides a basis for competitive advantage

---

formed in 1994, has gone on to win a string of Tony Awards and Gram-mys and is now a hugely profitable operation with productions playing all over the world.

Or consider ESPN. How did the company manage to transform what was originally a small, twenty-four-hour sports channel on cable televi-sion into one of the most powerful marketing empires in U.S. history and the world's largest distributor of sports information? It was pre-cisely by refusing to think of itself as merely a television channel. In-stead of accepting this narrow self-image, ESPN's leaders looked for ways to leverage the company's competencies (delivering sports cover-age) and assets (the ESPN brand) in all kinds of new ways, constantly stretching their definition of the business. Their vision was to build an omnipotent sports network. Thus, ESPN now has more than eight tele-vision channels, America's largest sports radio network, a biweekly magazine with a circulation pushing 2 million, lucrative licensing agreements for video games, one of the most popular Web sites in the United States, its own sports competitions and awards, a string of inno-vative programming concepts and movies, and a national chain of sports-themed restaurants. The company's annual revenues, which al-ready top $4 billion, are expected to grow to almost $7 billion by 2010.

This ability to leverage competencies and strategic assets in new ways or new settings serves to multiply the profit-making potential of these resources. Take Crest Whitestrips, P&G's popular teeth-whitening product. It was born out of the interaction between various competen-cies and assets inside the company—from the oral care unit (dental prod-ucts), the family care unit (substrate technology), and the fabric and home care unit (hydrogen peroxide bleaching).

The fact is, radical innovators tend to think of the *whole world* as a Lego kit of different competencies and strategic assets, owned by differ-ent companies, which can potentially be reconnected like building blocks or used in a new context to invent novel products, processes, services, and business models.

To illustrate the point, pretty much every Web-based business today is an example of "recombination." Take any e-commerce Web site, and you will probably find that the online merchant buys its credit clearance process from one company, another company runs its servers, another company provides the mapping service that helps customers locate physical stores, another company provides the software for searching the site, PayPal does all the money transfers, and a company like UPS or FedEx provides the shipping and the integrated package-tracking software. These capabilities are taken from a lot of different places and then seamlessly stitched together to deliver a particular type of value to the customer. It's a plug-and-play model that is rapidly bringing down the cost of new business creation, not just for Web-based companies but also for a new breed of "manufacturers."

Consider KEEN Footwear—a fashionable new kid on the block, based in Alameda, California. The company was founded in 2003 with nothing more than a big ambition and a now-patented toe protection technology. Using freelance shoe designers to provide the styling and manufacturing specs, two Chinese factories to make the shoes, and blog-based publicity to promote the brand, KEEN Footwear managed to go from nowhere to stealing sales from Nike in less than sixty days. To put this in context, it typically takes a traditional footwear brand about ten months to develop a new range of shoes. KEEN built its whole company and launched sixteen styles of shoes in just two months. It sold around $30 million worth of shoes—that's about seven hundred thousand pairs—in its first year, and its shoes are now available in retail locations all over the world. The lesson is clear: today's start-ups can effectively be born "full-size" by quickly and cheaply outsourcing everything from design, prototyping, and manufacturing to logistics, billing, sales, and support.

This, then, is the third perceptual lens used by radical innovators: the ability to see their own company—and the entire world—as a reservoir of competencies and strategic assets that can be recombined in different ways and used in different settings to create new value.

Getting Started

Your first task with this lens is to try to reconceive your company as a portfolio of embedded resources—core competencies and strategic assets—that can be recombined or leveraged in their own right to create wealth in interesting new ways.

This task is not as easy as it sounds. Why? Because most companies define themselves by what they *do* rather than by what they *know* or what they *own*. The tendency is to develop a self-image that locks up the organization's skills and assets inside a particular definition of the business.

Let's make the distinction clear. By core competencies we mean things that a company *knows how to do uniquely well*—its skills and unique capabilities. By *strategic assets*, we mean things that a company *owns*—brands, patents, infrastructure, customer database, proprietary standards, and anything else that is both rare and valuable.

Take Apple. Fundamental to the company's success in this decade has been the ability to look at itself not merely as a maker of personal computers but as a pioneer in cutting-edge, consumer-friendly technology. Making a move into MP3 players (iPod), online music and movie distribution (iTunes), and mobile telephony (iPhone) could easily have been construed as way "out of scope." But Apple's elastic definition of its own business made it possible to stretch into these new fields, harnessing the company's competencies (design excellence, user-friendliness) and assets (a brand name with cult status) to open up huge new opportunities in consumer electronics.

Or take Google. It started life as a search engine, but now it's a whole range of different Web-based services, and new ones seem to get added every week. This has only been possible by viewing Google's underlying software code as a powerful strategic asset that can be leveraged in a myriad of ways.

This principle—stretching the way you define your business; thinking of it in terms of what your company knows and what it owns rather than what it does—may sound fairly straightforward, but in our experience it is typically the hardest of the four discovery lenses for a company to work with.

Identifying Core Competencies

What exactly is a core competence? We define a *core competence* as a bundle of skills, technologies, processes, and values that has become part of the fabric of the company, and is difficult for others to copy. Good examples would be MTV's ability to understand Gen Y tastes, or Nike's ability to create emotional bonds between individuals and athletes. As a useful exercise, we usually express competencies as "the ability to . . . (do a particular thing uniquely well)."

It's important for a company to distinguish between core competencies and mere strengths. Unfortunately, since the notion of core competence was first introduced by Gary Hamel and C. K. Prahalad in 1990, the phrase seems to have taken on a life of its own.[8] Many executives we speak with will explain how their company has a core competence at market research (usually if we are talking to the vice president of marketing), or at logistics (if our interviewee is the head of that function), or at managing human assets (you can guess who that one usually comes from). We then ask them if they are as good as P&G or Kraft at market research. Or as good as FedEx or UPS at logistics. Or as good as GE or IBM at human resources management. We usually get an embarrassed "No, but . . ."

Here's what you have to keep in mind: the goal is not just to list your company's strengths—it is to identify *unique* strengths. To qualify as core competencies, those strengths have to meet the following five criteria:

Core Competencies

1. Create value for the customer

2. Are unique or at least scarce (at a minimum in your company's industry, and better yet, in the world)

3. Are sustainable over a significant period of time

4. Are important to the company's position today

5. Can be leveraged into new products, markets, or businesses

The third attribute in this list (sustainability) is particularly important and often overlooked. For a strength to be a true core competence, it needs to be *sustainable* for some period of time. In other words, your competitors shouldn't be able to copy it just by hiring away one or two of your employees or adopting a particular process that you use.

This doesn't mean that core competencies are static. Sometimes a core competence can deteriorate over the years. For example, FedEx's core competence was its ability to route and deliver overnight packages reliably.

This capability clearly created value for FedEx's customers, it was differentiated (FedEx was the only company able to do it), it was sustainable at least for a time (think of the investment others had to make in planes, trucks, sorting centers, information technology, and people in order to duplicate it), and it was central to the company's competitive position. But while FedEx still routes and delivers packages overnight reliably, today this competence is no longer "core" because others, such as UPS, DHL, and Airborne, have finally caught up.

A similar situation exists for CNN, whose core competence was once its ability to deliver live news from anywhere in the world at any time—a capability that other TV channels eventually copied, but only after awhile.

Clearly, then, core competencies have to be managed. Organizations need to continually invest in them—to maintain and enhance them in the face of competitive attacks.

Once you have listed some candidates for your company's unique strengths (be they technologies, processes, or skills), carefully compare each of them again with the five criteria for core competencies that we listed earlier. Apply these criteria stringently, and make sure you can state the evidence of why a candidate meets the criteria. Don't be alarmed if you come up with very few core competencies. It is a high bar, and in our experience, most companies really have only one to three true core competencies.

Having finalized your list of core competencies, begin thinking about your company's strategic assets.

Identifying Strategic Assets

There are many different kinds of strategic assets. For example, here are five categories that you could consider:

Strategic Assets

1. *Input assets:* Access to suppliers, supplier loyalty, financial capacity

2. *Process assets:* Proprietary technology, standards, functional expertise, infrastructure

3. *Channel assets:* Access to distributors, distributor loyalty, distribution networks

4. *Customer assets:* Customer information, customer loyalty, brand recognition

5. *Market knowledge assets:* Understanding of customer, competitor, and supplier behavior

Using these five categories, ask yourself:

- What assets does our company possess that are (a) rare, (b) valuable to customers, (c) transferable to new opportunities?

- Could we exploit our strategic assets in new ways to bring new value to customers?

- Could our strategic assets be valuable in other industry settings?

- Can we build new business models that exploit our existing strategic assets—that is, can we imagine alternate uses for our strategic assets?

These questions should help you appreciate strategic assets that may so far have been underleveraged or simply taken for granted inside your company because they have never been considered in this context before. Your aim should be to identify a comprehensive list of strategic assets (i.e., brands, patents, technologies, and so forth) that have the potential to be leveraged in new ways.

Borrowing Competencies and Assets

In the spirit of open innovation, some of the biggest opportunities can come from bundling your company's competencies and assets with those of other companies to produce radical new solutions. Take Procter & Gamble. Over the last few years, P&G has teamed up with a whole list of external partner organizations as well as individual inventors to bring a slew of product innovations to the market. For example, one of P&G's strategic assets is the Crest brand in oral care. It used to stand just for toothpaste. Now we find the Crest brand name on such things as Teflon-coated Glide dental floss (developed by W. L. Gore) or the SpinBrush—now the top-selling toothbrush in the United States—a low-cost, battery-powered disposable toothbrush that was developed by a small team of external entrepreneurs.

P&G's strategy is to search the world for ideas and technologies that can be packaged with its own competencies and assets to create new wealth. As an example, the Mr. Clean Magic Eraser is based on an innovative foam product developed by the chemical firm BASF. The strategy also works in reverse. P&G licenses some of its assets to other companies to develop revolutionary new products. For example, the Philips IntelliClean power toothbrush system dispenses liquid toothpaste that was specially formulated by Crest.

The point here is that you should learn to look not just at your own organization, but also at the world outside as a Lego kit of interesting skills, technologies, assets, brands, and so on—and start to think about all the exciting combinational and contextual possibilities.

UNDERSTANDING UNARTICULATED NEEDS

Radical innovators are deeply empathetic; they understand—and *feel*—the unvoiced needs of customers. They bypass traditional market research methods, relying instead on "getting into the customer's skin." They recognize needs that customers don't even know they have yet. Or they solve some common frustration in a way that people could never have imagined—which is precisely why they are not articulating the need or asking for a specific product, service, or business to address it.

Nobody, for example, was asking years ago for a global overnight courier service, or a way to buy made-to-order computers directly over

Customer Insight:

An unmet need or a customer frustration that can serve
as the basis for a new business opportunity

the phone, or a comfortable "third place"—somewhere between home and work to hang out and enjoy coffee, or an online store where you could find and purchase practically any book on earth. Yet visionary entrepreneurs gave us FedEx, Dell, Starbucks, and Amazon.com—new business models that solved problems or addressed needs we were not aware we had.

Look around your own home. Chances are, you have a lot of expensive IT equipment in one form or another. Ask yourself what is easier: getting somebody to come and service your $500 dishwasher or getting somebody to come and service your several thousand dollars' worth of IT? Who do you call when you need some help installing a Wi-Fi network in your house or getting rid of all the spam and spyware on your computer? Clearly, there is a need here, but have you heard masses of people crying out for a solution? Enter Geek Squad (now owned by Best Buy)—the 24/7 computer support task force, with its tongue-in-cheek "special agents" and "Geekmobiles." It's a company that has focused directly on addressing this unarticulated need.

Caroline Kovac runs IBM Life Sciences, a company she built from a two-person group in 2000 to a $1 billion, fifteen-hundred-employee business today. Kovac learned that her mother had developed health complications during hospital treatment when she reacted adversely to a particular medication. Although her records were updated to warn doctors not to repeat the treatment, just three days later another doctor missed that warning and gave her the very same medicine. Kovac was shocked to find out how common this experience is. Statistics show that around one hundred thousand people die every year in U.S. hospitals due to medical errors like false medication, incorrect dosage, inefficient diagnostics, duplicated procedures, operations on the wrong side of the body, and so forth. "It's an appalling safety record," says Kovac, "the equivalent of crashing a large plane every week." Yet, in health care, she argues, people accept this as "just part of the system."[9] Kovac saw the problem and started thinking about how IBM could solve it. She became convinced there was a big opportunity in using IT systems to help hospitals manage their patient data more effectively, in much the same way that companies manage their supply chains. And IBM responded.

These and many other examples teach us that uncovering unsolved problems, unvoiced needs, and market inefficiencies can lead to significant innovation opportunities. This is the fourth perceptual lens that innovators use to discover new insights—the ability to see an unmet customer need—not only before the competition, but before the customer is even aware of it or has articulated it.

Getting Started

Your mission with the fourth lens of innovation is to look for deep, unarticulated customer needs and frustrations—in an effort to uncover new and unexploited innovation opportunities. This is not about conducting traditional market research—that is, asking customers to go through a questionnaire, either on paper, online, or by phone. Neither is it about going out and directly asking customers what they want. Methods like these rarely yield the most useful customer insights. Typically, the answers they generate are the obvious suspects: "I want it cheap," "It should be easy to buy and use," and "Make it work really well, too."

If you truly want to understand customers' wants and needs, you need to remove the distance between you and them. You need to immerse yourself in their environment and make their needs, frustrations, and desires your own. That means getting out of the office and into the field, using a variety of tools and techniques to derive new customer insights first-person—from observation and direct customer experiences—rather than relying on others to conduct research. Somehow, you want to "become" the customer, to *feel* the customer's experience, to identify and understand the customer's problems, and then look for ways to solve them.

Here are three effective methods you can use:

1. *Direct observation:* "Shadowing" the customer from multiple vantage points; making photo or video diaries

2. *Customer experience mapping:* Developing a deep, empathetic understanding of what it feels like to be a customer at every stage of the demand chain

3. *Analogies from other industries:* Learning from other companies around the world—from outside your industry—that are dramatically reshaping customer expectations

1. Direct observation

Today, more and more companies are making an effort to understand the unmet needs of their customers by using the power of observation. Whirlpool's Hank Marcy, while president of Corporate Innovation and Technology, put it this way, "We spend a lot of time working with consumers. We get out into people's homes, into where they buy the products, and get to consumers at the front end of a product's technology string to understand consumers' wants and needs." He adds, "When we go through our innovation process now, we no longer are looking to improve the traditional white box with bells and whistles. Instead, we're looking for consumer solutions."[10] What companies are coming to understand is that many breakthrough innovation opportunities are found not by looking at the product, but by looking at the user.

To discover customers' deep, unarticulated needs, Procter & Gamble is increasingly shifting the focus from traditional market research (for which the company became famous) to "day in the life" observational research. In one exercise, P&G's designers went to various countries to look at the way people clean their bathrooms. After observing women in South America using brooms to clean their showers and walls, P&G developed the Mr. Clean MagicReach, which combines a cleaning pad with a four-foot extendable pole. Consumers loved it.

When P&G discovers a customer need, it goes out of its way to find possible solutions. The company calls this "matching what's needed with what's possible." Remember, for example, when you had to wash your hair first with shampoo, then apply a conditioner and wait around for it to set, and then finally rinse it all out? Nobody really has time for that in the morning—they need something quicker. So P&G spent three years developing Pert Plus: a two-in-one product that gives you a shampoo and a conditioner in one bottle so you can simply "wash and go." Then the company got to thinking about hairspray, which usually does a good job of holding your hairdo in place but tends to leave the whole thing stiff and sticky—yuck! Spotting an unmet customer need, P&G

scientists developed a special holding ingredient called Elastesse, which they added to the formula of their Pantene Pro-V hairspray. It gives your hair a flexible, almost natural hold, instead of all that stickiness—so you can still run a comb or your fingers through it. This was the first major breakthrough in hairspray technology for forty years.

At times, observation can uncover some very surprising things. Haier, the hugely successful appliance manufacturer from China, observed that customers in poor rural areas were using their washing machines not just to clean clothes but also to clean vegetables and even to make goat cheese! Instead of discouraging this practice, Haier recognized the unarticulated customer need, made some modifications to its washers, and put large stickers on them telling customers how to wash vegetables safely and how to make the cheese.

In the United States, Haier sent its product designers to visit college dormitory rooms and observe the way students used their refrigerators. One thing they discovered was that, in these cramped spaces, students were sometimes laying a board on top of the cooler to build a makeshift desk. Spotting a need, Haier introduced a new refrigerator with a fold-out worktop. The product took off immediately.

The point: developing an empathetic understanding of customers' frustrations and anxieties through the power of observation can be a great way to get deep insights into unarticulated needs.

2. Customer experience mapping

Look at the entire customer experience surrounding a particular product or service. Ask yourself what could be displacing or substituting for that product or service.

As an example, consider a major U.S. hospital—one of the largest and busiest hospitals in America—an organization that cares for more than 1 million patients a year. Some years ago, the hospital's leadership team was searching for ways to create a more serene, patient-centered experience. They knew it wouldn't be very useful just to ask patients what they thought could be improved. Most people are prisoners of their experiences (and their understanding of how a particular service or product is usually delivered), so most of those patients would have a preconceived idea about what a hospital should be like. What they did instead was to map the entire patient experience—from the first symptoms of illness right through to the final billing from the hospital.

At several stages, they found that the patient has significant needs, problems, and frustrations:

- *Stage 1:* "I've had an adverse health event, but how do I find the physician or the health-care provider who is right for me?"

- *Stage 2:* "I lead a busy life and have very little time for physicians' appointments, particularly if these involve long waits."

- *Stage 3:* "I need to feel I am getting the physician's full personal attention; I want to be treated with sensitivity, dignity, and compassion."

- *Stage 4:* "I need to feel that my privacy and dignity are being respected in the examination room."

- *Stage 5:* "Why is the hospital making me wait, and wait, and wait to get an appointment for surgery?"

- *Stage 6:* "How can I weave the treatment procedure into my busy life?"

- *Stage 7:* "I want a hospital room that reduces my anxiety and meets my family's needs."

- *Stage 8:* "During the hospitalization, I need timely and accurate information about various appointments, or visits by family members and friends."

- *Stage 9:* "Now that I've been discharged from the hospital, I don't understand all these bills. Why can't I get a bill that is simple to understand?"

Instead of looking at the whole experience in an abstract way, the hospital's leadership team focused on the realistic problems that certain individual patients would face. For example, they developed profiles like this one:

Joan is the linchpin of her family. Without her pushing, pulling, directing, or just flat-out "doing," nothing gets done in her five-person household. After the birth of her youngest, Emma, she developed back pain that has become progressively worse during the last year. Her physician, having exhausted medications, is recommending back surgery. Surgery will put her out of commission for at least a week. A week! And to make matters worse, the only available window the surgeon is offering is the week before school opens. How is she going to manage to work her way through this one?

Taking this profile, they began to ask themselves, How many of our patients are time-starved professionals who are single parents—people whose lives are already too hectic and complex, and for whom an urgent health-care issue causes even more chaos and disorder? What if we made their problem *our* problem? How could we show that we understand the patients' time constraints by coordinating the hospital's activities around *their* lives—and around their schedule—rather than ours?

3. Analogies from other industries

Another way to get at unarticulated needs is to ask yourself, What are the needs that other industries, products, or businesses fulfill that our company has not yet been responsive to? Are there analogies in the ways other industries and markets are solving customer problems? Could we use these analogies to create a more ideal customer experience in our own industry?

Let's look at how this method was used by the major hospital we described above. One thing the organization's leadership team came to appreciate was that they were never going to understand how to reinvent the hospital experience by looking at other hospitals. Instead, they would have to look outside their industry, try to identify what they thought were some of the very best customer experiences one could have in life, and then use these as analogies for what they could do differently.

Thus, team members said things like "Okay, let's spend a day at Walt Disney World," or "Let's fly British Airways first-class to London," or "Let's stay at the Four Seasons for a couple of nights." They decided to search out those really positive experiences and to capture what they saw and felt—using photos, or video, or just little note cards where they could write down what made the experience so special. Sometimes it was just the little things: "Everyone at the hotel addressed me by name, and they even pronounced it right," or "British Airways gave me these wonderful pajamas," or "Disney made sure everything was perfect, right down to the last detail."

Afterward, they came back and spent several days as "patients" in their own hospital. They had to use the bedpan; they had to walk around in those green hospital gowns that open up at the back; they were left sitting half-naked outside the radiology room for a few hours; and every time they had a negative feeling, they recorded it.

Finally, the team members put up all their photos and cards and stories around the walls of their room, and asked themselves, How can we take what we've learned about creating these positive and negative feelings, and start making changes to the hospital experience? What could we do to alleviate this particular negative and turn it into a positive?

ORGANIZING THE DISCOVERY PROCESS

Here's the core lesson: radical innovators build their game-changing ideas on the four specific types of strategic insights we have outlined in this chapter: unexamined dogma, unexploited trends, underutilized competencies and assets, and unvoiced customer needs. They discover those insights not by snatching them out of the air but by looking at the world—either consciously or subconsciously—through one or more of the lenses of innovation. You can do the same. And so can your organization.

What is missing in most large companies is a *theory* of innovation. They haven't yet grasped that these four kinds of insights are the building blocks—the raw material—for innovation breakthroughs. That's why they typically have no methodology for systematically generating them—no organized discovery process aimed at looking through the four perceptual lenses we have described.

Sure, they may already invest money in accumulating insights of one sort or another, but they usually don't invest enough in generating the *right kinds* of insights, and all too often their insights are neither fresh nor differentiated. Our argument is that you can't build a highly differentiated strategy—and this is the only kind of strategy that delivers above-average performance—with undifferentiated insights. Putting time, money, and effort into building a foundation of *truly new* insights is the critical starting point for any innovation process.

Without these insights, an organization can run plenty of off-site brainstorming sessions but will probably find that they produce few, if any, game-changing ideas. Why? Because, despite a wealth of industry data, customer data, market research reports, technology road maps, and trend surveys, their people will invariably end up addressing strategic issues from the same old perspectives.

Of course, it's not enough to just say "focus on the lenses" and hope for great things to happen. In our experience, the most effective way to start building a foundation of insights that can inspire breakthrough innovation is by engaging a core group of people that represents a diagonal slice of your company. The group should actively involve people from all across your organization, reflecting the diversity of thinking that was emphasized in chapter 2. From this core group, we typically create four dedicated "discovery teams"—one for each lens, or category of insights. So we have one team focused on challenging orthodoxies, another on harnessing discontinuities, a third on leveraging competencies and assets, and the fourth on understanding unarticulated needs.

Each team then goes off to do its own discovery work using one of these perceptual lenses—equipped with a specific set of tools (like the ones outlined in this chapter) for stretching their thinking, developing the right perspectives, and spotting new, unexploited opportunities. You may find it useful to organize the discovery process in a similar way inside your own company.

DRAWING ON COLLECTIVE WISDOM

The guidelines, tools, and techniques on the previous pages should help your discovery teams get off to a good start in accumulating and building new insights. As they go about their respective assignments, it's very important that they involve the rest of the organization, too. That way, they can not only engage people throughout the company in the strategic innovation initiative, but also tap into the collective wisdom of the organization about the orthodoxies that most deserve to be challenged, the trends that seem to have the most portent for industry upheaval, the competencies and strategic assets that could best be leveraged in new ways, and the customer needs that are currently going unmet.

One of the ways you can make that happen is by sending out members of the discovery teams to talk to diagonal slices of the organization for a few hours at a time, explain what they are trying to do, and ask other people to contribute their views. The input that is captured in these sessions can then be fed back to the rest of the team members to support them in the process of developing new insights. At a later stage, when the discovery teams are distilling out those insights, they should also go back to the organization to test and validate them, making sure there is nothing important they might have missed.

SELECTING AND USING "DISCOVERY INSIGHTS"

To help your discovery teams evaluate the quality of their potential insights and make a final selection, here is a set of criteria we often use:

- Does the insight allow you to see new opportunities and describe the strategic implications for disrupting or changing the rules of the game?

- Does each insight represent a unique point of view backed by documented learnings (data, observations, interviews, secondary research)?

- Does the insight challenge convention and not merely restate the obvious?

- Is each insight articulated well (leaving no room for multiple conflicting interpretations)?

- Does each discovery team have a *portfolio* of insights? For example, do the "orthodoxy" team and the "discontinuity" team have insights across each element of the business model? Has the "competencies" team gathered insights that reflect latent, core, and possible future competencies? Does the "customer insights" team have insights across the entire customer experience? Or across important target segments?

- Did the team step out of the comfort zone to generate this insight, or was the insight based on "outsourced" or "second-hand learning"?

At the end of the discovery phase, having made a final selection from perhaps hundreds of potential candidates, your four teams should be able to present the company with a potent collection of new strategic insights that can serve as the foundation for break-the-rules business innovation. We like to refer to these final findings as *discovery insights*. Usually, they come in three types:

1. That which was previously *unknown*—that is, "something we never saw before."

2. That which was previously *underappreciated*—that is, "something we saw, but, frankly, we discounted it or didn't do much about it, because it just didn't seem important to us until now."

3. That which was previously *underleveraged*—that is, "something we've been working on already and that we know is important . . . but wow, we ought to be really doing way more about it."

These important insights—which are intended to broaden the perspectives of the organization—should later be fed into a companywide conversation on innovation and strategy with the aim of inspiring a slew of new growth opportunities.

Ultimately, what you want from the discovery process is not just a collection of insights but a common point of view. You want your discovery teams to be able to say, for example, "Here are what we believe to be (a) the most important orthodoxies our company can overturn; (b) the discontinuities that have the most potential to upend our industry; (c) the core competencies and strategic assets we can best leverage into new products, markets, or businesses; and (d) the most significant unmet needs of customers—and *potential* customers—that we can address to create new value."

In the next part of the book, we will show you how to use your discovery insights to inspire literally thousands of new ideas and business opportunities. And we will explain why it pays to produce a whole torrent of strategic options rather than focusing all your attention and resources on finding one "big idea."

INNOVATION CHALLENGES AND LEADERSHIP IMPERATIVES

Innovation challenge: How do I (we) create the fresh new insights that lead to game-changing innovations?

Leadership Imperatives

- Use the four perceptual lenses to expand your thinking in four new dimensions: challenging orthodoxies, harnessing discontinuities, leveraging competencies and strategic assets, and understanding unarticulated needs.

- Make these four lenses the foundation of your company's proprietary point of view on the future.

- Engage a broad cross section of your organization in generating these insights and in validating them.

Innovation challenge: How do I (we) know if we are pushing our thinking—challenging our core beliefs?

Leadership Imperatives

- Analyze your company's market and competitive situation differently from the way you have done it in the past. Try to get different answers by asking different questions—using the four lenses of orthodoxies, discontinuities, competencies/assets, and customer insights.

- Systematically challenge the way business is done in your company and your industry. You may decide to preserve some of your existing practices, but you should do so knowingly and deliberately, rather than blindly on precedent.

- Include "outsiders" in your innovation process who can bring a fresh view to the table—one that is unbiased by industry conventions.

- Challenge yourself and others to create the richest set of focused discovery insights; have you described well the "unknown, the underappreciated and the underleveraged?"

PART TWO

ENLARGING AND ENHANCING THE INNOVATION PIPELINE

CHAPTER 4

Producing a Torrent of New Opportunities

I N CHAPTER 3, we outlined some principles and techniques for building a foundation of truly novel strategic insights. Developed well, such insights provide fresh, new perspectives that can open your eyes to significant opportunities for innovation—opportunities that other companies may have overlooked or ignored. They can help you develop completely new points of view about a particular product category or market segment, or an industry challenge you may be facing. They can provoke breakthrough ideas for transforming your core business model in some profound way, or for creating new, "whitespace" businesses that directly leverage your company's core competencies and strategic assets. This chapter describes how your organization can use these powerful "discovery insights" to generate a torrent of new growth opportunities across product, market, and industry spaces.

On the following pages, we suggest five design rules for enlarging and enhancing your *innovation pipeline* (not just your product development pipeline), so that it becomes capable of pumping out a continual flow of wealth-creating new products, services, strategies, and businesses.

The first three design rules are about *enlarging* the pipeline—building a high-yield process that generates and captures a flood of novel ideas from across the organization and beyond. They are:

1. *Involve many minds:* Find ways to harness all the latent creativity inside your own organization—and in your extended network of customers, suppliers, and partners—as you search for
   new growth opportunities.

2. *Sow enough seeds:* Recognize that innovation is largely a numbers game—you need to generate lots of ideas in order to yield a
   few big winners.

3. *Widen the front end:* Improve your chances of inventing new
   value by opening your pipeline to a broad range of innovation
   opportunities—not just new products, new technologies, and
   "cool" design.

Applying these rules can take your organization a long way toward
creating an innovation-friendly culture, which means that your chances
of spawning the kind of ideas that generate dramatic new wealth are
going to be much, much higher.

However, enlarging your pipeline—by increasing the sheer volume
of ideas—is only half the story. The simultaneous challenge is to *enhance*
the pipeline by improving the quality of those ideas, not just the quantity. That's what the last two design rules are about:

4. *Increase the combinations:* Look for ideas that have truly game-
   changing potential by "crashing" various types of insights
   against each other to see whether the collision opens up new opportunities for innovation.

5. *Ideate around specific themes:* Create "aiming points" for innovation by focusing your ideation efforts on clearly defined corporate challenges, customer problems, or industry issues.

Paying attention to these last two rules will help you produce bold,
unconventional ideas that are of far higher quality and strategic value
to your company than the ones you usually get from tired, more traditional ideation methods—brainstorming, creative thinking games, online suggestion boxes, and so forth. That's because the ideas will be
solidly grounded in your "discovery insights" and consistent with your
corporate strategy, rather than simply snatched out of the air.

Let's consider the five design rules in more detail.

INVOLVE MANY MINDS

In chapter 3 we described four "discovery lenses" that are highly useful for building a set of novel strategic insights. As you now go about using these insights as the foundation for generating breakthrough ideas, your objective should be to open up the process as quickly as possible so that more and more people in your company can get involved. Ultimately, the goal is to efficiently engage as many minds as possible across the organization—and even beyond it—in the search for new growth opportunities.

What companies seldom seem to recognize is that one of the best ways to get more ideas into the innovation pipeline is to ask for them. An organization that understands this principle is Best Buy, North America's leading consumer electronics retailer. The company has a systematic and highly disciplined program of bottom-up innovation that is open to every employee. Called the Customer Centric Cycle, this program encourages everyone in the company to dream up new ways of creating a differentiated, end-to-end shopping experience for customers—and to share in the financial rewards that come from pumping up the company's profits. The rollout of this program has unleashed a huge amount of store-level innovation, making employees alert to ways of serving customers better. It is also driving changes in everything from Best Buy's supply chain to the company's service offerings and marketing programs. Most importantly, these changes are being driven by empowered employees all across the organization, not by the board of directors.

Cultivating Innovators in Your Company

How many of your employees do you regard as innovators? Indeed, how many of them regard *themselves* as innovators? What percentage of your people would tell you that they are fully deploying their creativity every day on the job? While most companies tell their employees to bring their brains to work, many still limit the use of that brainpower to initiatives aimed at improving operational efficiency. They rarely ask all of their people to get involved in imagining new markets or new growth strategies. Instead of tapping into the huge potential for creativity that is latent throughout their organization, too many senior executives continue to view innovation as the exclusive province of one or two specialized departments (i.e., R&D, new product development, Skunk Works, incubators).

The problem is rooted in the widespread notion that "ordinary" employees are unlikely to be a source of wealth-creating innovation. Go back a few decades, and we find that a similar prejudice was hindering most Western companies from achieving dramatically higher levels of quality.

Before the Japanese introduced us to the processes and methods for making quality everyone's job, it was actually the responsibility of a very small group of people in most organizations. We called those people "inspectors," and quality was *their* job. Indeed, back then, the notion that "ordinary" employees could and should be responsible for quality would have struck most corporate executives as absurd.

For a great part of the Industrial Revolution, companies believed that the way to drive up productivity and efficiency was to steadily reduce the discretionary decision-making power of first-line employees. The idea was that it was the "expert" who was paid to think and to figure out how a particular job should be done. Ordinary workers, on the other hand, were paid to "do"; they were given lockstep procedures to follow and were expected to carry them out blindly and without question.

Then, in a radical departure from that paradigm, W. Edwards Deming and others came along and said that management should teach first-level employees about statistical process control—that they should actually *unleash* people's discretionary decision-making power—and that doing so would deliver a positive return on investment. Thus, the quality movement was born, initially heralding Japan's rapid economic rise, and later revolutionizing the relationship between American manufacturers and consumers.

If the answer to quality was tapping into the problem-solving skills of rank-and-file employees everywhere in the organization, why has it taken us so long to figure out that innovation should be approached the same way? Why, in other words, do so few companies make any serious attempt to deploy their employees' capacity for *innovation*? Instead of consigning innovation to a small cadre of "experts" in specialized departments, why don't companies provide easier opportunities for anyone in the organization to innovate?

Clearly, most companies lack the mechanisms and structures that are required for opening up innovation broadly to the organization—and to people outside it. As Gary Hamel observes, doing so requires fundamentally changing key management processes—and, indeed, challenging the very nature of how work gets done within large companies.[1] Perhaps, too, there is a belief among some managers that ordinary employees lack the necessary thinking skills to innovate. British historian Paul Johnson believes otherwise. Having studied great creators throughout Western history—from Beethoven to Disney—Johnson concludes that "there is creativity in all of us, and the only problem is how to bring it out."[2]

In the past, ordinary people never had the tools or the opportunities to unleash their creativity. Now they do. Look around today, and you see a world filled with bedroom DJs, amateur movie directors, podcasters, game developers, bloggers, and citizen reporters. Armed with new, easy-to-use software tools, ordinary people are proving that they are capable of the most amazing creativity. The challenge, therefore (and the opportunity!), is to "bring out" all of the latent creativity that currently lies untapped within your company's own organization—and indeed, across its extended network of customers, suppliers, and partners—and channel it into your innovation pipeline.

Just as it was ordinary employees who made quality happen, we sincerely believe it is ordinary employees who can make *innovation* happen, but only if your organization is willing to develop a social architecture that teaches and encourages them to be innovators, that unleashes the power of their imaginations, and that supports their innovation efforts in the appropriate ways.

Start by raising the ratio of innovators to the total number of employees. Simply put, the greater the number of employees who regard themselves as innovators, whatever their formal job descriptions may be, the greater the innovation yield. Set a specific goal. Identify the people in your company who have an innovation role (R&D personnel, product development staff, and so on). If this group comprises less than 10 percent of the employee base, commit to tripling it over the next twelve months—not by hiring more innovation specialists, but by involving existing employees in innovation processes or events.[3]

Send your employees the message that you *expect* them to generate new ideas—that innovation is at least part of their job, if not their whole job. Then give them the training, the time, the tools, and the space they need to exercise their innovation muscles. For every department and business unit, benchmark the percentage of employees who have submitted ideas or participated in innovation events. Give literally everybody in your company the opportunity to innovate. Do all this, and your innovation yields will soar.

Remember, at the heart of Deming's vision for Total Quality Management was a simple, yet profound notion—"quality starts with me." In an economic era where innovation, not quality, is the key competitive weapon, that notion needs to be reinterpreted for a new age. We believe that the cornerstone for making innovation happen is a deep, companywide understanding that "*innovation* starts with me."

Using the Power of the Net

A great way to get hundreds or even thousands of employees involved in the process of sharing insights and thinking up new ideas is to use the power of the Net. IBM, for example, often uses the Internet for on-line idea "jamming." On certain occasions, the company invites IBM employees from around the world—and sometimes even their family members and friends, as well as clients and consultants—to take part in a global, open-source ideation exercise. One of these exercises involved two seventy-two-hour sessions of innovation dialogue, based around using IBM's technologies in radical new ways. CEO Sam Palmisano told his employees it was the first time a technology company took its most valued secrets, opened them up to the world and said, "Okay, world, you tell us what to do with them."[4] He also announced that IBM would put $100 million behind the most promising concepts to come out of the online ideation process. In total, somewhere in excess of fifty-three thousand people participated in this particular IBM InnovationJam, contributing many valuable ideas for breakthrough innovations in areas such as transportation, health, the environment, finance, and commerce.

In the second round of the jam, they even got to rate the best ideas themselves based on their potential business value.

Look Beyond Your Organization

What else can you do in addition to asking for and expecting innovation from all of your people? One thing you can do is recognize the enormous potential for innovation that also exists outside your organization—across your extended network of customers, suppliers, and partners. As many other companies have done over last decade or so, you can put mechanisms in place that allow you to employ some form of "open innovation." Our colleague Amy Muller often describes this as "leveraging the global brain."

Of course, companies have long sought to complement their internal development efforts with external sources of innovation. Typical strategies have included licensing technology from more innovative firms, polling lead users for new ideas, outsourcing R&D to universities, or joining research consortia. However, what is new is the ability to use the Web to tap into the world's ever-expanding reservoir of human creativity—to engage the imagination and know-how of literally *millions of brains outside the organization*. It represents the power to open up your company's innovation processes for free trade with the rest of the world.

As an example, take Procter & Gamble. You might assume that the company has a long history of collaboration with external partners to bring product innovations to the market. This is not the case. Traditionally, P&G was more inclined take pride in its own innovation prowess, relying heavily on in-house R&D labs to develop its new products. Not anymore. In 2001, A. G. Lafley, P&G's chairman, signaled a fundamental shift in corporate strategy when he challenged his company to source half its innovations from outside the organization.

As part of the company's open innovation program, called Connect and Develop, researchers all across P&G can use a Web portal called InnovationNet to help them find solutions to scientific problems they might be grappling with. The Web site has a feature called AskMe, which allows them to post a question or a need to about ten thousand technical specialists around the world, both internal and external. P&G

also links to other networks like InnoCentive, NineSigma, or UTEK's U2B—online communities where tens of thousands of scientists, patents, and techologies are networked together, along with an inventory of their technologies. Yet even with all these links to qualified experts, researchers may well get the most innovative answer from, say, a graduate student in Bangalore. In addition, the company has assigned a large team of "technology entrepreneurs" from its business units, whose role it is to actively seek new ideas and solutions from the external world.

Larry Huston, former vice president for innovation and knowledge at P&G, put it this way: "You can't possess all the science and brilliant minds . . . In our R&D organization we have 7,500 people in 150 science areas, but there are 1.5 million high-quality people outside P&G. It doesn't take a genius to figure out that if you can engage the brains of your 7,500, plus the key ones from that 1.5 million, you can build better products."[5]

P&G has even entered into codevelopment agreements with archrivals like Clorox, in which the company shares its technologies and R&D pipeline in return for a stake in the new business generated by the collaboration. A recent success is GLAD Press'n Seal, an innovative plastic wrap from Clorox that's based on the same technology and sealant know-how as P&G's Impress. In fact, the company now gives its technology patents a "use-by" date—if they are not used within three years by the internal organization, P&G either sells, licenses, or donates them to the external market.

P&G also makes extensive use of the Internet for soliciting reactions from customers about new ideas. In the old days, the company would spend considerable time and money making physical prototypes and doing market testing. Today, what used to take about two months in the physical world can be simulated in the virtual world in one or two days using computational modeling—and customer feedback via the Internet is instant and direct.

Another example is IBM. The computer giant has had considerable success using its alphaWorks Web site to connect internal researchers and product groups with a large community of external software developers. The goal is to foster collaborative thinking and conversation around IBM's emerging technologies and to enroll outsiders in the work of fixing bugs, exchanging ideas, and looking for new applications. Early (alpha) versions of new IBM software are posted on the Web site for software developers to download, examine, and tinker with—either alone or in collaboration with others. Developers can then provide feedback to IBM via an electronic bulletin board, or an online questionnaire, or simply via e-mail. The alphaWorks site currently attracts hundreds of thousands of unique visitors per day.

Sometimes the site helps IBM to "unstick" innovation opportunities. One project that seemed to be going nowhere was posted on alphaWorks and, to IBM's surprise, generated an unusually high level of external interest. This prompted IBM managers to give the software a second thought. It is now known as XML (Extensible Markup Language), which is a central feature of IBM's WebSphere Internet software.

P&G and IBM are obviously massive, highly successful organizations with vast global reach and scale. Their particular approaches suit their respective business strategies and corporate cultures very well. However, as Northwestern University's Mohanbir Sawhney observes, what suits a company like P&G may not work well within another organization.[6] As Sawhney sees it, the particular approach your own company takes should be based on three factors:

1. *Your objectives:* Are you looking for raw ideas? Market-ready ideas? Market-ready products?

2. *Your industry's competitive dynamics:* What is the pace of technology and market-change?

3. *Your company's strengths and scale:* What is the extent of your global reach? How high is your brand awareness around the world?

Energizing a Community of Volunteers

The most exciting thing about the Web is that it allows your company to connect with people outside the organization "whose passions match your problems," as Gary Hamel likes to put it. Consider the way Linux, the open-source operating system, was developed. It is currently esti-mated that Debian GNU/Linux, which includes more than eighteen thousand software packages for eleven computer architectures, contains more than 213 million source lines of code. This translates into tens of thousands of person-years in terms of development time. If Linux had been developed by software coders who were compensated for their work, it would have cost billions of dollars. Instead, it was created for free by a worldwide community of volunteers, in a similar way to Wiki-pedia, the online encyclopedia.

Google is another company that understands how to engage zealous volunteers from outside the organization. In its annual Code Jam com-petition, Google gives developers from around the world the chance to work on its toughest software problems. Cash prizes are modest—the real incentive for contestants is the chance to see their code incorpo-rated into Google's ubiquitous search engine. The company has also opened up some of its programming interfaces (called APIs) to the pub-lic, allowing the propeller-head community to produce their own "mash-ups" using data from other Web sites. In addition, Google runs a public Web site called Google Labs, where staffers with zany ideas can post their prototypes and solicit feedback on using or improving them. This is where services like Google Maps, Google Desktop, Google News Alerts, and Google Video first started out. Because the company publishes ideas on Google Labs at an early stage and lets outside inno-vators play around with them, there is a much bigger chance that these pilots will one day become real products and real services.

MIT professor Eric von Hippel points out that "innovation commu-nities are by no means restricted to the development of information products like software."[7] He cites user innovation communities that have been instrumental in improving or customizing *physical* products as diverse as sports equipment (e.g., surfboards, snowboards, mountain bikes), surgical equipment (e.g., clinical chemical analyzers), and food products for major restaurant chains (e.g., sauces).

If you want to energize a community of innovation volunteers, con-sider the following questions:

- Who out there cares about the problems my company cares about?

- What kind of investment in this community would be required to build goodwill and trust?

- What nonmonetary incentives might engender the volunteers' contributions?

- What mechanisms—Web sites, peer review processes, discussion forums, standards and protocols, design toolkits, and so on—can we use to structure their contributions?

Make it your company's goal to raise the ratio of externally sourced innovation to internally sourced innovation. The better an organization becomes at harnessing ideas and energies from outsiders, the better its innovation yield.

SOW ENOUGH SEEDS

At its core, innovation will always involve an element of serendipity. But your company can dramatically improve the odds that serendipity happens by understanding that innovation is largely a numbers game— it takes a lot of acorns to grow an oak tree. You have to ensure that your innovation pipeline has a large number of ideas coming in at the front end in order to yield an adequate number of successes at the back end.

The point is, whether you are trying to innovate in consumer packaged goods, pharmaceuticals, financial services, or industrial equipment, you are going to be faced with an inescapable arithmetic: it takes a thousand ideas to find a hundred with enough commercial promise to merit a small-scale experiment. From those one hundred experiments, only ten projects will be judged worthy of pursuing seriously with a substantial financial commitment, and of those, only one or two will turn out to be unqualified successes. In other words, to find those few ideas that have the transformational power to change the fortune of your company, you must first dream up thousands.

Think about those entrepreneurial adventurers who went off to seek their fortune in the California Gold Rush. They literally had to sift through tons of mud and muck to find a few valuable nuggets. The same principle applies in the search for golden business opportunities—whether you like it or not, your company is going to have to sort through a huge amount of ideas to find those one or two hidden gems.

As an analogy for this "innovation arithmetic," think about the venture capital business. Most good venture capitalists will give you numbers similar to the ones above: for every thousand business plans they receive, around a hundred would-be entrepreneurs will be invited for a meeting, and out of those one hundred potential ventures, the VC will eventually fund about ten. From the ten opportunities that are funded, the VC expects two or three to go out of business, five to seven to do okay and produce middling returns, and one or two to be a home run.

Very few companies are willing to accept this arithmetic—even though there is little reason to believe that the odds should be higher for a global firm looking for growth opportunities than for a VC. Indeed, in the pursuit of efficiency, most large organizations end up driving out the "waste" and "extravagance" from their ideation efforts—the very fuel of innovation.

Many CEOs seem to think that a team of the organization's smartest senior execs, aided by some even smarter consultants, can quickly come up with that one killer idea that will produce hundreds of millions of dollars in incremental revenues and profits. Or they leave the innovation imperative to a small cadre of "experts" working in R&D labs, incubators, new-venture divisions, or Skunk Works, hoping that somebody will eventually hit on the "big idea" as much by accident as by design. But these enclaves, divorced as they are from the rest of the company, usually produce very few ideas that ever make a big impact on a company's profits. They are no substitute for an innovation pipeline filled with novel strategic options for revitalizing the core business.

Granted, it may be difficult to accept (and to argue internally) that from all the ideas you generate, only 10 percent will warrant experiments, and roughly 90 percent of those experiments won't give you the learning you expected. But, as our VC analogy illustrates, the real issue is not how many times you fail but the value of your successes. What counts is how the *portfolio* of ideas and strategic options performs as a whole rather than whether any particular experiment pans out. The chance that any single new idea fails may be high—say, 80 percent. Yet in a portfolio of ten such experiments, each with a one-in-ten chance of success, the likelihood is that one of them will pay off handsomely. There is simply no way around it: your chance of finding the next big opportunity is largely a function of how many seeds you sow and how many new things you try.

Once again, Google is a good example. Its founders—Larry Page and Sergey Brin—grasp the arithmetic of innovation. They came out of that exciting cauldron of experimentation called Silicon Valley, and they understand that the way to spawn the next Google is to try to replicate the same environment inside the company. Their goal is to constantly create new "Googlettes"—novel business ideas, services, and software applications that may start small but that one day may grow into significant sources of revenue. Staff are permitted to spend at least 10 percent of their time on whatever interests them. This gives them the freedom to create a lot of new ideas and then to experiment with those ideas to see whether they go somewhere—which, as we noted earlier, is what led to many of the Google services we now use every day.

WIDEN THE FRONT END

Remember GE's innovation goal described in chapter 1—to deliver at least $15 billion or more in annual growth? Allow us to put this figure in context. In the United States, it would be equivalent to the annual combined revenue of the entire bookstore industry, or the entire fitness center industry, or the entire music production and distribution industry. Not exactly peanuts! Granted, your own growth goals may not be quite as ambitious as GE's, but if you want to be confident of producing meaningful earnings impact at the back end of the innovation pipeline, you need to ensure that your company doesn't constrain the flow of new ideas entering at the front end.

Some companies unwittingly do this by defining innovation too narrowly, limiting their innovation efforts to the search for nifty new product ideas or disruptive new technologies. While there is nothing wrong with these types of innovation per se—indeed, they can be highly lucrative—it is important to understand that they are not the only types of innovation that can help your company drive growth and strategic renewal.

In order to steer clear of this "innovation myopia," try to widen the front end of your innovation pipeline so that it becomes open to a whole range of different innovation opportunities.[8] For example, consider the following innovation categories:

- *Technology innovations:* These are new-to-the-industry technology breakthroughs that cause fundamental shifts to the way we do things. For example, they might displace entire product sets, or reinvent the customer experience in some way, or open up substantial new markets, or dramatically disrupt existing industry structures. Think of things like the Internet, the PC, the digital camera, the ATM, the air bags and navigation system in your car, e-mail, voice mail, flash memory, or the Dyson vacuum cleaner. Technological innovations can have a big impact on any given industry. In health care, for example, innovations like telemedicine (remote health monitoring, diagnostics, and treatment), electronic medical records, handheld scanners, mobile digital assistants, drug-eluting stents, and surgical robotics are currently transforming the quality of both the health-care service and the patient experience.

- *Product innovations:* These would include revolutions like Apple's iMac, iPod, and iPhone; the Toyota Prius; Segway; the new MINI Cooper; a blockbuster drug like Viagra; or less glamorous but still very impactful innovations such as Fresh Express's prewashed, precut salad in a bag, or Crest's disposable SpinBrush.

- *Service innovations:* These would be things like PayPal, or Charles Schwab's online equity trading, or Enterprise Rent-A-Car's decision to take car rental to the local neighborhood rather than merely concentrating on airports.

- *Operational innovations:* These are things that refine or reconfigure a company's operational processes to give it a competitive edge. Examples include Wal-Mart's supply chain management, Cisco's approach to M&A, or FedEx's use of information technology.

- *Cost innovations:* These create a substantial cost advantage for particular companies, often based on their geographical location in a low-wage economic region with a well-developed industry cluster. In consumer electronics, for example, first Japanese and then Korean companies proved adept at establishing a manufacturing cost advantage. Over the last ten years, Chinese firms have been extending cost advantages in stepwise fashion to revolutionize entire business models—and are now successfully competing at the "high end" of major industries like appliances (Haier), energy (PetroChina), computers (Lenovo), and even fashion (Ports 1961).[9]

- *Experience innovations:* These improve or reinvent the customer experience in the purchase or usage of a product or service. Examples include Midas bringing car care to the public parking garage, sleeping on a Heavenly Bed at Starwood Hotels, shopping at an American Girl store with your daughter, or visiting a MinuteClinic at CVS for fast treatment of nuisance illnesses. All of these provide distinctive experiences when compared with the "old way" of doing things.

- *Management innovations:* These are about innovating around a company's core management processes in the hope of creating an enduring source of competitive advantage. Examples of management innovations from the past would include strategic planning, scenario planning, brand management, Total Quality Management, lean manufacturing, and Six Sigma.

- *Business model innovations:* These are about reengineering existing business concepts or creating entirely new ones. IKEA, eBay, Apple, Dell Computer, and Spanish clothing retailer Zara are all companies that have successfully innovated at the level of the business model. Sometimes a powerful business model can be built around a product innovation. Consider, for example, Nespresso—Nestlé's capsule-based coffee system—where, in addition to purchasing the coffee machine itself, consumers also need to continually buy the capsules, and can even join a user community (the Nespresso club).

- *Industry innovations:* these have to do with building new industry architectures. For example, to revolutionize the way people listen to radio in the United States, XM Satellite Radio had to orchestrate three or four different components across several different industries—that is, entertainment content providers, car companies, satellite companies—all of which adds up to an entirely new industry ecosystem. Likewise, Apple had to bring together a collection of players from several different industries to build and continually enhance the iTunes/iPod platform.

Obviously, there is much more complexity as you go from, say, product innovation to business model innovation to industry innovation. On the other hand, the potential for building competitive advantage and generating new wealth increases as you move up the scale. Disruptive business models and industry architectures are typically the most difficult kinds of innovation for rivals to replicate.

Though our list of various types of innovation is by no means exhaustive, it serves as a reminder that stretching your thinking beyond new products and technologies or just "cool" design will significantly extend your scope for innovation.[10] So, as a practical step, ask yourself: Does our company's search for strategic opportunities currently encompass many of the above and perhaps other types of innovation? If not, could we widen the front end of our innovation pipeline by considering and pursuing more types of innovation—those that are best suited to our business context?

Simply put, the broader and less constrained you make your search for innovation opportunities, the more chance you will have of discovering potential avenues for inventing new value. Later in this chapter, as well as in chapters 5 and 7, we will provide some guidance on how and when you should narrow things down again by bringing more strategic focus into the ideation process.

INCREASE THE COMBINATIONS

Sometimes, a single strategic insight can be all it takes to stimulate ideation, inspire fresh thinking, and allow you to see an exciting new opportunity. However, in our experience, the innovations that have truly game-changing potential are those that are born at *the intersection points between various types of insights*.

As we pointed out earlier in this book, radical business innovations are almost always the product of "creative collision"—that is, they are based on a combination of insights from the four different categories we have identified: unexamined dogma, unexploited trends, underutilized competencies or strategic assets, and unvoiced customer needs.

Your objective should be to take various discovery insights from these four distinct lenses and play them off against each other to see whether the collision opens up new opportunities for innovation. We call this process *crashing*.

To illustrate how combining or crashing various insights can lead to the discovery of breakthrough business ideas, let's take a look at two cases: PECO Energy and Whirlpool.

Rethinking Energy

PECO Energy Corporation, today owned by Exelon and formerly known as the Philadelphia Electric Company, had successfully operated within the public utility paradigm since its founding in 1881. However, in 1996, PECO's leaders could see that their old regulatory strategy was not going to be of much value in what was rapidly becoming a deregulated market. Annual growth was already slow—hovering at about 1 or 2 percent. They knew they needed to transform their strategy and their corporate-wide growth agenda if they were going to survive and thrive in the new competitive environment.

In an effort to abandon its strategy-by-habit ways, PECO embraced the task of building a foundation of discovery insights in much the same manner we described in the previous chapter. PECO's teams worked hard to examine widely shared *orthodoxies* in the company and in the industry, asking what would happen if they overturned these "rules." They set out to identify deep *discontinuities* at work in the marketplace with the goal of harnessing change to the company's advantage. They took a comprehensive look at their *competencies and assets*, searching for ways to leverage them into new growth opportunities.

And they deliberately tried to uncover unvoiced and unmet *customer needs*. Here are some of the key insights they generated:

Orthodoxy: It was believed that, in the future, all the real money in the power generation business was going to be made by moving downstream—from the "dirty old business" of managing power plants and networks into the exciting new business of "retail wheeling" (selling energy services to consumers—primarily corporations—in any geographic region). PECO challenged this orthodoxy (which had become almost conventional thinking in the industry) and developed a contrarian point of view about the attractiveness of the retail opportunity. Its focus became, How can we build a strategy that is clearly based around the unique or at least rare competencies and assets that we possess?

Orthodoxy: Another widespread industry orthodoxy at the time was that energy companies should tread carefully in the nuclear sector. At the time, the industry's largest stranded asset costs were linked with these plants, and there was a general wariness of taking on the presumed regulatory and consumer resistance to nuclear power generation. However, where other firms saw liabilities, PECO saw an opportunity.

Core competence: One of the things PECO'S discovery teams uncovered was the company's distinct *core competence* in managing big, mission-critical, and relatively older power plants very efficiently. This grew out of PECO's experience with its own Peach Bottom nuclear power plant, which the company had transformed from a "problem plant" a decade earlier into a model of high-capacity performance with low operating costs. It led the company to ask, What would happen if we took our core competence into a place where rival energy firms are increasingly reluctant to go: the efficient management of old nuclear power plants that other companies are not very interested in?

When the discovery teams finished their work and "crashed" their new insights together, what emerged was a bold and highly unconventional growth strategy. While everybody else in the industry seemed to be moving downstream into retail, PECO made the decision to actually dismantle the retail consumer marketing organization it had begun to build, and instead, tried to become *the* low-cost wholesale provider of energy in the United States. As part of this strategy, the company went on to buy and turn around several nuclear power plants in North America, including Pennsylvania's notorious Three Mile Island reactor, which PECO purchased for just $23 million instead of the plant's $640 million book value (at the time, nobody else seemed very interested in it).[11]

The results of PECO's strategy transformation speak for themselves. In 2000, the company merged with Unicom to form the Exelon Corporation, which today is the largest producer of nuclear energy in the United States. Exelon's seventeen nuclear facilities generate a full 18 percent of all U.S. nuclear power.

Reinventing Appliances

In another industry—this time domestic appliances—consider the origins of a novel dishwasher from Whirlpool called Briva. The idea for this highly innovative product came from combining or crashing different types of insights: a discontinuity, an unmet customer need, an orthodoxy, and a competence.

Discontinuity: The fastest-growing demographic group in basically every developed country over the last twenty years has been single-person households. This is not an invisible development; it's something that is blatantly obvious, but the whole "white goods" industry seems not to have noticed, or at least not to have paid any attention to it. Look at the average appliance—say, a dishwasher, a refrigerator, or a washing machine. Who is it built for? Judging by the size of it, probably the mythical family of four. Yet we all know that this just isn't the way the world works anymore.

Unmet customer need: The fact that most appliance manufacturers have ignored this deep, fundamental sociodemographic change has created an unmet customer need: household appliances designed for single people. Traditional appliances are way too big—for example, if a single person is working long hours, and probably eating one meal at home during the day, it would take a week and a half to fill up the dishwasher, by which time all kinds of other things would be growing on the dishes! Single people also tend to live in smaller apartments, where space, particularly in the kitchen, is limited.

Orthodoxy: Dishwashers are big boxes that sit under the kitchen work surface near the sink. Recognizing that this doesn't make sense for single people, Whirlpool challenged company and industry conventions by asking, "Why shouldn't a dishwasher be more like a microwave oven—very small, very compact, very fast?"

Core competence: One of Whirlpool's core competencies is in designing, producing, and marketing low-cost, high-quality appliances. The company asked itself how it could use this competence to create and market a dishwasher that would perfectly fit a single person's lifestyle.

By crashing all of these insights, Whirlpool saw the opportunity for Briva: a mini, high-speed dishwasher that could be integrated on one side of a double-tub sink, saving a lot of space in the kitchen. The product is specifically designed for small loads—the kind that would typically meet the needs of a single-person household. Briva completes a wash cycle in about fifteen minutes, versus traditional dishwashers that grind away for an hour or two. And because it's a top-loading appliance, as opposed to the conventional front-loader, its lid comes down and doubles as a drainer or a chopping-board surface. When not in use, the whole wash mechanism can even be lifted out to provide a fully functional second sink.

IDEATE AROUND SPECIFIC THEMES

One of the concerns that managers often have about the ideation process is that if they open it up and go too wide, the company will end up "boiling the ocean," and the ideas that are generated will be all over the map. Their fear is that people will waste time, energy, and resources by going off in all kinds of crazy directions, potentially taking the company into a lot of areas it knows nothing about. Here are three reasons why they need not worry.

First, in our experience, organizations are usually so caught up in their own orthodoxies—their own narrow view of their company and their customers—that they are reasonably focused anyway. It's not as if people are already thinking way out there on the fringe and they need to be pulled back; on the contrary, most of the time people have to be pushed to get far enough *out on the edge.*

Second, if your company has already done the kind of disciplined discovery work that we described in the last chapter, your ideation efforts will be reasonably grounded. In other words, the ideas that get generated will be based on things you know for sure about your industry, things that are definitely changing in the world, real competencies and strategic assets in your organization (or in potential partner companies), and real customer needs. Although the discovery insights may not have been necessarily data driven or analysis driven, they are certainly in a sense data *based*—they all represent realities, things you can test and validate. That means that the ideas they inspire will be connected to the real world, not just some crazy, unbounded creative space.

Third, while it is possible to give your ideation a very wide perspective—for example, if your entire company is looking for a whole new strategic direction—it is also possible to narrow the scope by focusing your ideation on very specific corporate challenges, customer problems, or industry issues. Our colleague Gary Getz calls these "aiming points." Examples would be one financial service firm's objective to "own retirement" or McDonald's goal to "recapture breakfast."[12] In some cases, the aiming point might be a broad product platform, such as P&G's "oral care." In other cases, it might be a customer-focused issue, such as an electronic retailer's push to make its stores more "female friendly."

As an illustration of how this works, Royal Dutch/Shell will sometimes identify a big problem in search of new solutions and then invite people from around the world to spend a few days thinking boldly about that problem and contributing their ideas. One example is "Urban Utopia"—an ideation project that focused on the problems big cities face due to issues like overcrowding and pollution. It produced all kinds of potential opportunities for Shell to provide pathbreaking answers.

Sometimes, a company sets out to generate a portfolio of options around some predefined opportunity domain—almost like going to a fishing hole to find out what is in there. For example, one global food and beverage company decided it wanted to develop a portfolio of opportunities around "water." The company's leaders knew they were interested in getting into that particular opportunity space, but at the outset they were not exactly sure what they wanted to do there—whether it was making water portable in the third world or competing with industry incumbents like Perrier in some new and different way. Initially, they just wanted to generate a lot of strategic options, and the discovery and ideation process we have outlined in this book became the rod and tackle they used to fish for potential opportunities.

In chapter 3, you learned how to generate rich and very grounded strategic insights. With this chapter, we have outlined some ways to develop a large number of quality ideas from those insights by following our five design rules for enlarging and enhancing the innovation pipeline. Applying these rules should help to ensure that your company is thinking broadly enough across types of innovation and, equally important, encouraging and enabling broad involvement throughout the organization and beyond it.

In chapter 5 we turn to the business model—an excellent way of focusing your ideation efforts while simultaneously increasing your scope for innovation. We explain in some detail how to unpack your company's business model and examine each component as a potential opportunity for challenging industry rules.

INNOVATION CHALLENGES AND LEADERSHIP IMPERATIVES

Innovation challenge: How can we increase the volume of ideas to consider?

Leadership Imperatives

- Open up the ideation. Post your discovery insights on a company Web site, and invite all employees to contribute ideas.

- Don't reject ideas at the early stages because they are too small, won't work, or have been tried before. Ideas generated at this stage could spark other bigger and better ideas.

- Accept the arithmetic of innovation: to create one successful large-scale business, you need to generate hundreds of new ideas.

Innovation challenge: How do we improve the quality of the ideas generated?

Leadership Imperatives

- Focus your ideation on specific platforms or "aiming points."

- Generate ideas based on discovery insights rather than unstructured brainstorming.

- Seek ideas at the "intersection" of various types of insights. Ideas that leverage multiple insights are the most powerful.

- Be specific when generating ideas. Each idea should specify *who* the customers would be and *what* benefit you would provide.

- Look for "open" market spaces. Don't chase the next billion-dollar opportunity that many other competitors are already pursuing.

CHAPTER 5

Innovating Across the Business Model

W HEN YOU MENTION THE WORD *innovation*, most people immediately assume you are talking about new product development, or cutting-edge technologies that emerge from traditional R&D departments. Yet some of the most successful innovations of our time have been *business model innovations* that break from company or industry norms in meaningful and perhaps even radical ways. They do so by:

- Serving unmet or unsatisfied customer groups

- Providing new or different benefits

- Delivering and/or extracting value in an unconventional fashion

Take eBay's peer-to-peer, Web-based marketplace, Apple's iPod/iTunes platform, IKEA's assemble-it-yourself furniture model, Dell's made-to-order computers, BMW's customize-your-own MINI Cooper, or Zara's continuous product line updates. These are all examples of dramatically different business models (or *existing* business models that have been dramatically reengineered) that create substantial new value for customers and shareholders. What's clear from these examples is that they go beyond pure product or technology innovation. Rather, they create wealth by pushing the boundaries of one or more dimensions of the company/industry business model in a sustainable and profitable way. The problem for many organizations is that they never even think about innovation in this context.

Consider a familiar example: Apple. If someone asked you what has made Apple so successful in recent years, your tendency might be to think right away about a *product*—the iconic iPod. This is quite understandable, given the iPod's highly visible role in Apple's meteoric comeback. But the iPod is actually just the front end of the success story. Less visible than redefining the size, look, and functionality of an MP3 player, Apple's real innovation was creating a digital rights management system that could satisfy the music industry (assuring its members that they were not going to lose control over their intellectual property) while simultaneously creating a legal music download service that would satisfy consumers (giving them a way to browse hundreds of thousands of songs and to buy individual tracks or whole albums at a very reasonable price).

Apple's genuine breakthrough was not good product design; it was a revolutionary business model—one that allowed people to find and legally download high-quality music files extremely easily, transfer them to different iPods, and make a few copies for their friends by burning a limited number of CDs, but that wouldn't allow them to start pirating whole albums and exporting music from China. This was a major reason why the iPod took off as it did: it was the front end of a very smart and highly differentiated platform that worked for both the music industry and the consumer. That platform, the iTunes Music Store—which now also offers digital music videos, television shows, iPod games, and feature-length movies—is at the very heart of Apple's strategic move into consumer electronics, allowing more recent Apple products like the iPhone and Apple TV to sync with PCs as easily as the iPod. In fact, iTunes is the Trojan horse with which Apple plans to capture a significant share of the home entertainment market.[1]

In their book, *Dragons at Your Door*, Ming Zeng and Peter Williamson describe another type of business model innovation—cost innovation—that is currently emerging among dominant Chinese firms like

Haier, Lenovo, and Pearl River Piano. These firms and others share three principal characteristics:

1. High technology at low costs

2. Unmatched choice of products in standardized, mass-market segments

3. Specialty products offered at dramatically lower prices, turning niche segments into volume businesses

As the authors remark, "Imagine a world [in which] high technology, variety and customization, along with specialist products, are available to customers at dramatically lower prices; a world where the value-for-money equation offered to global consumers [is] transformed by Chinese multinationals."[2]

The point we are making here is not that product innovations per se are unimportant. Far from it. Radical product innovations—like the Toyota Prius, the Nintendo Wii, or a blockbuster drug like Viagra—can change customer expectations and behaviors, alter the basic conception of a product or service category, and occasionally even change the future of an industry. Rather, our argument is that taking a holistic view of innovation at the level of the business model is likely to bring more returns for your company in the long term than just thinking about innovation in terms of products, services, technologies, or operations.

WHAT IS BUSINESS MODEL INNOVATION?

At its essence, business model innovation is about creating fundamentally new kinds of businesses, or about bringing more strategic variety into the business you are already in—the kind of variety that is highly valued by customers.

These days, the term *business model* is thrown around very loosely, so you would assume that it is widely understood. The reality is that if you asked a few people in your organization to describe your company's business model, their answers would most likely lack clarity and consistency.

Chances are, everyone would have a vague picture in their minds, but it wouldn't be the same picture—and it would probably not be a complete picture, either. Even if your employees were able to identify some key components of your business model, they might still be unable to recognize or articulate the interrelationships between those components.

A definition would obviously be helpful at this point. We define a *business model* as a conceptual framework for identifying how a company creates, delivers, and extracts value. It typically includes a whole set of integrated components, all of which can be looked on as opportunities for innovation and competitive advantage. In order to innovate at the level of the business model, you first need to unpack it into these individual components and understand how all the pieces fit together in a holistic way.

Figure 5-1 shows a simple framework for unpacking the key components of a business model.[3] It breaks the whole thing down into five basic components: who you serve, what you provide, how you provide it, how you make money, and how you differentiate and sustain an advantage. Considering these components one by one will help you to unpack your business model and articulate it more clearly in its entirety.

To build a breakthrough business model that rivals cannot easily emulate, you will need to integrate a whole *series* of complementary, value-creating components so that the effect is cumulative.

A classic example is Southwest Airlines. Essentially, Southwest offers customers an alternative to traveling by car, bus, or train, giving them a no-frills flight service they can still enjoy through a whole set of complementary activities.[4] The key point is that Southwest's business model differs from those of other major U.S. airlines along several dimensions. It's not just about low fares, point-to-point connections, and the use of a standardized fleet of aircraft (all Boeing 737s). Another dimension is the way Southwest treats its employees—putting them first

Business model:

A conceptual framework that describes how a company creates, delivers, and extracts value

FIGURE 5-1

Unpacking the business model

Who do we serve?	What do we provide?	How do we provide it?	How do we make money?	How do we differentiate and sustain an advantage?
Who are our customers? What market segments do we serve, in which geographies? Who are the buyers of our products and services?	What are the products and services we sell? What benefits and solutions do we deliver to our customers?	What distribution channels do we use? How is our value chain configured? What are the core processes and activities that translate our competencies, assets, and other inputs into value for customers (outputs)? Who are our partners? How do our suppliers and partners help us deliver value?	What do we charge our customers for? What are the major costs we incur in delivering our offering? How do we extract value? What is our pricing model? (e.g., flat rate versus subscription, own rate versus customized, direct versus indirect through third parties, bundled versus priced separately à la carte, set prices versus market-based prices, etc.)	How are we different from competitors? How do customers experience this difference? What differences do they value most? How sustainable is our differentiation? Is it protected by core competencies and strategic assets that we and only we have?

Source: Strategos analysis.

with profit-sharing and empowerment programs. Another is the fun experience Southwest creates on board and in the terminal, with jokes, quizzes, and goofy behavior by the cabin crew and ground staff. Another is the legendary care and attention Southwest puts into its customer service. All of these elements compound to create a business model where, as authors Kevin and Jackie Freiberg put it, "love plays a part in running the airline" (the company even uses LUV as its stock ticker symbol!).[5] Love aside, Southwest's demonstrably successful business model has spawned numerous imitators around the world, including Ryanair, easyJet, JetBlue, and AirAsia.

TWO DISTINCTLY DIFFERENT OBJECTIVES

There are two objectives to innovating at the level of the business model.

One objective is to find breakthrough growth opportunities by *inventing entirely new business models*, never before seen in a particular industry. For example, when the University of Phoenix set out to educate midcareer adults instead of eighteen- to twenty-two-year-old students, or to create campuses in business parks across the United States instead of a single campus in Phoenix, Arizona, or to use Web-based learning rather than bricks-and-mortar classrooms, it was inventing an entirely new business model that in many respects redefines the adult education industry.

The other objective is to drive growth by *evolving the business model you already have*. An example would be Whirlpool's creation of Gladiator GarageWorks: a new business model for Whirlpool based on garage appliances. This growth opportunity leveraged the company's core competencies not just in a new product category (modular storage units and accessories for organizing the garage) but in a new customer segment (male do-it-yourselfers) that was historically underserved by Whirlpool, and in a new "room" of the home (i.e., the garage) that has traditionally been ignored by white goods manufacturers, who tend to focus on the kitchen or laundry room.

Where many companies go wrong is in vigorously pursuing one of these two objectives (i.e., trying to invent entirely *new* business models), while forgetting to pursue the other (i.e., continuously evolving the *existing* business model).

Two distinct objectives of business model innovation

- Trying to invent entirely *new* business models, never before seen in an industry
- Continuously evolving your company's *existing* business model

For example, while Intel was off chasing all kinds of new businesses in other industries, the company came under quite intense criticism for taking its eye off the core microprocessor business and losing ground to rivals like AMD.[6] The important point here is not that Intel ended up neglecting its core business *operationally*, but that it forgot to *innovate* and *evolve* fast enough in the core business to stay competitive.

Conversely, we sometimes see companies—and even whole industries—that put a lot of effort into evolving the core business but that fail to take advantage of some of the more radical business opportunities that present themselves outside the core.

Consider the telecom industry. A few years back, most telecom companies were giving plenty of thought to innovation in things like products and pricing (coming up with "friends and family" packages and so forth), but how many of them were thinking about telephony switching to a completely different kind of network—like VoIP?

Likewise, most airline companies were focused some years ago on how to innovate in things like their loyalty programs, or their onboard catering, or their first-class seating, but how many were thinking about inventing a completely new, low-cost business model for the airline business?

Our argument is that companies need to continuously do both of these things—they need to be evolving the core business at breakneck speed while simultaneously searching for innovation opportunities outside the core.

THINKING HOLISTICALLY

Whether your goal is to invent a completely new business model that revolutionizes your industry or to continuously evolve your company's existing model, you will find that your ideation efforts can be dramatically enhanced by systematically considering each component of the business model as an opportunity for game-changing innovation.

We could illustrate this using the same two examples cited above. The University of Phoenix's rule-breaking innovation emerged from focusing explicitly on several components of the business model that traditional universities had largely taken for granted—that is, who our customers are, which geographies we serve, and how we deliver our service—and then asking whether things could be done radically differently. Similarly, Whirlpool came up with Gladiator GarageWorks by thoughtfully challenging core dimensions of their existing business model—that is, who the customer is, what benefits we deliver, and how we go to market—and then overturning orthodoxies along each of these dimensions. In either case, the challenge is to think holistically about every component of the business model (either your company's existing model or the traditional model of the industry) and then to try to innovate in as many of these components as possible. This helps to ensure that you will be comprehensive in your innovation efforts. It forces you to systematically explore all the potential avenues for business model innovation.

More importantly, thinking holistically helps you to avoid innovation "blind spots" that may be exploited by competitors. Most companies have certain areas in which they innovate a fair amount and other areas that almost never get any attention. This can open up significant opportunities for rivals to innovate along a particular dimension of innovation that has long been overlooked—and thereby gain an advantage.

Take Wal-Mart. The company appears to be very good at innovating along many dimensions of its business model but not so good at others. This has created innovation blind spots that major competitors have been only too glad to exploit. A good example is U.S. retailer Target, a store that generally attracts younger, more educated, and more affluent customers than Wal-Mart. Fans of the store even refer to it as "Targé" (a trend Oprah Winfrey is supposed to have started), giving the name a French-sounding pronunciation to emphasize its more appealing image.

Instead of trying to out-innovate Wal-Mart on things like pricing, supply chain management, or IT, Target has focused on a dimension of innovation that Wal-Mart seems to have overlooked: the overall shopping experience. While it couldn't exactly be described as deluxe, Target's store design offers customers a more upscale environment that generally feels friendlier and more inviting than Wal-Mart's. For example, the aisles are wider, the ceilings are lower, and the merchandise is presented in a friendlier, more attractive way.

Beyond this fundamental difference, Target was a pioneer in making exclusive deals with fashionable designers—like Mossimo, Michael Graves,

Liz Lange, and Isaac Mizrahi—and convincing them to design low-cost lines for its stores. It also partners with big brands like Sony to create products that are exclusive to the store, sometimes colored red to match the company's corporate identity. Thus, Target is not just about just low prices; its business model innovation has to do with customer-friendliness, trend awareness, and an ability to *set* design trends through an innovative supply chain model. As a result, it can deliver "proprietary" products rivals can't match. Taken together, these factors mean that Target is competing on entirely different dimensions of the business model relative to Wal-mart—dimensions that Wal-Mart has largely chosen to ignore.

As this example illustrates, your company must learn to view every component of your existing business model as:

- A potential opportunity to create value by departing from industry norms

- A potential blind spot or Achilles' heel that competitors could use to undermine or devalue your position

Rarely do managers look at the logic or architecture of each component as something that represents a designed *choice* that could have been done differently. After a while, it's just "the way we do things around here." And as we saw in chapter 3 of this book, all too often "the way we do things" becomes a set of rigid orthodoxies that are rarely revisited or challenged. Companies tend to stop asking themselves how they could innovate along these long-unexamined dimensions.

Thinking holistically about every component of the business model— and systematically challenging orthodoxies within these components— will significantly extend your scope for innovation and improve your chances of building a sustainable competitive advantage.

ASKING NEW QUESTIONS

The challenge, then, is to take your business model (or your whole industry model) apart, as we outlined earlier in this chapter, and think about every single component as a potential candidate for innovation and industry reinvention. The way you do that is by examining each component of the business model from new perspectives, asking yourself how it could be dramatically redesigned to create new value for the customer.

In particular, you should look at any aspect of the business model that has remained essentially unchanged for five or more years, or where progress has been slow and incremental, or where there has been little or no innovation. The goal is to open up "long ago" choices to scrutiny: to generate a whole set of *why* questions about the taken-for-granted aspects of the business model. For example: Why do we target only these types of customers? Why do we price this way? Why do we sell through these channels? Why are we this vertically integrated?

Here are some focusing questions you can use to drive innovation in the various components of your own business model:

Who Do We Serve?

- Are there types of customers that have been ignored by companies in our industry?

- How might we target a different buyer who values our offering more than the existing buyer?

What Do We Provide?

- Could we deploy the customer benefits we provide in new ways or settings?

- Can we change the benefit bundle in ways that will surprise customers and frustrate competitors?

- Have we defined the customer need we are trying to address broadly enough? Conversely, are we delivering benefits that customers don't really care about?

- Have we looked critically at where we draw the boundary between what we do and don't do as a company?

How Do We Provide It?

- Could we make the process of fulfillment and support substantially easier or more enjoyable for customers?

- Could we reinvent the customer experience in ways that would strengthen the sense of affiliation the customer has with us?

- Are there opportunities for step function improvements in the efficiency or effectiveness of our processes?

- How might we reposition ourselves in the value chain to our advantage?

- What partners or suppliers might we work with to enhance our ability to deliver value to the customer? How might we redefine what each party brings to the table?

How Do We Make Money?

- Can we more closely align what we charge for with what customers actually value?

- How can we improve our cost position without jeopardizing the value we provide to customers?

- Does our existing pricing structure implicitly penalize some customers and subsidize others? Can we change this?

- Can we break the predominant pricing paradigm in our industry?

How Do We Differentiate and Sustain an Advantage?

- How sustainable is our differentiation? Is it protected by core competencies and strategic assets that we, and only we, have?

- Are there any dimensions of differentiation that we or our competitors have not yet explored?

- Have we searched diligently for differentiation opportunities in *every* dimension of the business model?

- Can we exploit our core competencies and strategic assets in new ways to bring value to customers?

- How might we leverage our core competencies and strategic assets in other industry settings?

Finally, you should also ask yourself whether all the components of the business model positively reinforce each other. Are some components of the business model at odds with others?

STRETCHING YOUR BUSINESS MODEL

An excellent way to "stretch" your business model—making it more differentiated and harder for rivals to replicate—is to reexamine every component using your foundation of novel strategic insights (the four kinds of insights we discussed in chapter 3) to spot new opportunities for innovation.

Of course, it is quite possible to ask new kinds of questions about your business model without having done any of the discovery work we outlined in that chapter. However, in our experience, it is much more effective to consider the focusing questions listed above in light of what you have learned about orthodoxies, discontinuities, core competencies and strategic assets, and unmet customer needs. This usually produces better, more grounded answers and prompts much more radical thinking.

For example, you can challenge the internal mind-sets that have built up around your business model by using the *orthodoxy* insights. For each component of your business model, think about the deeply held dogmas or orthodoxies that are related to it (e.g., what orthodoxies do we have about who our customers are, how we interact with them, how we define our products or services, how we make money, how we configure our value chain, etc.?). Now think about what would happen if you overturned or challenged those orthodoxies. What would the new business model component look like?

Next, do the same exercise using the *discontinuity* insights. Pick one or two discontinuities—deep, fundamental changes already at work in the external environment—and ask yourself how they might be leveraged to improve each business model component. How might they require you to rethink or reinvent this component? Look for ways in which you could use these discontinuities to substantially change the way things are done in your industry.

Now look at your insights into *core competencies and strategic assets* vis-à-vis your business model. Ask yourself whether any assets or competencies could be recombined to create new value, or leveraged in their own right to generate growth, or transferred to new opportunities. Think about how you might combine other companies' competencies and assets with your own to radically change the way you do business.

Last, consider the various components of your business model from the point of view of your *customer insights*. Using insights into existing or emergent customer needs that are currently unaddressed, think about how you could change the various components of your business model to meet these needs. How could you create the kinds of benefits that a currently underserved customer group would value?

THE ACID TEST

The exercises we have described in this chapter are designed to help you inject innovation into every component of your business model, making the whole thing more robust. They can be applied to both an existing business model that is in need of some fresh thinking and *entirely new* business models that may emerge from your ideation.

The business model framework brings discipline, clarity, and reality to the task of innovation. It serves as a forcing function to stretch and elaborate your thinking along all these different dimensions, and to check whether there are any avenues for innovation—or any blind spots—that you may have missed.

Whether you are trying to invent fundamentally new business models or evolve the one you already have, the acid test of any business model's potential for creating above-average customer value—and thereby new wealth—is the degree to which it is "radical." Chapter 6 explains why radicalizing ideas, business strategies—and, indeed, business *models*—is so crucial for dramatically enhancing your innovation pipeline.

INNOVATION CHALLENGES AND LEADERSHIP IMPERATIVES

Innovation challenge: How do I keep my current business model fresh and innovative?

Leadership Imperatives

- Make sure that everyone in the company has the same definition of *business model*. Clarify what you mean and adopt a common definition.

- Don't assume that your current business model is the only viable way to do business. Keep challenging it and seeking alternatives.

- Challenge each of the core assumptions of your current business model. Are yesterday's assumptions still valid, or have they become today's orthodoxies? Are they blind spots that your competitors could exploit?

- Innovate new business models while continuously challenging and evolving your current business model.

Innovation challenge: How can I make sure that we are thinking expansively enough in searching for new opportunities?

Leadership Imperatives

- Escape the narrow view of innovation as "R&D" or "new product development." Learn to consider all aspects of the business model as targets for innovation.

- Don't assume that product or service innovation is "better" than innovation in other elements of your business model.

- Use novel strategic insights (i.e., the discovery findings we outlined in chapter 3) to challenge and evolve each element of your business model.

PART THREE

EVALUATING AND ALIGNING NEW GROWTH OPPORTUNITIES

CHAPTER 6

Asking the Right Questions at the Right Time

MANY EXECUTIVES SAY that their problem is not a shortage of ideas, but knowing which ideas are the right ones to execute. Where companies tend to go wrong is in prematurely deciding that an idea is either "good" or "bad" and then overcommitting resources to the so-called good ideas while weeding out the bad ones. Instead, we believe it's better to think about new ideas and opportunities as being on a continuum from "embryonic" to "fully mature."

To this end, what criteria should your company be using to evaluate new opportunities? And how do you know whether you are asking the right questions at the right stage of the idea development process? This chapter will provide you with some useful guidelines in this regard.

EVALUATING IDEAS

All too often, great ideas get prematurely squashed. The typical innovation killer is a question like "What's the expected ROI?" or "How profitable is this opportunity?" Of course, asking detailed questions about profitability is not wrong, but many companies tend to ask these questions way too early—at a stage when they are sometimes impossible to answer.

It's worth remembering that no big new idea ever starts out as a 90 percent sure thing. Take eBay. Go back to December 1995, when eBay was only a few months old. Who would have thought that this fledgling online auctioneer would one day have a market value surpassing $50 billion?

Demanding a lot of financial precision about a nascent idea—particularly during the embryonic stages of experimentation—is very counterproductive. It's almost like looking at a human baby when it is only a couple of months old and saying, "Well, it can't walk. It can't talk. What kind of value is there in this?"

Rather than making a quick decision about an idea at a very early stage, the goal should be to create an extremely fast iterative cycle—one that allows prospective innovators to get started, quickly test whether their hypotheses are valid or invalid, see what they learn from their experimentation, and rapidly iterate that learning.

In our experience, the first things a company should ask when evaluating a new opportunity are: How *radical* is the idea? How big—or how important—could it be? What kind of impact could it have on customers, on the competition, on the whole industry? How big is the potential market? Would customers actually want it? How much would they care about it? In other words, the evaluation criteria should initially be focused on assessing the upside—how interested the company should be in an idea, how hard it should work to push the idea forward, and how committed it should be.

Sequentially, the next questions to consider are: How feasible is this? How mature is the technology? Do we have the resources, the competencies, the capabilities to make this happen, or can we get them somewhere else—that is, through partnerships? Do we have the distribution channels to bring this to the market?

As these questions of feasibility get resolved, the final questions to start asking are those that concern business model economics: Can we actually make it profitable? What sort of revenue might this idea generate? What are the costs involved? What sort of margin can we put on this?

This sequence—asking first about the size of the idea, then about the feasibility, and only then about the profitability—is one that many venture capitalists understand, but many companies don't. Large organizations are often so afraid of overinvesting in a lousy idea that they fail to appreciate the concomitant risk of prematurely killing a great, but immature idea. By asking the profitability questions first instead of last, they make it almost impossible for the innovator to present a compelling case to those responsible for budgeting. As a result, the project either gets flatly rejected at its embryonic stage—as a "bad" or "uncertain" idea—or, alternatively, the innovator is forced to create some false certainty about the project that can later blow up in people's faces.

Asking the right questions in exactly the right sequence will help you avoid the premature culling of promising opportunities. It will also help you identify the ideas that—if they worked—would be most likely to give your revenues a *dramatic* boost.

In this vein, let us return to the primary question in our evaluation sequence: How *radical* is the idea? For the remainder of this chapter, we will look at why this question is crucial to producing wealth-creating innovations, and how you can use it in a practical way to evaluate the portfolio of ideas in your pipeline.

THE LIMITS TO INCREMENTALISM

Most companies are under intense pressure to meet relentless growth targets. Yours is probably no exception. But what do you do if your organization is experiencing *deteriorating growth rates*, as current business models mature and consolidation runs its course?

Perhaps you've been able to perform well so far through continuous operational improvements—but now you are faced with *decelerating efficiency gains*, having already "squeezed most of the juice out of the lemon," or you've come up against legacy costs you just can't get around (as Detroit's Big Three automakers have with their health-care programs). Add to this the pressure of declining real prices and the bargaining power of today's customers, and it's no wonder so many big companies find that they have hit a wall. Today's growth-charged executives face some very difficult challenges in this regard.

The hard reality is that "incrementalism" is not going to solve any of these problems. Companies can no longer hope to significantly grow revenues by coming up with a slightly improved version of the same old thing and then selling it to the same old customers through the same old channels in the same old way. A different flavor of Coke, an additional razor blade for Gillette, or the next version of the BMW 3 Series sedan—these can only take a company's revenues so far. If you're in a mature industry, the only way to meet *radical* top-line growth targets is by stimulating demand with products, services, or business models that are truly *radical*.

The logic of radical innovation also applies on the cost side. In most companies, it simply isn't possible to eek out much more efficiency from the existing business model. Rather than focusing on incremental cost improvements, what you really should be doing is looking for ways to *radically reinvent* the cost structure—as IKEA did in home furnishing, or as Wal-Mart did in retail, or as Southwest did in air travel, or as Dell originally did in computer distribution.

What we are arguing, in short, is that the only way to meet today's formidable growth challenges is not through incrementalism but through radical, game-changing innovation.

RADICAL INNOVATION DEFINED

By our definition, an idea is truly radical if it passes one or more of the following three tests:

1. Does it have the power to dramatically reset customer expectations and behaviors?

2. Does it have the power to change the basis for competitive advantage?

3. Does it have the power to change industry economics?

Let's consider each of these questions in turn.

Does It Have the Power to Dramatically Reset Customer Expectations and Behaviors?

Remember when a personal computer only came in varying shades of gray and was the ugliest thing in your home? That was before Apple hired the edgy young British designer Jonathan Ive, the man who put the *i* in the iMac. By redefining the PC as a jazzy work of art, Ive completely changed customer expectations about how a computer should look. And Apple has continued to change those expectations with each successive generation of the product. But why stop at computers? Remember when an MP3 player was an MP3 player was an MP3 player? That was before the iPod—as much a lifestyle statement as a music device. From that moment on, there was only one way to be seen listening to music on the go. Indeed, remember when music was something most of us bought on CDs in music stores? That was before iTunes made it legal and fashionable to download almost any track we want for just 99¢.

Another example would be PayPal, eBay's user-friendly payment system. By making it safe and easy to move money around online, PayPal has dramatically altered the way customers and vendors go about their Internet transactions. And the impact goes way beyond eBay. PayPal is by far the most popular online-payment service on the Internet—generating billions of dollars in payment volume every year—and is now featured by many other companies (e.g., Dell, The Sharper Image) as a payment option on their Web stores.

Finally, the Lexus RX 400h, a great-looking SUV with a hybrid gas-electric motor, shows how raising the bar for consumer expectations can really pay off. This SUV is as comfortable and powerful as any other luxury SUV, but the difference is that you can drive it from Los Angeles to New York and back nine times and produce fewer smog-forming emissions than painting a room in your house. After announcing its intention to launch the new car, Lexus took more confirmed presold orders than for any other vehicle in the company's history. Waiting customers were invited to take part in the birth of their own car by assigning their name to a specific RX 400h before production and then tracking it through delivery, just as you would track a FedEx parcel. Meanwhile, with demand far outstripping supply, would-be buyers were willing to pay up to $10,000 over the list price to go to the head of the line and get their car sooner. This at a time when Ford and General Motors were fighting a price war and struggling to see who could survive on the lowest margins.

These are all examples of radical innovations that fundamentally reset customer expectations and behaviors.

Does It Have the Power to Change the Basis for Competitive Advantage?

Think about the way pharmacogenomics—the study of how an individual's genetic inheritance affects the body's response to drugs—is changing the basis for competitive advantage in the pharmaceutical industry. The traditional pharma model is focused on drug *discovery*—testing thousands of compounds in an almost brute force way and seeing whether any of those compounds makes a measurable difference. It's a model that has essentially remained unchanged since the industry got started in the early nineteenth century—the only difference being the scale and efficiency with which today's pharma giants can manage the compound-testing process. Today, however, a new set of players has emerged—companies like Amgen, Genentech, and Genzyme—where the business model is focused on understanding disease *mechanisms* (i.e., genetic diseases, immune system disorders, heart disease, cancer) and creating targeted products that address those mechanisms. Their promise is "personalized medicine," in which the therapy can be matched to an individual's own unique genetic makeup. Interestingly, whereas drug companies are filled mainly with chemists, as opposed to biologists, the rapidly growing pharmacogenomics sector is hiring huge numbers of microbiologists, geneticists, and so on. By innovating around gene-based therapy, which is based on completely different skills and assets from conventional drug-making, the new breed of pharma companies is fundamentally changing the game.

Does It Have the Power to Change Industry Economics?

Netflix, which was launched in 1999, transformed the way we rent movies by challenging the conventional thinking held by Blockbuster and other incumbents. Instead of customers being required to rent and return movies to a physical store, they would be able to rent online and receive as well as return their choices by mail. Coupled with a user-friendly site, a wide collection of titles, and effective promotion in retailers like Best Buy, Netflix quickly gained ground and today has upwards of 7 million members.

Netflix radically challenged the pricing structure of the existing industry, where late fees accounted for $1 billion of the $8 billion industry. Instead of requiring customers to pay per movie and charging people "an arm and a leg" for late fees (founder Reed Hastings himself had previously racked up $40 dollars in late fees), Netflix adopted a subscription model where customers could select how many movies they wanted to rent at a given time and have the flexibility to return those movies on their own schedule. Customers would not be held liable for late fees, though of course, the faster they could watch a movie, the sooner they'd be able to return it in order to receive another one. With this new business model for online DVD rentals, Netflix leaped ahead, while Blockbuster delayed five years to enter what it considered to be an unproven market. Wal-Mart also entered the market but discontinued its operations in 2005, deciding instead to throw its weight behind Netflix.

RADICAL DOESN'T HAVE TO MEAN RISKY

For many executives, the word *radical* is too, well . . . radical. It makes them feel nervous and uncomfortable. They tend to equate it with ill-conceived and highly speculative projects, or major high-tech developments that can indeed take on radical dimensions. But "radical" innovation doesn't necessarily mean making "risky" (i.e., uncertain and expensive) investments. Clearly, when a company moves outside its core business and tries to innovate in entirely new product categories and markets, the risks generally go up. Why? Because these are fields the company knows little or nothing about—that is, where it has no competence foundation (the skills that are necessary to compete). Yet what many senior managers need to realize is that you can innovate in a radical way without going off and doing something completely crazy.

Take the Starbucks debit card, for example, which allows regular customers to purchase their daily fix of caffeine without fumbling through their pockets for cash. It was clearly a radical innovation for the quick-serve restaurant industry, where nobody had ever before asked, "How do we get people to happily pay days or weeks in advance for their coffee?" By our definition, the idea was radical because it had the power to change both customer behavior and industry economics. Yet, was it *risky*? The card offers customers a solid benefit. It relies on an established technology (magnetic stripe credit cards), which is well known and well proven. It's also a concept Starbucks could easily test in a few stores first before deciding whether to launch a big rollout. So the risk was actually quite small, but the payoff has been huge. Within sixty days of its launch, convenience-minded customers had snapped up 2.3 million cards and provided Starbucks with $60 million in prepayments. Since then, more than 26 million cards have been sold. This single innovation now accounts for 10 percent of Starbucks' sales.

Another example is Travelpro. It was the first company to put wheels on luggage. This all started with the Original Rollaboard, which was a great solution for airline pilots and is now standard equipment for hundreds of thousands of flight crew members around the world. When other travelers saw it in the airport, they would say, "Wow, where did you get that?" and that's how the idea spread. It's certainly a *radical* innovation, because it completely changed people's expectations about luggage—why would anyone want to haul a heavy suitcase around when they can just roll it? Yet, was it *risky*? The idea didn't require any materials breakthrough—in essence, it was just about screwing some wheels onto a piece of luggage. No doubt the results were pretty crude on the first few attempts, but it didn't matter—Travelpro's innovation was more conceptual than anything else; it was about coming up with a way to transport luggage more conveniently.

WILL IT HAVE *IMPACT?*

If you still can't stomach the word *radical*, try using *impact*. When you look at a new idea or business opportunity, ask yourself: Is this idea going to have *impact*? Our argument is that if an idea does not meet the test of being truly radical, it is not going to have very much impact on either the top line or the bottom line. It still may be something that is perfectly worthwhile to do, but it's unlikely to make much of a difference to revenue growth. The challenge, as we have outlined above, is to come up with ideas that are high impact but that don't require a company to "bet the farm."

As you screen through the ideas that find their way into your innovation pipeline, ask yourself the following questions to evaluate the potential impact of each idea:

- If we succeeded at this idea, how many people would actually care?

- How much would people's lives be changed or improved as a result of this idea?

- How much productive change would it bring to the industry as we know it today?

- How much would company and/or industry economics change?

Or if you prefer, think of it as a "mathematical" formula. The degree to which an idea is radical—or will have impact—can be measured by the percentage of people who would consider it important, multiplied by the magnitude of difference it would be likely to make in their lives, or the degree of difference it would make to the underlying industry economics.

As an exercise, try to recall some examples of both radical and incremental innovation, and then evaluate them against this formula. Which ones get the highest score on the impact scale (see table 6-1).

To increase the potential impact of a new idea, try to "stretch" it, just as we suggested "stretching" the various components of your business model in chapter 5. You may find that by "radicalizing" a new idea, or by

TABLE 6-1

Rating ideas in terms of their impact

Idea	Impact	
	Low	High
A new version of the BMW 3 Series	X	
Yet another blade on a Gillette razor	X	
Bringing back the popular MINI Cooper automobile	X	
Reinventing the way personal computers look		X
Changing the way we buy and listen to music		X
Providing a safe, easy online-payment system		X
Matching therapy to an individual's own unique genetic makeup		X
Dramatically cutting the cost of air travel		X
Making it "easy" for consumers to find a good deal		X

recombining it with other idea fragments, it can be built into a much bigger business opportunity.

Unfortunately, some managers do exactly the opposite. When confronted with somebody's nascent idea—especially one that sounds a little wild or rough around the edges—they automatically try to tame it, or dilute it, or make it "safer." They believe that by making it less radical, they can make it less risky. What they haven't yet understood is that radical and risky are two completely different notions.

INNOVATION CHALLENGES AND LEADERSHIP IMPERATIVES

Innovation challenge: How do I get a good balance of incremental and radical ideas into my portfolio?

Leadership Imperatives

- Generate both incremental and radical innovations. Radical innovations are likely to be harder to generate, so the tendency is often to focus on the easier, more incremental goals. Instead, challenge your teams to get a good balance of both radical and incremental ideas by giving them a specific target (e.g., 50/50, or 70/30—whatever works best in your organizational context).

- Test whether an idea is radical by asking yourself whether it has the power to dramatically change the "rules of the game." If it doesn't, try to make it more radical by "stretching" it with the four discovery lenses (chapter 3).

- Don't assume that just because an idea is radical, it is also risky. There are many examples of innovations with big impact that did not involve a lot of risk.

- Don't dilute the radical ideas in an attempt to make them less risky.

Innovation challenge: How can I make sure that radical innovations survive in my company?

Leadership Imperatives

- When evaluating ideas, first focus on the potential market impact of the idea and the demonstrable customer need which is currently going unmet, and only then start applying feasibility screening criteria and financial criteria.

- Be clear about the definition of radical innovation: does it have the power to reset customer expectations, change the basis of competition, or change industry economics?

CHAPTER 7

Constructing an Innovation Architecture

ONE OF THE KEY ARGUMENTS of this book is that successful innovation is a numbers game. As you've learned so far, the chance of finding a big new opportunity is very much a function of how many ideas you generate, how many you pick out and test with low-cost experiments, and how many of the most promising projects you get your resources behind. That's why throughout the pages of this book, we recommend that companies create a diverse portfolio of ideas and experiments, with a view to pushing up the odds of finding some winners.

Importantly, we are not suggesting that your company should pursue a mixed bag of completely unrelated opportunities, in the hope that a small percentage of them turn out to be strategically and financially rewarding. On the contrary, we believe that strategic innovation requires a high degree of focus. Competitive advantage does not come from a "full speed ahead in all directions" approach. Rather, it comes from narrowing your focus in a "don't get distracted, get all the wood behind one arrow" sense—on either a corporate level, or a divisional level, or a business unit level. It requires coherence, consistency, and specialization.

So how can these two opposite and seemingly contradictory requirements—"diversity" on the one hand and "coherence" on the other—be reconciled? How should you manage the paradox? This chapter explains why an innovation architecture can be a big help in this regard—and how your company can effectively build and deploy one to create a powerful strategy for revolutionizing your industry.

Here is the point: while you need a lot of ideas and experiments to increase your chances of success, you also want your company's innovation efforts to *compound*—to be cumulative over time—so that you can build a strong, defensible and differentiated competitive position in the marketplace.

Once again, Apple is a good example. The company has produced a steady flow of exciting innovations over the last few decades—from the original Macintosh and the Mac operating system, to the iMac, the iTunes music platform, the iPod, the iPhone, and the Apple Store—but a quick glance will tell you that there is a coherent logic to all of these innovations. They compound and reinforce each other. This coherence has made a great contribution to Apple's meteoric comeback.

There is a compelling need, in other words, to bring focus to the innovation process, so that the ideas and opportunities you generate become *connected* in some way and can build on one another, maximizing your skills and resources rather than fragmenting them. However, there is an equally compelling need to avoid the other extreme, where your innovation becomes *too* focused and you end up with "all your eggs in one basket." This can be very dangerous in a world of hyper-accelerating change, where strategies and business models are rapidly rendered obsolete. The art in all of this, therefore, is to find a way to both unleash and focus innovation at the same time. You want a lot of diversity, but you also want some things that constrain that diversity. You want your innovation to be broad enough so that you avoid closing off innovation opportunities and strategic options prematurely, yet narrow enough so that you are not trying to "boil the ocean." Walking between these two sides of the road is a delicate balancing act.

FOCUSING THE INNOVATION PROCESS

The goal with innovation is not simply to "let a thousand flowers bloom" but to make sure those flowers get planted in an orderly fashion—in the same garden, if you will. Instead of a thousand different crazy directions, what you really want to produce is a thousand high-quality ideas and opportunities within a few discrete areas of strategic focus.

In chapter 4 we discussed the importance of "aiming points" that can help your company to focus ideation and the rest of the innovation process, thereby increasing the odds of success. These aiming points should be broad enough to invite contributions from across the firm—and beyond—yet specific enough to channel your organization's innovation efforts and investments.

Here are three mechanisms for creating such aiming points.

A Portfolio of Growth Platforms

Some companies identify three or four fairly broad growth platforms or innovation themes on which they decide to focus strategically as an organization, and they continue to work at those platforms consistently year after year.

GE, for example, has defined a limited number of major challenges it wants to go after—like "How could we improve the world's water supply?"—and this has helped the company generate a multitude of focused ideas and initiatives within these platforms.

CEMEX has also chosen to focus its innovation on a relatively small number of specific growth platforms—particular domains within which the company is looking for innovative, new ideas. These include things like "housing for the poor" and "solutions instead of cement"—which are broad enough to invite a lot of innovation but narrow enough to rule some things out of scope. The company assigns dedicated "platform teams" to innovate for several months within these broad opportunity areas, after which the team members finish their assignment and new members come in to work further on the same platforms. This has provoked innovation after innovation inside the company, sometimes resulting in the creation of completely new businesses.

A Portfolio of Customer Problems

Another mechanism for creating aiming points is the one used at P&G. The company focuses on building "brand equities" by creating products that make a meaningful difference to the customer experience. Every year, within each business unit, P&G generates a list of what it sees as the ten most important customer problems the organization should be trying to solve.[1] The implicit message to its people is quite clear: Innovation that's focused on these customer problems is going to get more resources faster, because there's an inherent logic to ideas that tackle these issues, and the burden of proof on you as an innovator will be lower.

An Innovation Architecture

A third mechanism—which we often use ourselves—is an "innovation architecture," where a company defines the three or four vectors of innovation along which it intends to transform its existing business model or reinvent the rules of its industry. We use the metaphor of architecture because when an architect sits down to design a new house, for example, he or she does not start by trying to work out where every piece of furniture is eventually going to go. The first step is to think broadly about what kind of house it is going to be—whether it should be a bungalow or a two-story structure, for example, or how many bedrooms it should have, and so forth. Then, over time, the design becomes more and more detailed as it continues to evolve. Likewise, the objective here is to create a broad strategic rationale for the company's innovation efforts—one that provides focus and clarity and that stretches the organization in an aspirational way. In the sections that follow, we'll walk you through the process of creating an innovation architecture and show how one company—Nokia—has used this focusing mechanism to distance itself from its competitors.

SHAPING YOUR INNOVATION PORTFOLIO

The process of creating an innovation architecture involves both divergence and convergence. First comes the *divergent* phase—that is, generating a rich and diverse portfolio of ideas and strategic options (see figure 7-1a). Then comes the *convergent* phase: looking across those options to find the patterns and themes—creating clusters of ideas that can reinforce each other and lead the firm in a clear strategic direction (see figure 7-1b).

The objective of the *divergent* phase is to identify and define your alternatives—to create a universe of strategic options that could take

FIGURE 7-1A

Divergent phase of innovation architecture process

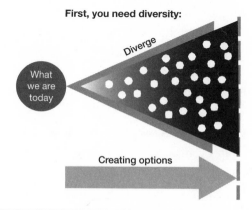

FIGURE 7-1B

Convergent phase of innovation architecture process

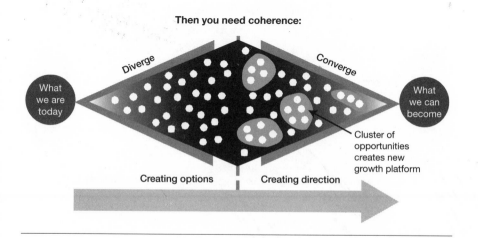

your company in many new directions from where it is today. The objective of the *convergent* phase is to make selective choices about which particular strategic direction your company should be moving in, with a view to differentiating itself from the competition.

The goal, in other words, is not only to ensure that a lot of experimentation is going on across the organization, but also to create an explicit, compelling, and widely shared sense of what the company is *becoming*—and what it is *not* becoming. Managers need to shape the company's innovation portfolio in a way that brings consistency and coherence to all those diverse ideas and opportunities, and that keeps innovation from splintering the company's resources.

This is exactly what an innovation architecture can do for you. It helps to create a shared and proprietary point of view about your company's future that will guide your decisions about the particular *kind* of growth opportunities your organization wants to pursue. Thus, instead of going after hundreds of unrelated things, your company will have some broad, consistent themes within which it is innovating.

"The key to strategy making," as Henry Mintzberg once put it, is "synthesis."[2] The task of shaping your innovation portfolio—so that individual instances of innovation compound on each other over time—requires you to condense and synthesize a whole population of interesting ideas into ten or fifteen different clusters or domains, and out of these, to eventually choose just three or four as the main components of your innovation architecture. We refer to these domains as *vectors of innovation* in that they define the ways in which your company intends to shape the future of your industry and set itself apart from the competition.

Some possible vectors of innovation include:

- *Customer types:* What segments of potential customers will we focus on?

- *Customer benefits:* What are the primary benefits we will offer to the customers we want to serve?

- *Product/service offering:* What offering areas will we dominate?

- *Geography:* Do we have the ambition to be a local leader? A regional leader? A global leader?

- *Core competence:* What core competencies do we want to master and leverage?

- *Economic or profit model:* What revenue and profit model will we use? For example, moving from a purchase model to a subscription model.

These vectors can be expressed as "from-to" statements, suggesting a continuum of progress. For example, a vector of innovation based on geography could be "from local to global." If it's about customer benefits, it might be "from convenience to indulgence." Or if it concerns your offering, it might be "from product to service" or "from product to experience." We like to illustrate these vectors of innovation in a simple graphic diagram, shown in figure 7-2, where we plot them as trajectories along which the company wishes to compound its innovation efforts into the future. They represent the vectors of transformation or innovation for the company.

Of course, the process of building an innovation architecture—of deciding exactly which three or four of these vectors of innovation to include—is quite a challenge. There are usually many heated discussions

FIGURE 7-2

Three vectors of innovation

The goal is to define the specific vectors along which a company intends to transform its existing business model or reinvent the rules of its industry.

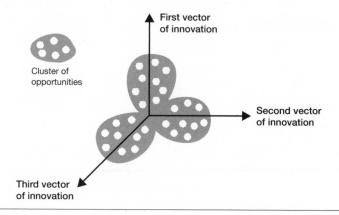

about what should *definitely* be included in the architecture, what could *possibly* be included, and what is eventually *left out*. These are strategic decisions of the highest level with long-term implications for the company, which is why they are very difficult to make. But once the architecture is in place and you have a view of innovation priorities, a lot of subsequent decisions become much easier. For example:

- Every project or initiative within the company can be assessed in terms of how well it is aligned with the organization's innovation focus.

- Each decision for where resources should be dedicated can be evaluated against these same dimensions.

Ask Yourself

Are we building an "innovation architecture" that gives our opportunity portfolio coherence and consistency and that defines what we want our company to become?

Example: back in the 1990s, Nokia successfully managed this systematic process of innovation divergence and convergence. The primary goal was to beat Motorola, which meant that Nokia had to develop greater industry foresight across the company and work out how to access the exciting new growth opportunities that were emerging in multimedia. Instead of making this a traditional top-down, forecast-laden "strategic planning" exercise, Nokia set out to involve the whole company. It was not aiming to come up with a new plan; it was aiming to create a highly inclusive and democratized process of strategy innovation. The hope was to generate a companywide perspective on truly unconventional strategic options. As Chris Jackson, former head of strategy development at Nokia, put it, "By engaging more people, the ability to implement strategy becomes more viable."[3]

In the first stage of the process—the divergent stage—Nokia's teams developed a set of novel strategic insights using the four perceptual lenses we outlined in chapter 3. This opened their eyes to *industry orthodoxies* that deserved to be challenged, deep *discontinuities* that could potentially re-shape the business landscape, *competencies and assets* that could be leveraged to create opportunities beyond the boundaries of their existing business, and emergent *customer needs*. Next, literally hundreds of Nokia's people—from top management to newcomers who had been with the company for only a few weeks—got involved in generating ideas and opportunities based on these insights. Out of all this thinking came a diversity of ideas—everything from mobile phones with built-in digital cameras, to face-plates in wildly different colors and designs, to mobile phones that could be used to buy things from vending machines. Some of the ideas seemed quite wacky at the time but have since become commonplace. A few were just downright crazy. But the important achievement was creating the cultural conditions that could spawn lots of new ideas about how to differentiate the company and shape the future of the industry.

The next phase in the process—the convergent stage—was where Nokia's managers could start to sift through all those ideas and opportunities and say, "Where are the patterns? What are the fundamental themes that would give overall direction to our company?" That was when the ideas began to be clustered into domains, and when strategic choices had to be made, because one cluster of ideas—one domain—would lead the company in one direction, whereas another domain would push it down a different route. In its search for a highly differentiated strategy, Nokia had to decide what kind of company it wanted to become.

In the end, Nokia's innovation architecture coalesced around three themes: *humanize technology*, *seamless solutions*, and *virtual presence*, with a collection of ideas and opportunities grouped around each of these respective domains.[4] *Humanize technology* was a cluster of ideas that focused on how to make a mobile phone easier and more intuitive to use, how to personalize it and make it more fun and more colorful, and how to make the interface friendlier. Another set of ideas came to be called *seamless solutions*—these ideas explored ways to offer network operators complete packages that would integrate the mobile phone with the software that provides a particular set of services, as well as the network equipment behind that. A third set of ideas looked at ways to extend the functionality of the phone beyond voice to give the user a *virtual presence*—for example, turning the phone into a kind of electronic credit card that would allow you to make purchases from vending machines, or into a security device, or into a more comprehensive communication device. These three domains became the vectors on which Nokia's innovation architecture was built, making it very simple to understand for everyone in the company (see figure 7-3).

From that point in 1996, Nokia began to innovate persistently along each of those trajectories. For example, the company worked hard to humanize and personalize the mobile phone in many imaginative ways. Nokia was the first to come up with colored faceplates that could be changed according to the outfit the customer was wearing on a particular day, helping to reposition the cell phone as a fashion accessory rather than a purely functional device. Nokia provided network operators like Vodafone with innovative and seamlessly integrated packages of services. And Nokia expanded the phone's capabilities to offer virtual presence much faster than anybody else—for instance, it was the first company to introduce a mobile phone with a calendar, e-mail, and Internet access features. In essence, Nokia's innovation architecture allowed the company to rewrite the rules of its industry.

FIGURE 7-3

Nokia's innovation architecture

Nokia redefined the cell phone industry with a consumer-centric strategic architecture.

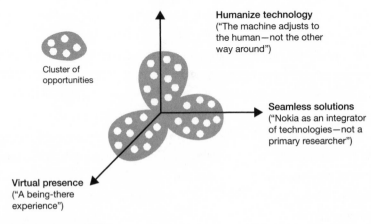

Source: Nokia annual report, 2000.

SCREENING AND SEQUENCING IDEAS

Having an explicit innovation architecture is a huge help when sifting through potential opportunities. It becomes a screening mechanism that sorts out those ideas that make sense for the company from those that may be attractive in the abstract but that don't fit the overall strategy. If anyone suggests pursuing an idea or a new business opportunity that doesn't drive the organization down one or several of the desired vectors of the innovation architecture, he or she will naturally have a much higher burden of proof. The general reaction is, "Why should we do this? It doesn't fit our strategy. It's not where we've decided to go." Thus, the innovation architecture provides ongoing guidance for daily operational and strategic decisions.

On the other hand, it should not become so set in stone that it causes you to ignore fundamental marketplace shifts that you hadn't anticipated when the architecture was developed. Your company has to stay open to ideas that match changing market conditions and customer needs, as well as to radical ideas that don't quite fit your strategy but that are too good for you to pass up—perhaps even under a different brand name. These may include, for example, ideas that could potentially have a transformational impact on your customers, or on your business model, or on your industry. In other words, the innovation architecture acts as a very useful guide that will help your innovation efforts compound consistently over time, but it also needs to be occasionally challenged and refreshed.

Another benefit is that having decided on the three or four dimensions of your innovation architecture, you can go back to that large portfolio of ideas that people have generated, and you can start to sequence all the ideas on those vectors over time. For example, Nokia could see that making a cellular phone available in a range of new colors was not a difficult thing to do—it could achieve this objective in about six months. However, some of the other ideas presented a much bigger challenge (e.g., the technology was not yet mature), which meant they would take a lot longer to implement. By looking at each idea in this way, you can plot a step-by-step migration path to your company's future along your chosen vectors. The innovation architecture allows you to plan what you are going to do this year or next, and what will be pushed back to subsequent years.

One of the major advantages of this approach to strategy—generating a big portfolio of ideas, grouping them into domains, and then crafting an innovation architecture—is that it tells your organization not only where it should be going but *how* it is going to get there. Instead of starting with some grand vision of the future and then trying to work backward, looking for ways to make it possible, your strategy grows out of a rich population of ideas and opportunities that you have already identified. Having all those ideas at your disposal makes it easy for everyone in the company to see how to make the strategy a reality.

A SHARED POINT OF VIEW

The real power of an innovation architecture is in the collective understanding it develops inside an organization about what the company wants to become. The actual process of building the architecture generates a high level of dialogue throughout the company about how the industry may be different in the future and about what the organization intends to do to shape and take advantage of that future. In most organizations, this collective understanding—this shared point of view about the company's future—is simply not there.

We often conduct an exercise that can be quite revealing. We take a random sample of a company's senior managers (say, ten to fifteen of the top one hundred people in the company), and we ask them a question that every senior executive group should be able to answer: What are the three to four ways in which you are going to reinvent your company and your industry over the next few years? We ask the executives to write their answers on a piece of paper. What we are looking for from each person is just three to four simple, declarative "from–to" sentences— "We are going to go from being this kind of company to that kind of company." Then we collect those sheets of paper, dig through the answers, and ask the following:

1. Did we find a consensus? Is there a shared point of view about what this company is becoming?

2. Would these answers surprise competitors? Or are these the same kind of things we would hear if we went to an industry conference—that is, "We need to be more environmentally conscious," "We need to be more customer driven," etc.?

3. Are these answers reflected in the short-term priorities of the company? Can you point to things you are doing right now—this quarter or this year—that are starting to move you in that direction? For example, building new competencies, pursuing new markets, developing new services, hiring new kinds of people, taking on new partners—specific steps that connect you with that longer-term point of view about how the company wants to change itself in the world.

In situations like this, many senior executives simply repeat their company's mission statement—there is usually some consensus in the organization about that. But just how unique is their mission statement? To find out, we usually conduct another exercise: we go to the Web sites or annual reports of a few of the company's direct competitors as well as some *indirect* competitors—companies in the same "space" but with a different focus or approach (e.g., same service to different customers, same customers but different style, etc.)—and we write down all of these companies' mission statements. Then we post them on the walls of the meeting room, but without the name of the company they belong to. We ask those senior executives to match the mission statements to the right companies. And what do we find? Quite often, the executives can't identify their *own* company's mission statement, let alone match all companies and all statements—which illustrates just how similar most of them are.

This exercise is not meant to challenge the value of or the need for a mission statement, but rather to point out its limitations. If the corporate mission statement suggests a level of consensus around *who* a company is or *what* it wants to be, then what represents the consensus of *how* it is going to get there? If we agree with the definition that strategy is the "art of differentiation," then exactly *how* does the company intend to become different? What steps will it be taking to amplify or extend its difference?

As an example, consider how Apple's innovation architecture, illustrated in figure 7-4, is helping the company to differentiate itself as it sets out to redefine and expand the digital media category. Does your organization have such a powerful and shared point of view about how it intends to redefine its own industry?

MORE THAN A MISSION, A VISION, OR A PLAN

An innovation architecture is more than a corporate mission. It's a blueprint for strategic and industry transformation—an explicit and widely shared point of view about how the company will strive to differentiate itself now, and five to ten years into the future. That makes it more compelling, more radical, and more transformational than a business plan. Yet, at the same time, it's more practical than a vision because it is connected with day-to-day activities and guides decisions on what to do next.

FIGURE 7-4

Apple's innovation architecture

While not the first, Apple redefined and expanded the digital media category.

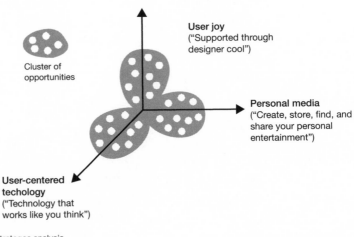

Source: Strategos analysis.

We like to describe an innovation architecture as being:

- Grounded in original, deep insights . . . *that are viscerally understood*

- Distilled from many competing options . . . *in a transparent process*

- Boldly aspirational . . . *and immediately practical*

- Engendered from deep commitment . . . *yet still appropriately tentative*

Would you describe your own company's mission statement or corporate strategy in that way? How grounded in reality is it? How many people were involved in creating it? How compelling is it? How practical is it for guiding day-to-day decisions?

STRATEGY FROM THE BOTTOM UP

Historically, most mission statements and corporate strategies have been created by small groups of top executives who go away for a few days, sit in a hotel, and brainstorm. When the members of that executive committee have finished deliberating, they typically launch an internal campaign that says, "Here is our strategy. Here is our vision. Go forth and implement it."

We believe that strategy should emerge from both the bottom up and be driven from the top down. It should come from the minds and hearts of your people. It should grow out of their passion and their insights. It should emerge from an inclusive and visible process that allows people to see where the strategy came from.

IBM, for example, has made a concerted effort in recent years to engage all of its people in an ongoing, global conversation about the company's strategies and purpose. In one seventy-two-hour online session, all 319,000 IBMers around the world were invited to engage in an open "values jam" via the company's global intranet, to discuss what they themselves thought should set the company apart and what should drive each individual's actions as an IBMer. Chairman and CEO Sam Palmisano describes how employees reacted:

They were thoughtful and passionate about the company they want to be a part of. They were also brutally honest. Some of what they wrote was painful to read, because they pointed out all the bureaucratic and dysfunctional things that get in the way of serving clients, working as a team or implementing new ideas. But we were resolute in keeping the dialogue free-flowing and candid. And I don't think what resulted—broad, enthusiastic, grassroots consensus—could have been obtained in any other way.[5]

Even if you assign specific teams in your company to do insight discovery work and to take the lead in generating new ideas and opportunities, as much of their work as possible should be published (in real time or near real time) on your intranet. Why? Because every single person in your company should be part of the conversation about what kind of future you are building.

In this emergent, bottom-up approach to strategy making, top management is less the author of strategy and more the *editor* of strategy. Its role switches from generating the company's new thinking to "connecting the dots"—sifting through a wide variety of options and ideas bubbling up from below, and searching for the patterns and fundamental themes that would give overall direction to the company.

One of the classic problems in strategy has always been the gap between formulation and implementation. Often, people say that formulation is the easy part and implementation is the hard part. We believe this is wrong. In our view, formulation is only easy if you are willing to have a strategy that is a derivative of everyone else's strategy. And implementation is typically a lot harder than it needs to be because people have not been brought along in the learning process; they don't have a deeply shared sense of what the company wants to become in the future—and why.

When you develop strategy in a way that has a high level of transparency and involvement, you find that you no longer have to sell some official point of view to the organization. Instead, it's already *their* point of view, because that's where it originated. The organization's future has become *their* future—it now seems inevitable to them; they know exactly what they are going to do, and in many cases you find that they are already racing off to do it.

Some executives worry about overresourcing and overinvesting at the strategy formulation stage—by involving so many people, doing so much insight discovery work, going out to visit places where change is happening, and so forth. But this usually pays huge dividends at the implementation stage, because people now know where the company is headed, and they understand where that point of view came from. It's as if they now have the DNA of the company's future embedded inside them, and they can't wait to go out and act on it.

PROPRIETARY—BUT NOT CONFIDENTIAL

"Hang on," you might be thinking, "if we make our strategy development process completely transparent, then it won't be long before the competition knows what our strategy is." And you would be absolutely right. But the reason that shouldn't worry you is that even if your competitors looked at your innovation architecture, those three or four vectors—or "dimensions of industry reinvention"—that you have defined would probably mean very little to them. They would read a few interesting-sounding phrases, but they wouldn't see all the learning, all the insight, all the ideas and opportunities, all the passion and energy behind them. In fact, if your innovation architecture didn't fit the mental model inside their own company, they would probably just discount it.

We might illustrate this with a movie. Imagine you walk in at the very end of a film, and all you catch is the final scene. Let's say it's Hugh Grant kissing Julia Roberts on a beautiful balcony. The scene might strike you as romantic, but it wouldn't really mean much to you emotionally—after all, it's just a kiss. However, anyone who has watched the whole movie might have tears in their eyes at this point because they know what led up to that scene; they know all about the impossible struggle those two characters have gone through to be together; they know the whole story behind how they got to the balcony and the big kiss. Likewise, if competitors come across your innovation architecture once it is finished, all they will see is a neat little diagram that could have come from any consulting group. They will see all those little dots clustered around a few vectors, but they won't have any idea what they are. Only people who were part of the process will have a visceral understanding about the opportunities that ended up in that cluster.

As an example, a term like Nokia's *virtual presence* wouldn't have meant a great deal to Motorola or to Ericsson, because they were not part of the process that created it and would therefore have no deep understanding about that particular opportunity space. The fact is, a few years after Nokia had defined its innovation architecture, the leadership team even went so far as publishing it in the company's annual report. Now you might say, "Why on earth would Nokia want to publish its innovation architecture if it is supposed to be its key to differentiation? Why would anyone publish something that is supposed to be proprietary?" The answer is this: it's the process of *creating* the architecture—the depth and breadth of the analysis, as well as all the discussions and decisions around it—that is proprietary; it's not the architecture itself. If the only requirement for an innovation architecture were to label the three legs on a tripod, then the power of that architecture as a guide for decisions would be miniscule. The innovation architecture would become a mere "check box" as opposed to a means for critical and informed dialogue across the company.

CREATING AND TESTING A TRIAL ARCHITECTURE

If you are ready to start trying to build an innovation architecture, keep in mind that it will rarely just fall into place the first time around. After all, there are so many possible permutations, and there is no "right" answer to the puzzle. You will probably identify quite a number of potential vectors of innovation around which to cluster the ideas your people have generated. And there are quite a number of considerations to be made before you finally decide which of these vectors to include in your innovation architecture.

To make the job easier, here's some advice: once you have identified, say, ten to fifteen possible dimensions of industry reinvention for your company, try putting three or four of these potential vectors together into a trial architecture. Experiment with several different combinations. Then evaluate each combination by asking yourself whether this architecture is:

- *Forward looking:* Does it represent our unique point of view about the future we want to create?

- *Distinctive:* Is it clearly different from the strategies of our traditional competitors and the threats from our nontraditional competitors?

- *Fact based:* Is it well grounded in proprietary insights on orthodoxies, discontinuities, competencies/assets, and customers?

- *Inspirational:*

  - Does it provide a stretch for the organization?

  - Will it foster passion among current and future leaders?

- *Practical:* Does it provide:

  - A clear guide to positioning, budget allocation, acquisitions, managerial efforts, and allocation of talent?

  - Targets for experimentation and learning?

- *Cohesive:* Does it bring the organization together by bounding the scope of debate about what we are becoming and about what we are and aren't going to do?

- *Cumulative:* Does it provide consistency and cumulativeness over time?

A BLUEPRINT FOR BUILDING THE FUTURE

An innovation architecture is not just a highly effective approach for synthesizing all the ideas and options your organization can imagine for its future. It's also a blueprint for actually *building* that future. It tells you what you should be doing right now to manage the migration path to future opportunities. It becomes the link between your present and your future. For example, it tells you things like:

- Which existing competencies you should be leveraging

- Which new competencies you should be acquiring

- Which new functionalities you should be deploying

- Which new customer groups you should be trying to understand

- Which new distribution channels you should be exploring

The process of building an innovation architecture can provide your entire organization with the emotional and intellectual energy to make the journey from where you are to where you want to be. It creates a shared a sense of direction—a sense of destiny—by engaging and mobilizing every person in the company. The role for your senior management team is to lead this inclusive, companywide process, not to go away in a little group and come up with the strategy on its own. Over time, its responsibility is also to make sure your innovation architecture is continually challenged, reinterpreted, and refreshed—in a world where the goalposts are constantly moving.

Creating an innovation architecture is not a typical consulting job that ends with a report about what your company should do. It's a process that produces a deeply and widely shared view of your company's future *throughout* the organization—among the people who have the power to make it happen. And it invariably unleashes talents and energies that would otherwise have remained untapped if those people had been disenfranchised from the process. As one pharma client remarked, "The involvement of hundreds of employees at all levels has allowed our senior management to discover talent previously below their radar screens."

Sometimes we use an innovation architecture to help an entire organization (e.g., Nokia) make the necessary strategic choices about what it wants to become—that is, what are the three or four vectors along which it wants to reinvent itself and the rules of its industry over the next few years? Then there are times when we use the innovation architecture process to define and crystallize the primary innovation themes that will help a company "unlock opportunities" within a broad new *growth area*— that is, an opportunity domain that has been predefined by corporate headquarters, or a division of the company, or a business unit or team.

In each case, creating an innovation architecture helps our clients to narrow their focus, develop a shared point of view about future opportunities, effectively screen and sequence ideas, and give a coherent logic to their innovation efforts so that they compound and reinforce each other over time.

INNOVATION CHALLENGES AND LEADERSHIP IMPERATIVES

Innovation challenge: How do I set the framework for innovation so that my innovation efforts have direction and coherence?

Leadership Imperatives

- Try focusing your ideation on "aiming points" such as a portfolio of specific growth platforms (innovation themes, important challenges) or customer problems.

- Build an innovation architecture for your company to help all employees understand "what we want to become." Use this architecture as a guide for choosing innovation opportunities that will bring you closer to this view of your future.

- Use the architecture as the foundation for ideation—to generate additional opportunities and to set boundaries for your ideation process.

- Don't adopt an innovation architecture that is so vague that everything can be included in it. Make sure it provides clear guidance on what you *won't* do.

- Challenge and refresh your architecture periodically. Make sure it reflects any fundamental marketplace shifts that you hadn't anticipated when the architecture was developed.

- The power of the architecture is in the deep tacit understanding of it by those who created it. Don't assume that competitors can act on your architecture if they see it.

Innovation challenge: How do I get buy-in and ownership at all levels for our innovation architecture?

Leadership Imperatives

- Involve more than the top executives in building the innovation architecture. Wider participation will build understanding and ownership. Don't make the architecture a top-down, executive-only strategy exercise.

- On the other hand, don't let the organization assume that the architecture will be selected by a vote. Ultimately, the decision about what strategy to pursue remains with top management.

PART FOUR

MAXIMIZING THE RETURN ON INNOVATION

CHAPTER 8

Managing and Multiplying Resources

OFTEN, THE MOST DIFFICULT CHALLENGE to innovation is not how to generate a lot of new, unorthodox ideas but how to quickly get enough talent and capital behind those ideas to start turning them into viable business plans and scaleable opportunities. Within most organizations, there are formidable barriers that prevent would-be innovators from getting access to the resources they need to execute their ideas.

Of course, removing these roadblocks to innovation is easier said than done. As every manager knows, reallocating resources is an intensely political and difficult process. In this chapter, however, we share examples of companies that have successfully overcome the barriers to funding radical innovation—by instituting processes that help them effectively manage and multiply their available resources.

The fact is, there are several different ways to think about funding game-changing innovation in a large company, from using the existing budgeting process to establishing Skunk Works and incubators, right through to creating budget set-asides and grassroots funding models. On the following pages, we focus on these mechanisms and examine why some of them are better than others.

BARRIERS IN THE BUDGETING PROCESS

Traditionally, the only way to get anything funded in large organizations has been through the traditional budgeting and resource allocation processes. These are usually among the most disciplined processes in the company, and in many respects, they work quite well: detailed proposals are submitted, senior management reviews the portfolio, and allocation decisions are carefully made. Projects and initiatives that are deemed critical to the organization are likely to get funded. Projects that are a bit farther off in time scale—or perhaps on the fringe of the core business—tend to receive few or no resources.

This practice is quite an understandable way for a company to set its financial priorities. Since the vast majority of the organization's revenues are coming from existing customer segments and distribution channels rather than from new ones, it is natural for senior managers to allocate capital accordingly. Thus, the "innovations" that end up getting funded are typically the incremental product enhancements within established businesses rather than the rule-breaking strategies out on the edge.

Being the single source of funding in most large companies, the budgeting process is, in effect, a monopoly: there is only one "seller" of capital. "Project advocates" have no alternative but to go hat in hand to the guardians of formal planning and ask them for money. They do not have multiple sources of capital available to them.

Contrast this with Silicon Valley, where some of today's hottest tech companies started out by pitching their idea to a breadth of angel investment networks and venture capital firms. On average, many had their proposals rejected at least ten times before they ultimately got funded. The entrepreneurs behind these start-ups had lots of choices about where to obtain seed capital, because in Silicon Valley—although not infinitely so—there always seems to be somewhere else to take an idea. However, in a large company, if your boss doesn't think it's a very interesting idea, it is probably going to die right there.

This highlights another pervasive barrier to innovation. In most organizations, there is not only a "monopoly" on capital but also a "monopsony" on ideas—there is only one *buyer*—and that is up the chain of command. There is simply nowhere else in the organization to take your idea except to the boss, and if business history is anything to go by, this is about as far as many ideas are ever going to get.

INCUBATORS AND SKUNK WORKS

One solution to the challenge of allocational rigidity is to create a corporate incubator or Skunk Works with a dedicated budget for "fringe" ideas. But all too often these incubators end up as orphanages—a refuge or last resort for ideas that can't find sponsors elsewhere.

By their very nature, incubators and Skunk Works lead a solitary existence, operating as an adjunct to the real work of the company. The fact that they are sequestered from the core business is often self-defeating, since the core business typically controls many of the key resources that are essential to innovation—for example, cash, talent, customer relationships, and core competencies. Thus, they are forced to pitch their ideas to business unit leaders who may have no emotional equity in those ideas, and who would frankly much rather dedicate their limited resources to existing strategies and tactical needs than to sponsoring seemingly irrelevant projects. That's why the fringe ideas and business concepts associated with these groups are rarely adopted or commercialized by the rest of the company. Most Skunk Works and incubators produce little in the way of new shareholder wealth.

The classic example is Xerox PARC (Palo Alto Research Center), where the company's innovators and dreamers were consciously separated from the managers, product engineers, and accountants who were running the rest of the firm. Lacking the power to leverage any of the resources in the core business, this small group of creative thinkers ultimately failed to create any real value for Xerox. Ironically, it was other companies—most notably Apple—that went on to commercialize some of the group's best ideas.

Having said that, there are cases—Lockheed's famous Skunk Works unit comes to mind—where being isolated from the rest of the organization has led to significant breakthroughs. However, it should be noted that the small team of engineers who were gathered at what was officially called Lockheed Advanced Development Projects Unit in 1943 were not being paid to just tinker with new technologies and dream up novel ideas (which was to some extent true of the researchers at Xerox PARC). Instead, they were given big, ambitious, and highly specific goals—like developing the U.S. Air Force's first operational jet fighter at the end of World War II in the face of the German threat, or building a spy plane that could fly over the Soviet Union during the Cold War, or building a Mach 3.0 aircraft out of titanium.

The reason the engineers at Lockheed's Skunk Works were given a lot of autonomy was to enable them to focus all their attention on these highly advanced (and often secret) projects, unhampered by organizational bureaucracy. As a result, they were able to produce both their prototypes and their finished products in record time.

To be sure, incubators and Skunk Works do attract a high percentage of the "lunatic fringe" inside a company, and they are probably the first places to look for your innovation mentors and champions. However, segregating innovation into these separate units—with limited funding and staffing—has very often proven to be counterproductive.

A MARKETPLACE FOR IDEAS, CAPITAL, AND TALENT

In most organizations, certain people have a much greater chance of getting heard than others. Usually a person's share of voice diminishes proportionately to their distance from corporate headquarters and their level in the corporate hierarchy. For example, if you come up with an idea and you happen to sit next door to the chief technical officer, there is a big chance you will get your idea heard, and you may even get it funded. But if you are working seven levels down in a large company—in some department or retail outlet or remote regional office—you are likely to have very little chance of getting heard, much less of winning some funding for a small-scale innovation experiment.

What companies really need is a mechanism for connecting an idea—wherever it originates and whoever thinks it up—with the money and the talent required to start pushing that idea forward. Prospective innovators should be able to get fast, easy access to experimental capital that has been set aside in the company for funding breakout ideas. And they should also get access to human skills—to a few smart people who can help advance, develop, and test the idea, perhaps by building a prototype. Instead of talking to the boss or to some incubator, the would-be innovator should be able to pitch his or her idea to an open internal *marketplace* for capital and talent that runs all across the organization—and even beyond its borders.

Markets are better mechanisms than hierarchies for getting the right resources behind the right opportunities at the right time. Nobody would seriously contend that a centrally planned economy—like that of the old Soviet Union—could compete with the speed and fluidity of capitalism's free markets. Yet, more often than not, a company's innovation processes are run more like a socialist state than, say, the New York Stock Exchange. Instead of creating a vibrant and unfettered marketplace where ideas, capital, and talent can find each other quickly and easily, most large companies create a centralized innovation process that moves as slowly and surely as an advancing glacier.

"Bringing Silicon Valley Inside"

Silicon Valley is a great example of an effective innovation marketplace. In Silicon Valley, capital and talent flow rapidly and freely to the best new opportunities, melding into whatever combinations are most likely to create new wealth. In most large companies, capital and talent don't move unless someone orders them to move.

What's more, in Silicon Valley, there is no prejudice about who can be an innovator. It doesn't matter whether you are old or young, whether you have an academic degree or you dropped out of college, whether you spent the last two years in a world-class company or working in a garage—what matters is the quality of your idea.

Gary Hamel argues that Silicon Valley's phenomenal wealth is not being generated by a group of geniuses, but by the valley's marketlike business model.[1] His clear prescription for large companies is this: try to "bring Silicon Valley inside" by replicating the region's economic model within your organization—that is, set up mechanisms that connect ideas, capital, and talent much more fluidly than traditional organization structures and management processes.

Connecting Ideas and Capital

There are various ways to build a marketplace for ideas inside a company. One way is to set aside a certain percentage of the budget for funding break-the-rules business concepts, and invite people to pitch ideas from anywhere in the organization. At one large company, the budgeting process has been changed to make this a reality. Top management has earmarked 10 percent of its $1 billion-a-year capital budget for funding projects that meet the test of being radical innovations. To qualify, a project has to be truly unconventional and have the potential to substantially change customer expectations, or industry economics, or the basis for competition in a given space. Divisional executives have been told that if they don't bring in such projects, they will slowly be starved of capital. This approach demonstrates a deep recognition that if the company is not funding breakout projects, it is never going to achieve breakout results.

Another possible way to redesign resource allocation processes—so that they work more like Silicon Valley and less like centrally planned economies—would be to say to anyone who has a discretionary budget of more than, say, $100,000 (of which there are sometimes hundreds or perhaps thousands in a big company), "You can take 1 percent or 3 percent or 5 percent of your budget, and you can invest it in any project anywhere in this company that interests you." In other words, those managers could get to play the role of angel investors, pooling their resources with a group of other corporate "angels" to provide seed funding for attractive strategic experiments and initiatives. And to the extent that a project, or a portfolio of projects, produces a positive return—in terms of new revenues or big cost savings to the company—a bonus could go back to those who provided the funds and served as sponsors and mentors. This would give the prospective innovator access to a multitude of potential investors across the company to whom he or she could appeal when seeking to raise funds, just as any start-up would have in Silicon Valley. Thus liberated, capital could flow to the most intriguing new possibilities for transforming the core business, unfettered by executives' protectionist tendencies.

Shell "GameChanger"

An excellent example of a marketplace for ideas is to be found at Royal Dutch/Shell, the Anglo-Dutch oil giant. This may not be a name that immediately comes to mind when you think about fast, flexible resource allocation—indeed, an employee once described the company as "a maze of 100-foot-high walls."[2] But for several years now, a radical culture shift has been under way.

Royal Dutch/Shell has instituted a companywide process called GameChanger, which solicits and funds breakthrough ideas from all across its global enterprise—and beyond. Started initially as an ad hoc, internal process only, GameChanger is now open to anybody, anywhere in the company (whether sitting at corporate headquarters, or working on an oil platform somewhere in the South China Sea) as well as to people and organizations outside the corporate boundaries. Founded on the notion that ideas and entrepreneurial talent lurk everywhere, the system was designed to break down the company's famous organizational "walls" and create a climate more hospitable for innovation—a climate that completely dissociates a person's capacity to be heard from their political and geographic position inside or outside the organization. Just as in a democracy, where everybody's vote counts, what counts in the GameChanger process is the quality of the idea, not who or where it comes from.

As described by Shell, the purpose of GameChanger is to "invest in technology or business ideas from inside or outside of Shell that either (a) fundamentally reshape one of our primary existing businesses, or (b) allow us to explore wholly new directions."[3] Here's how GameChanger works: any employee (or outsider) with a promising idea can go online, fill out a very clear form, and submit it electronically. The primary criteria for assessing these ideas are:

1. *Novelty:* Is the idea truly and fundamentally new and different?

2. *Value:* Could the idea create substantial new value if it works?

3. *Why Shell?:* Does Shell enable the idea to become bigger, and do we care if it does?

4. *Credible plan:* Is there a plan to manage primary risks prudently by qualified people?

Once an idea is submitted, it completely bypasses the hierarchy and instead goes straight to a six-person peer review panel that meets once a week and that is refreshed with new people every six months. The panel looks at every single idea that comes in, and when an idea looks as if it has potential, the panel members discuss it in more detail with the innovator. If an idea is given the green light, the innovator can receive initial funding of $25,000 in less than a week. Along with that money, the innovator is given thirty days off to design an experiment that will either validate or invalidate the idea's most critical hypotheses. This is based on the recognition that one of the innovator's biggest challenges is not just finding experimental capital but finding the experimental *time* to test an idea by being released for a while from his or her current responsibilities.

After the critical hypotheses for an idea have been ranked, it becomes quite clear which fundamental questions have to be answered first. So with $25,000 and thirty days, the innovator sets out to address those issues. It might be as simple as going off to talk to some people who are subject area experts to see whether they think the idea is feasible. Or it could be setting up a lab experiment to test whether something is technically possible. Or it could be mocking up a prototype to gauge people's reactions.

After thirty days, the innovator comes back and presents the learning. In many cases, it already becomes obvious at this stage whether or not an idea has the potential to eventually go somewhere. Alternatively, it may be that while an idea was not exactly validated, it certainly was not *invalidated*. So the GameChanger panel may say, "OK, how about another $25,000 for the next thirty days?" Or the panel may say, "This looks really promising, so we'd like to give you $50,000 for ninety days." A subsequent proof-of-concept review determines whether a plan is workable and deserves further funding. In the end, the average GameChanger grant is $100,000, but some projects have received as much as $600,000 in funding.

The panel will also try to connect the innovator with a broad range of other company resources, including company experts who can serve as technical advisers, mentors, and coaches, or other talented individuals and teams who can get involved in developing the project. Later, if a project is gaining serious momentum, they will bring together a panel of business leaders from all across Shell and give them the opportunity to adopt the new idea.

So far, the system has been a magnet for thousands of new ideas from employees in all parts of the organization—as well as from external sources—hundreds of which have been funded. Many of these ideas are later moved into an operating unit or one of Shell's growth initiatives. Still others are carried forward as R&D projects. In the last few years, some of Shell's largest growth initiatives had their origins in the Game-Changer system, and a large percentage of the company's R&D budget goes to ventures that started in GameChanger. Those ideas that don't pass muster enter a database that is accessible to anyone within Royal Dutch/Shell—it's a kind of "idea bank" that allows the company's world-wide base of potential innovators to further shape their own ideas by comparing them with earlier submissions, or bring new insight to those existing ideas.

It is also noteworthy that, beginning as an initiative in Shell's largest division, Exploration & Production (E&P), the budget assigned to the first GameChanger panel for allocating to new ideas was $20 million. That figure represents less than 0.1 percent of E&P's earnings in 2000. The process has therefore delivered a lot of bang for comparatively few bucks and is based on small increments of capital and experimental time rather than big, bet-the-farm investments.

This approach to innovation has imbued what used to be a bureaucracy-burdened industrial giant with the kind of passion for innovation that you would expect to find in a Silicon Valley start-up. In fact, that's what makes GameChanger all the more interesting. If it were happening at

Google, a lot of people would say, "Oh, but that's Google. We couldn't do a thing like that here. We're too big and bureaucratic and cumbersome." Well, they don't come a lot bigger, more bureaucratic, and more cumbersome than Royal Dutch/Shell. If this sort of thing can be done at Shell, it can be done in your company, too.

GameChanger works incredibly well, yet in its essence the process is very uncomplicated; it's something that would not be hard to duplicate inside any other company. So why have so few organizations decided to adopt a similar approach? The reason has little to do with the difficulty of implementing such a scheme. It has more to do with the difficulty of changing the locus of power and influence inside organizations, because at its heart, a process like GameChanger puts power in different hands—it shifts the authority to make some resource-allocation decisions away from the traditional budgeting process and gives it to another set of people. Understanding the potential benefit from changing the locus of power—and exactly how best to make the change—is the real issue behind the current organizational inertia.

CREATING A PORTFOLIO OF PROJECTS

Shell's GameChanger process illustrates the importance of recognizing that there is enormous potential value in radical, rule-breaking ideas—even ones that would appear to have only a 10, 15, or 20 percent probability of success. Trouble is, nobody knows exactly which ideas will turn out to be duds and which ones will emerge as winners.

Too often, companies tend to review and fund projects based on the individual merits of each project proposal: is this a "good" idea or "bad" one? Is it a safe investment opportunity or a big risk? Does it have a 90 percent chance of success or a 20 percent chance? No wonder radical, rule-breaking ideas seldom get corporate funding; judged against these evaluation criteria, almost all of them are deemed to be losers.

Venture capitalists think differently, investing in perhaps a dozen or so companies *within the same market space*, knowing that six will lose everything, three might break even, one or two will double the investment, and one could turn out to be the next Google, returning fifty to one hundred times the investment. A VC's goal is not to weed out the losers but to make sure there is a big winner. It's not about the return on each project; it's about the return on a *portfolio* of projects—all of which have only a 20 percent chance of success—where most of those projects will probably fail, but the upside on the one or two projects that succeed is potentially enormous.

This is the logic behind the GameChanger model. Unlike a traditional resource allocation process, in which each project has its "owner" or sponsor, GameChanger is a panel that owns and manages a *portfolio* of projects. And instead of performance being assessed on a project-by-project basis, it is assessed across the whole portfolio. The fact is that GameChanger has become one of the most profitable investment portfolios anywhere in Shell.

REALLOCATING TALENT

In Silicon Valley's marketplace model, talent is just as mobile as money; it migrates to the companies offering the most exhilarating work and the greatest potential rewards. In the valley, the market for talent works with brutal efficiency, and it operates through resource *attraction*, not resource allocation.

Why not create an internal market for talent in your organization that functions on the same principle? Why chain some of your brightest people to old, established businesses when they could be adding untold value to a new breakthrough project? Why not free up the "A" people to work on the "A" opportunities? Why not make divisional vice presidents, project leaders, and others bid for the best employees in the company?

Here's the good news: you don't have to be in Silicon Valley to manage by these principles. Chuck Knight, the now-retired and deeply respected former CEO of Emerson Electric, writes that the ability to see talented managers as "assets of the corporation—not of the divisions or other units in which they happen to work" is a key management principle for fostering innovation.[4] Great companies are increasingly learning to view their employees this way. Many are currently busy breaking down the walls between business units and national organizations in order to let human capital flow more freely to the most promising growth projects.

Consider Whirlpool. Instead of relying on a forced talent-pool system to assign people to innovation projects, Whirlpool allows its employees to "vote with their feet." The company's intranet-based Innovation E-Space allows employees to see all the innovation projects that are currently under way across the organization and to volunteer to join one of those projects (either full- or part-time) if they are excited by the idea and feel they can make a valuable contribution. Innovation E-Space also has a section called MyPage—which works in a similar way to popular Web sites like MySpace.com—where individual employees can describe themselves, their experience, their skills, and their interests. This creates not only a vibrant online community around the globe but a very effective internal marketplace for talent.

TOWARD THE HYBRID ORGANIZATION

Clearly, getting the right resources behind the right ideas requires companies to take on new ways of thinking, new management processes, and new organizational forms. While the hierarchical "command and control" paradigm was indispensable to the evolution of the large-scale industrial organization—which was built for efficiency—it is proving to be a less appropriate form of governance for an organization that is built for innovation.

Hierarchies put managers in control of considerable economic resources, but they simultaneously create the allocational rigidities that hamper creativity and the development of radical ideas. They exhibit a systemic bias against the exploration of the new. Markets, on the other hand, are becoming increasingly attractive as a form of organizing innovation, precisely because they offer the promise of disrupting these rigidities. They allow companies to tap the imagination and creativity of *all* their employees, and they enable ideas, capital, and talent to find each other swiftly and easily.

What is needed, in our belief, is a hybrid organizational form that combines elements of both a hierarchy and a market—with a view to improving the innovation capacity of a firm. We need to rebalance the use of corporate resources through new mechanisms—ones that release the creative energy of an enterprise in a way that pure command-and-control organizations never could. We need organizations that believe in *innovation democracy*—the notion that ideas with billion-dollar potential can come from anyone and anywhere.

Instead of fearing that this will put them out of a job, managers should be exploring and embracing these new governance structures, recognizing their pivotal role as champions of the new innovation process. Rather than painstakingly sifting through ideas and trying to decide which one represents the biggest new investment opportunity, executives should be looking for ways to invest incrementally in the opportunities that employees are already exploring. They should be reading the business plans that employees are writing in their spare time. They should be asking where employees would invest their own time, enthusiasm, and attention if only they had the chance. They should be encouraging all of their people to think like entrepreneurs, and making it possible for them to sell their ideas in the corporate marketplace. They should be diverting at least a small amount of their resources away from legacy programs and into experimental alternatives—new products, distribution channels, customer groups, pricing strategies, and so forth.

Just as most companies reengineered their business processes to reduce the time between order and cash flow, they now need to reengineer their management processes—like capital budgeting and strategic planning—to reduce the time between *idea* and cash flow. The race is on, not just to dream up new possibilities and recognize nascent opportunities, but to capture them all efficiently and then quickly get enough capital and talent behind them to transform promising ideas into new sources of profit.

MULTIPLYING THE AVAILABLE RESOURCES

Many managers would argue that the biggest difficulty is not how to reallocate resources from legacy businesses to new growth opportunities, but how to find enough resources to work with in the first place. With every budget in every company under intense and perpetual scrutiny, and with the screws being turned down all over the organization, where exactly are the resources for innovation supposed to come from?

If executives believe that innovation requires them to take a big hit to short-term earnings, freeing up the necessary cash and talent will always be something they do reluctantly. While this reluctance is understandable at some level, the implicit assumption here is that radical, game-changing innovation only happens if a company invests substantial resources. This is not necessarily true. Sure, innovation takes resources, but in many cases it doesn't take anywhere near as much in the way of resources as most managers assume.

As an example, consider the University of Queensland's HyShot program, which was responsible for the world's first successful test flight of a scramjet engine (considered to be the future of commercial aviation). How could a small team of scientists in Australia—working with a shoe-string budget of less than $2 million and a rocket built mostly from off-the-shelf parts—achieve such an impressive breakthrough? How could they go up against mighty NASA, which had already spent a hundred million dollars on its own scramjet project, and beat it to the punch?

The answer is this: the correlation between innovation resources and competitive outcomes is much weaker than most people imagine. The fact is, you don't have to have a budget like NASA's to produce great ideas and to pull off incredible innovation achievements. On the contrary, you can innovate very successfully on the cheap. Indeed, you *should* innovate on the cheap! If your organization is turning down the screws on everything else, then innovation budgets should be no exception. Innovation must be run just as efficiently as any other process in the company.

In practice, there are many ways of multiplying your available resources to deliver a whole lot more bang for the innovation buck. One way, as we pointed out in chapter 4, is by involving many minds across the organization—and beyond its borders—in your company's innovation efforts. Shell's GameChanger process, as we described a few pages earlier, is a very good illustration of this. Creating an open door to ideas from anyone and anywhere is literally the cheapest way to dramatically push up the number of ideas entering your innovation pipeline. It's worthy of note, for example, that P&G's open innovation program—"Connect and Develop"—has not only produced a slew of successful new products from outside the firm, but has simultaneously helped P&G slash its own R&D investments by around 20 percent, giving productivity a tremendous boost.

To innovate on the cheap, you need to break with the notion that pathbreaking innovation requires your company to do everything itself. How is it possible, for example, that Apple makes arguably the world's most advanced personal computer operating system, despite having a tiny 2.5 percent market share and just a fraction of Microsoft's $6 billion annual R&D budget? It's not as if Apple makes up for the resource gap by selling Mac OS X Leopard at a premium price—like, say, Ferrari does when it asks a quarter of a million dollars for a beautifully crafted, high-performance sports car. Here's the answer: the core software code behind Apple's operating system is UNIX—it came out of the public domain. Essentially, Apple layers its own proprietary "skin" over this core—the interface, the Finder, and other components that make the operating system so wonderfully cool and easy to use.

The same thing is true if you look at the iPod. Apple may have developed the ultimate circuitry for the device and added the iconic look and the friendly user interface, but at its heart, the iPod relies on a reference platform designed by a company called PortalPlayer Inc. This helps explain why Apple was able to develop the original iPod in less than a year.

If Apple had chosen to develop Mac OS X Leopard or the iPod completely on its own, entirely from scratch, the challenges would have been much greater, the costs would have been much higher, and the time frames for these projects would have been much longer. Instead, it chose to be innovative where it matters—in things that add unique Apple-type value—and source the rest from outside the organization. This is a hugely important method for multiplying resources.

Even organizations with gigantic budgets and big, ambitious goals are coming around to the idea that innovation doesn't have to eat up piles of money. Take the U.S. Department of Defense. One of its priorities is to develop battlefield robots that can take over some of the ground-based reconnaissance tasks that are highly risky for human soldiers. The ultimate goal is to make one-third of ground military forces automated by 2015. When that job landed on the desk of the Defense Advanced Research Projects Agency (DARPA), what did it do? Try to fight for a sizable slice of the U.S. defense budget for funding extensive R&D into robotics? No.

It launched the "DARPA Grand Challenge"—a government-sponsored competition, open to anyone, where the aim is to build a completely autonomous ground vehicle that can find its way, unmanned and unguided, across a long stretch of the Mojave Desert in the fastest time. The annual event, which offers prize money of $2 million, attracts hundreds of teams from universities, high schools, colleges, businesses, and other organizations—either based in the United States or abroad—all willingly contributing their technical skills just for the fun of it.

A second way to improve your innovation efficiency, as the Shell Game-Changer example also illustrates, is to make sure your innovation experiments are initially based on small increments of capital and time rather than hefty, bet-the-farm investments.

A third and closely related way to multiply your available resources is to keep your innovation commitments consistent over time. Think about Toyota's patient, multiyear program to develop eco-friendly cars—resulting in its hugely popular range of hybrid vehicles. It was managed as a stepwise migration path, with investments gradually increasing in stages as the company's learning and experience compounded and as competencies grew stronger. By contrast, GM made a big, expensive start in the early 1990s in pursuit of the same goal, eventually investing a billion dollars on EV-1, an egg-shaped, all-electric (as opposed to hybrid), zero-emissions vehicle. The car was a commercial flop. Three years after its fanfare launch in 1996, having produced only seven hundred vehicles, GM's CEO decided to pull the plug. The lesson here is that it's fine to have revolutionary goals, but the best way to achieve those goals is usually by taking consistent, evolutionary steps, not by making big shifts in innovation priorities with start-again, stop-again investments.

By focusing on critical productivity drivers like these—freeing your employees' imaginations, looking for external innovators, investing incrementally, and keeping your commitments consistent—you should be able to significantly multiply your financial and human resources.

But how can you make sure you are matching the level of your investment to the pace at which a particular opportunity is likely to evolve? And what can you do in practical terms to derisk your innovation investments? These are the key questions we will consider in chapter 9.

INNOVATION CHALLENGES AND LEADERSHIP IMPERATIVES

Innovation challenge: How can I make sure that sufficient funding and talent flows to the best ideas?

Leadership Imperatives

- Rethink your current budgeting process: is it geared to encourage new ideas or to preserve the status quo?

- Consider creating a central pool of money earmarked for game-changing innovation and use it to fund radical ideas from anywhere within the company—or from outside.

- Don't chain your brightest people to the old established businesses. Instead, emulate and apply the principles of free-market economics by creating an internal marketplace for talent based on talent attraction rather than talent allocation.

- Combine elements of markets and hierarchies to maximize your innovation potential. Rebalance the use of resources through new market mechanisms that release creative energy in a way that pure command and control never could.

Innovation challenge: How can I best nourish the early ideas and give them a chance to grow rather than prematurely killing them?

Leadership Imperatives

- Recognize that even ideas with a "low" probability of success are worth experimenting with—albeit in a limited way—to learn more about the opportunity space.

- Don't isolate innovations in an "innovation orphanage." Make sure that new ideas are connected to corporate resources, assets, and competencies.

- Focus on the portfolio of innovations and seek to maximize the number of winners versus losers. Don't use traditional financial metrics to judge individual embryonic ideas.

- Don't stick to a budgeting system that encourages innovators to overhype and overpromise new ideas in order to get them funded.

Innovation challenge: How can I innovate with limited resources?

Leadership Imperatives

- Embrace the fact that it is possible to innovate on the cheap. There are many ways to multiply innovation resources to deliver more bang for each innovation buck.

- Don't use "lack of resources" as an excuse for poor innovation performance. Remember that the correlation between innovation resources and outcomes is much weaker than most people imagine.

- Accept the notion that "ordinary" employees can be a source of extraordinary innovation. Don't delegate innovation responsibility to a small cadre of "experts."

- Look outside your company for innovation ideas and talent— the way companies like P&G are now doing.

Innovation challenge: How do I maintain innovation momentum?

Leadership Imperatives

- Commit to a small number of medium-term innovation goals, and maintain that commitment.

- Don't continually make big shifts in innovation priorities. Start-again, stop-again investment programs tend to undermine innovation credibility and productivity.

CHAPTER 9

Pacing and Derisking Innovation Investments

TAKE A LOOK at the portfolio of new growth opportunities you have generated through your innovation efforts, and you are likely to find a diverse set of opportunities with very different time frames and risk profiles. This diversity is not inherently bad—though managers often view it as such. However, to create sustainable value from your innovation efforts, it's critical for you and your company to understand these differences and to manage both your learning and resource investment accordingly.

In this chapter, we will show you how to distinguish between different kinds of opportunities in terms of time frame and risk profile—initially as they are conceived through your innovation efforts and then as you manage them over time—and we suggest some practical guidelines for pacing and derisking your commitments. Our goal here is to help your company create the optimum strategy for realizing and capturing the value of each individual innovation opportunity.

KNOW THE RACE YOU RUN

C. K. Prahalad and Gary Hamel characterize opportunities with different time frames as "sprints and marathons." *Sprints* are opportunities that seem to take off overnight—where the customer benefit is both obvious and substantial, the technology is already available, and a large potential market is just sitting there waiting for the idea to happen. Think Netflix, Hotmail, Skype, MySpace, YouTube, PayPal, or DirecTV.

Marathon opportunities have a much slower buildup. It may take quite a number of years to get the technology right, or the business model right, or to penetrate the public consciousness, before an idea takes off in a significant way. Think high-definition television, gene replacement therapy, speech recognition software, or fuel cell–propelled automobiles—these have turned out to be hugely difficult, long-term challenges. There are also radical product concepts and business models that fall into this category—examples would be Nespresso (Nestlé's capsule-based coffee system), or the organic supermarket chain Whole Foods Market; both of these opportunities were decades in the making.

Of course, in hindsight it is not hard to see which opportunities were sprints and which ones were marathons. But companies often find it difficult to distinguish between sprints and marathons at their nascent stage—to judge whether a new business idea will take off very fast or will need much longer to gain market penetration. As a result, they can find themselves investing too much too soon—racing to the market with an idea that is extremely premature; or, conversely, investing too little too late—chasing an opportunity when it has already been cornered by a competitor and there is very little chance of catching up.

How can you work out the optimum pace and the scale at which to invest resources in a particular opportunity? The answer is by paying great attention to the external factors that can either accelerate the time frame for commercializing a new idea or dramatically slow it down.

As you assess a new opportunity, ask yourself probing questions like these:

- Are there substantial technical hurdles that need to be overcome?

- Does market takeoff depend on complementary products or services?

- Will a new infrastructure be required for this market to develop?

- Will customers need to learn new skills or adopt new behaviors?

- Are there going to be high switching costs for customers?

- Will competing standards confuse customers and delay adoption?

- Does success depend on aligning the interests of diverse constituents?

- Are there powerful competitors that will seek to delay or derail us?

If your answer to one or more of these questions is "yes," it's very likely that this opportunity is going to be a marathon. Your company should be very careful not to overcommit resources by investing too much too soon.

UNDERSTANDING MARATHONS

Let's look at a good example of a marathon, perhaps with a cup of coffee. Consider the development of Nespresso—the capsule-based espresso system from Nestlé. After Nestlé bought the original patent in the 1970s, it took the company's R&D department over a decade to perfect the extraction pump, the capsules, and other parts of the system that were needed to make it function properly. Subsequently, in the mid-1980s, Nestlé moved the idea outside its core organization structure and created a 100 percent–owned affiliate called Nespresso. Initially, the business went nowhere. In fact, it would take another fifteen years before the market penetration curve went from horizontal to vertical, and during much of this time, Nespresso was not much more than a loss-making embarrassment to Nestlé. A critical lesson here is that throughout the whole three-decade marathon, Nestlé never gave up on the idea. Just as importantly, the business—though small—was managed for profit and learning. The company was convinced that the concept would one day have the potential for mass-market appeal—and it was right. Today, Nespresso's coffee machines and little capsules are a fixture in homes and offices all over the world. Annual revenue, which has been growing at rates of 25 percent to 30 percent each year, is now heading for $1 billion.

Why did Nespresso take so long to take off? First, there were technical hurdles to be overcome just to make the system work. Second, there were relatively high switching costs—customers had to replace their coffee machine. Third, customers had to adopt a new behavior—literally learn a new way to make coffee—which was quite a tough sell. But Nestlé knew that if it could make Nespresso work, it had the potential to be a *big* opportunity. After all, how many people drink coffee around the world? And how many people would like to enjoy a really good cup of Italian-style espresso without all the typical mess?

Early on, Nestlé could see that as consumers became more affluent, they would grow increasingly dissatisfied with granules of instant coffee from a jar. And that was long before there was a Starbucks on every corner. But it took years for everything to come together in the right constellation: the customer demand for better-quality coffee, the design and colors of Nespresso's machines, the public awareness for a new capsule-based system, the widespread presence in distribution channels, and the right kind of advertising strategy (featuring an ultra-suave George Clooney).

It was Nestlé's vision—about the size of the opportunity—that fueled its commitment for so long. Importantly, this was not the kind of commitment that is measured by the size of the budget and head count that a company invests in a project. It was the kind measured in terms of how *persistently* a company pursues success—the depth of belief and the level of perseverance it brings to the project.

Nespresso illustrates that innovation is often a game of successive approximation over an extended period of time, where a company is gradually trying to find the right combination of value, price, technology, and marketing to make an opportunity happen. It also illustrates that some ideas need considerable time to reach their profit-making potential. Companies need to be extremely careful not to pull the plug on a genuinely big opportunity before it fully matures, based on the reasoning that it is not yet delivering significant returns or, worse, making a loss.

Let's be clear: no company should run a marathon unless it believes there is an enormous prize at the end of the race. There is simply no point in persevering over many years for an opportunity that is trivial. But if the prize appears to be worth all that effort and commitment over the long term, you need to ask, What are the natural barriers to getting this thing done? And if those barriers are relatively substantial, then the next questions are, How do we conserve our resources for what may be a very long journey? How can we be extraordinarily committed to a new opportunity space, and yet, simultaneously remain extremely tentative in terms of investment?

Pacing Your Commitment

Clarity is not the same thing as proximity—your organization may have a crystal clear vision about a potential new opportunity, but it might still take several years to make that opportunity happen. Think of it like driving toward the Swiss Alps or the Rockies: you can see the mountains long before you can actually touch them and start to climb them. As Institute for the Future founder Paul Saffo frequently declares, "Never mistake a clear view for a short distance."

Most people would agree, for example, that there is a huge potential opportunity in speech recognition. We can all see the goal—it could be the next killer app—but technically we are just not there yet, despite the fact that software companies have been working on it for years already. Even Microsoft—no lightweight when it comes to throwing resources around—has so far not been able to make speech recognition happen in a big way. Whether we like it or not, some opportunities simply have a long lead time.

This is something that is deeply understood at W. L. Gore, where there is no pressure inside the company to rush a premature idea to the market. Bob Doak, a W. L. Gore business leader in the United Kingdom, says, "Gore has immense patience about the time it takes to get it right and get it to market. If there's a glimmer of hope, you're encouraged to keep a project going and see if it could become a big thing."[1] By taking the long view—knowing that it can take years or even decades to turn a revolutionary idea into a profitable new product—W. L. Gore gives its people the time they need to nurture these slow-burn opportunities to their proper fruition, while simultaneously making sure that they are not overresourcing them.

UNDERSTANDING SPRINTS

There are other opportunities, of course, where the challenge is not to move too *slowly*; otherwise, one or more competitors may get there first. To find out whether your organization should be rapidly ramping up its investment in a particular opportunity, ask yourself another set of questions:

- Are the customer benefits clear and substantial?

- Are there potential network effects that will accelerate takeoff?

- Are competitors already aiming at the same target?

- Are there clear "analogies" or "exemplars" from other industries—companies with analogous business models and opportunities that suggest the portent for success?

If the answer to these questions is "yes," make sure that your company does not undercommit resources by investing too little, too late. This opportunity is going to be a sprint, and you'd better move fast—if it's not too late already.

Consider eBay as an example. Think about how you might have answered the above questions in the early 1990s, before the opportunity took off. Were the customer benefits clear and substantial? Yes. Were there potential network effects that would accelerate takeoff? Yes, huge ones—people would be eager to sell their stuff on the auction site that has the most eyeballs looking at it. Were there clear analogies to follow? (In other words, could you have pointed to similar ideas or business models that had worked out well—perhaps in another industry or another context—giving you evidence that this opportunity could also be viable?) Again, the answer would have been yes. At its heart, eBay was not a new idea; it was a totally *old* idea—flea markets, auctions, classified advertising—but applied in a new technological context. The global, peer-to-peer, Web-based marketplace was an opportunity that was just waiting to happen, but it was not going to wait for long.

Another good example is PayPal. Launched in the late 1990s at the height of the dot-com bubble, PayPal offered a fast, easy, and, most importantly, *secure* way to send and receive payments online—something scores of e-commerce companies and millions of Internet-savvy consumers were looking for at the time, most notably the online auction crowd. With the volume of online payments rising exponentially, PayPal rapidly became the payment method of choice with an exploding crowd of users, and in 2002, was acquired by eBay in a deal valued at $1.5 billion. Today, PayPal manages well over 100 million accounts in more than 100 markets and handles a total payment volume of tens of billions of dollars annually (currently growing by over 30 percent each year).

Again, it was a case of a sprintlike opportunity. The customer benefits were clear and substantial—PayPal immediately offered a safe and simple electronic alternative to traditional paper methods of payment, like checks and money orders. The network effect was there, too, with Internet usage going through the roof. And PayPal did not require any new infrastructure—it could piggyback on the existing financial infrastructure of bank accounts and credit cards. The system was also incredibly easy to use—nothing to do but fill in a few fields on an online transaction form and press a button—and it involved absolutely no switching costs for the customer. In terms of market penetration, these factors gave PayPal the acceleration power of a Lamborghini.

BECOMING A "SMART MOVER"

Innovators and academics have long debated the optimum speed with which an organization should move to capture a particular growth opportunity. They are still divided into two camps: those who believe innovators should try to build a "first-mover advantage" and those who argue that "fast followers" end up making all the money.

Our belief is that the debate about first-mover versus second-mover advantage is actually misframed. Instead of first-mover versus second-mover, a more accurate framing would be "Are we a *smart* mover?"

A company can be the first mover and be *smart*—think Amazon.com or eBay. But a company can also be first to market and be *dumb*—think Pets.com. Being first is of no value if the destination isn't worth the trip. Or, as Apple's fiasco with the Newton demonstrates, you can be first to market with an idea whose time has not yet come.

With sprintlike innovation opportunities, as we illustrated above, it's smart to move fast. With marathons, on the other hand, the smart thing to do is move slowly. Companies that are smart movers have impeccable timing. They match the pace of their investment to the underlying pace of market development. Companies that are not smart movers let their financial commitment and the pace of their learning get out of sync with the natural time frame of an emerging opportunity.

Asking the probing sets of questions we listed above can help you to recognize whether an opportunity is going to be a sprint or a marathon, and thus, to pace your investment accordingly.

AVOIDING RISK

Emerging opportunities have not only different time frames, but also very different risk profiles. Learning to distinguish between betting the farm and betting a pig—or several piglets—is another crucial piece in the innovation puzzle.

Without a doubt, innovation can be a risky endeavor. Companies have sometimes used this argument to justify their instinctive fear of novelty. But what many fail to understand is that novelty actually implies nothing about risk. As we discussed in chapter 6, an idea can be new, and even radical, without being inherently risky. Risk is a function of uncertainty—or the probability of failure—multiplied by the size of one's financial exposure. Newness is a function of the extent to which an idea defies precedent and convention. The persistent failure to distinguish between new ideas and risky ideas reinforces a company's tendency to overinvest in the past.

Actual Risk Versus Perceived Risk

There is an important difference between the actual risk associated with pursuing a new opportunity and the *perceived* risk. *Actual risk* is determined by four factors:

1. The size of the irreversible and nonrecoverable financial commitment that must be made to get the project off the ground

2. The degree to which the new opportunity departs from the company's existing base of technical and market understanding

3. The amount of irreducible uncertainty surrounding critical project assumptions (particularly with respect to the nature of customer demand and technical feasibility)

4. The time frame required for ramp-up (the longer the time scale, the higher the risk)

Perceived risk, on the other hand, is a function of ignorance—it is based on a pure lack of information, evidence, or experience. It is determined not by what the risk actually is but by what a company *thinks* it is. This can create a significant disparity between the actual risk and the perceived risk, which we call the *ignorance gap*.

The ignorance gap breeds two dangerous effects. First, it can cause a company to *overestimate the total risk* of doing something new. In this instance, managers are afflicted with a kind of uninformed pessimism about new opportunities: "We can't make products that look like that," "We can't get into the consumer business," "We mustn't upset our partners." The problem in such cases is usually that managers are too "distant" from the opportunity to make an informed assessment—too far from the leading edge of customer demand, too far from the trends that will shape the future. The farther you are from a hands-on, first-person understanding of a new opportunity, the greater the perceived risk.

Second, the ignorance gap can cause a company to *underestimate specific risks*. This usually happens at the middle management/project management level, where we typically find a high level of uninformed, "go for it" optimism about a new opportunity: "Yeah, and then we'll develop and run a joint venture with Microsoft," ". . . And then we'll get a permit from the Chinese government," ". . . And then we'll recruit some local management talent." This is an equally dangerous pitfall.

To close the ignorance gap, and thereby derisk innovation, a company needs to do everything it can to reduce uncertainty. It needs to be excruciatingly clear about the assumptions or hypotheses that are critical for an opportunity's market success, and then focus on testing the validity of these assumptions to see whether they can be confirmed. For example, assumptions about:

- Who the customers are

- What benefit the new product or service will offer them

- Whether customers would actually want or value it

- How much they would be willing to pay for it

- What product or service configuration would work best

- How much it is going to cost to produce

- What kind of technical competencies will be required

- Which distribution channels would be most effective

Too often, companies launch a new business based on a very faulty set of assumptions about what it will take to be successful in that particular market. Maybe the opportunity arena itself is relatively uncharted territory—perhaps few if any companies have tried anything like this before, so there is very little information to go on. Or a company is entering a new business but bringing along a lot of unstated assumptions from its existing business, some of which may no longer hold true in the new area. One example of taking things for granted is the initial launch of Euro Disney, which struggled at first because the business model was built on some untested assumptions—that is, that European employees and European consumers would behave in much the same way as their American counterparts. This turned out not to be true. Disney later recovered, turning around Euro Disney based on a more insightful understanding of customer needs.

The greater the initial uncertainty surrounding critical project assumptions, the greater the number of experiments that should be launched. Each experiment should be set up to rigorously test an explicitly stated hypothesis about what must hold true for a project to succeed. This experimentation—and the learning associated therewith—is vital for creating a deep, shared, and most importantly, *informed* understanding about any given project.

MAXIMIZING LEARNING OVER INVESTMENT

When companies assess new opportunities, the emphasis tends to be on their financial earning power: "How do we maximize return over investment?" However, in the early stages of any new business concept experiment, the emphasis should be on *learning* rather than earning—on maximizing the ratio of *learning over investment*. Companies invariably make huge mistakes when their spending on a new opportunity gets too far ahead of their knowledge base.

The way to alter that ratio is by accelerating the pace of learning (i.e., increasing the level of knowledge) while making experimentation cheaper (i.e., decreasing the level of investment). The more efficient a company is at exploring new opportunities, learning much while risking little, the more efficient its overall innovation efforts will be.

Ask Yourself

Do we really know enough about this opportunity yet to invest substantial resources? Are we letting our investments get too far ahead of our learning?

Example: let's imagine it's the late 1990s—the height of dot-com mania—and you come up with an idea that could radically reinvent the grocery business. Your reasoning goes like this: many consumers say they dislike the current supermarket experience and would be willing to pay a little more to improve it; all of us are living busier lives and have less time to do grocery shopping; more and more people are going online, so they could easily order their groceries from home or from the office and have them delivered. Groceries are a low-margin business, but technology allows us to gain some efficiencies by rethinking the distribution system. And "Hey, everyone's gotta eat." So wouldn't "online ordering and home delivery" make a huge amount of sense in the grocery industry?

The founders of Webvan thought so. And their investors agreed. So what should a company do at this point? Let's have a little quiz. Should you:

A) Hire a high-profile CEO from Andersen Consulting—at the time the largest consulting firm in the world—who has no management experience in the supermarket industry?

B) Put your newly hired CEO in charge of a group of senior executives who also have zero experience in the grocery business, award them huge options, and promise them employment for life?

C) Hire Goldman Sachs to pump up the helium and float a high-flying IPO?

D) Bring on Bechtel—the world's largest civil engineering company—to build twenty new distribution centers ASAP to a total tune of $1 billion?

E) Buy a fleet of shiny new delivery trucks, thirty Sun Microsystems Enterprise 4500 servers, and over a hundred oh-so-dot-com Aeron office chairs?

F) Try to learn as fast as you can about whether consumers would really be willing to pay more for home delivery? Or about the percentage of their shopping dollars they might dedicate to this new channel? Or whether you can really improve a low-margin business by adding costs? Or why two other competitors have yet to make money (with a five-year head start)? Or whether it would make more sense to go it alone or to partner with an existing grocery retailer?

Unfortunately for Webvan, it chose everything but F. The venture capitalists who had funded the company were more interested in rapid *earning* than in rapid *learning*. They urged Webvan to scale up at lightning speed and start delivering groceries in as many U.S. markets as possible—again, the belief was that being the "first mover" to achieve critical mass in that opportunity space would provide an unbeatable advantage. But it turned out to be simply a way to lose more money, faster. Webvan's gigantic investment in all that infrastructure was not only out of all proportion to its level of knowledge and learning; it also far exceeded sales growth, which is why the venture quickly went bankrupt.

There was nothing fundamentally flawed about the idea of online grocery shopping, as a host of other retailers have since proven. Instead, Webvan's massive failure was based on a whole series of flawed and untested
assumptions around the idea's *value proposition*. These included:

- The assumption that a very large segment of consumers would
  prefer to order their groceries online and have them home-
  delivered (not true)

- The assumption that Webvan would be able to generate rapid
  awareness and trial through traditional media (not true)

- The assumption that Webvan would achieve up to 20 percent
  penetration in the markets it served (not true)

- The assumption that once they tried it, consumers would dedicate 75 percent of their grocery shopping requirements to the
  service (not true)

- The assumption that consumers would pay a slight premium in
  price for the convenience (not true)

- The assumption that Webvan would scale up to a large consumer
  base within six months of introduction (not true)

In addition, there were the untested assumptions about Webvan's
economic engine:

- That the grocery industry was so inefficient that it was necessary
  to rebuild the whole infrastructure (in fact, it would have been
  much better to partner with an existing supermarket chain)

- That high-tech warehouses were needed to revolutionize distribution and reduce labor costs (actually, labor is relatively cheap)

And the untested assumptions about *partnerships*:

- That Webvan needed to move up the value chain and cut out
  wholesalers (not true)

- That it could derive significant research money from food manufacturers (not true)

And the untested assumptions about *products and services*:

- That warehouses would scale up to eight thousand orders per day (average daily orders were less than half that amount)

- That high-tech frozen conveyance would work

- That low-wage temporary workers would have enough incentive to pick the best groceries for customers

Contrast Webvan's approach with that of the United Kingdom's leading supermarket, Tesco. While Webvan raced to go national, Tesco started with a single Web site for just one store in Osterly, England. Rather than building a huge new infrastructure, Tesco used its existing stores and infrastructure for the first two years. Instead of betting on one business model, Tesco experimented with alternative approaches—that is, customer pickup at stores as well as home delivery. Unlike Webvan, which largely went it alone and eschewed partnerships with supermarkets, Tesco announced a partnership with rival Safeway in 2002 to crack the U.S. market. The figures speak for themselves: whereas Webvan burned through $1 billion and went belly-up, Tesco has since built an online grocery business with annual sales of almost $2 billion and profits of more than $100 million. Tesco.com currently has a 66 percent share of the U.K. online grocery market. The Web-based store takes over two hundred thousand orders a week, and sales are currently rising by over 30 percent from year to year (see figure 9-1).

Webvan could have avoided a huge, costly, and embarrassing disaster by clearly identifying the opportunity's critical hypotheses (the assumptions that could make or break the business concept), creating small-scale, low-risk experiments to validate those hypotheses, assessing the learning and making adaptations, then deciding whether to scale up or instead to go through another experiment cycle, and another, and so on.

This continuous process of experimentation, assessment, and adaptation—with each experiment designed to test some particular aspect of a new business concept—should stop you from ever completely misreading the customer or from misreading the basic economics of an opportunity. It will progressively close the ignorance gap, which in turn

FIGURE 9-1

Experimentation matters—not "trial and error"

Webvan's approach	Tesco's approach
• Raced to go national	• Started with a single Web site for one store in Osterly, England
• Built a huge, new infrastructure	• Used existing stores/infrastructure for the first two years
• Bet on one business model	• Experimented with customer pick-up at stores and home delivery
• Largely went it alone, eschewing partnerships	• Announced partnership with Safeway in 2002 to crack U.S. market

Webvan results: Burned through $1 billion and went belly-up	Tesco results: A $2 billion business earning $100 million

Source: Strategos analysis.

reduces the decision risk associated with each aspect of the project. It will ensure that hubris never gets the better of humility.

LEARN FASTER, LEARN CHEAPER, LEARN BETTER

Your experiment cycle time has to get faster as the world changes faster. Today's innovation leaders are testing and refining new ideas at a speed that leaves traditional competitors breathless. P&G, for example, used to take an average of two months to create prototypes and test them with consumers; in some instances, it now does it in just one or two days, thanks to computational modeling and simulation, along with use of the Internet.

Experiment, assess, adapt. Experiment, assess, adapt. The faster a company can go through this recursive cycle, the faster it can resolve the uncertainty that inevitably surrounds a new and unconventional business concept, and the faster it can get to a viable, cash-generating business model.

Testing in the Real World

It is crucial to test ideas as early as possible in a *real-world environment*—or as close as possible to marketlike conditions—and get feedback based on actual experience, not just lab results. This might mean conducting a market experiment where an inexpensive prototype is put into the hands of a small number of customers. Or the "market" could initially consist of employees in your company. For example, if Apple had given a prototype of the Newton (instead of a Newton T-shirt!) to two hundred employees for six months and asked them to be really honest about it, rather than just listening to the development team telling everyone how "insanely great" the Newton was, the company would quickly have been able to see the glaring problems with the product. In this case, Apple might have decided to wait a year or two and take the Newton through a few more iterations.

One of Procter & Gamble's innovation mottos is: "Make a little, sell a little, learn a lot." The company often manufactures a small quantity of an experimental new product, launches it in a test market, and watches closely to see how consumers react to it. This enables the company to make any necessary adjustments early on, before the product launch has gone full-scale.

MANAGING A PORTFOLIO OF EXPERIMENTS

When we look at the future, there are many uncertainties and a widening spectrum of possibilities. Nobody can predict what the world will look like in ten years, so the only option companies have is to *try a lot of things*, many of which will fail, but some of which will work. To maximize the chances of future success, a company needs to build *a portfolio of experiments*. But in order to afford such a wide portfolio, an organization has to be able to experiment at low cost.

Unfortunately, many large companies have almost no patience with "small things" and have not given nearly enough attention to managing a portfolio of small-scale experiments over a reasonably long period of time—the kind of time period that some of these ideas are going to need in order to have a chance to grow. Large companies often argue that the problem is not necessarily a lack of capital but a shortage of management bandwidth. Their concern is that keeping track of a wide portfolio of small-scale, slow-burn experiments could very easily fragment the organization's already limited management resources. Instead, the attitude of many such companies seems to be, "We'll just let some upstart do the experimentation and innovation, then we'll buy them and quickly scale them up"—which is not an entirely irrational argument.

However, we believe it is entirely possible to track and manage a diverse collection of strategic experiments over quite an extensive period of time. Take IBM. Back in 2000, J. Bruce Harreld, IBM's senior vice president for strategy, set up twenty-five relatively small-scale venture groups called Emerging Business Opportunities (EBOs). He was looking for a way to get more management time, energy, and resources behind potentially big opportunities that didn't fit neatly into the company's existing business units. When these groups started, they had virtually no revenue and very limited staffs, so they were not exactly big blips on IBM's corporate radar screen. But every single month, all twenty-five of those groups were reviewed by a small corporate committee responsible for strategic growth opportunities—a committee headed up by the vice chairman of the whole company. Simultaneously, IBM's finance function was tracking the spending going into these new projects month by month.

In other words, it was the people at the very top who were constantly tracking and reviewing these findings and making all the investment decisions. That meant that nobody else in the organization could kill off one of these projects by taking away its funding or robbing it of people. If anybody tried to do that, then somebody at the top would immediately notice.

The program turned out to be extremely successful. Of the original twenty-five EBOs, three were eventually discontinued, but the other twenty-two went on to collectively contribute $15 billion in annual revenue to IBM's growth—and EBO revenue has been growing at the rate of more than 40 percent a year. This illustrates that, over the longer term, managing a portfolio of experiments can be a very profitable initiative.

SHARING RISK WITH PARTNERS

Another option for derisking innovation is sharing risk with strategic partners. Though this option is not readily considered, some companies know how to use smart partnering to their advantage. For example, when Virgin launched its financial services business, Virgin Money, it relied on an Australian insurance company for most of the initial capital and on a British bank for back-office support. In fact, nearly all the successful companies that Virgin has spun off—Virgin Atlantic, Virgin Money, Virgin Mobile and Virgin Trains—have involved outside investors and strategic partners. Virgin's comment on this approach: "We're very adept at managing the downside. We usually take someone else's skills and someone else's money."[2] Virgin also has an exit plan for every business it enters— one that minimizes the potential damage to the Virgin brand.

There are three primary factors to consider when deciding whether to partner, and how many partners to have:

1. *Financial commitments:* If scaling requires large, irrevocable financial commitments, partners can help by providing capital.

2. *Range of skills or critical assets required:* If your company doesn't have the skills or critical assets (e.g. particular distribution channels) in-house, you may need to find partners that have these skills and assets.

3. *Size of the strategic window:* If the risk of preemption is high, partners might be needed to help accelerate market penetration.

At times, you may decide that the solution is to join up with other, like-minded competitors in a coalition. This is particularly likely to be the case where investment or technology hurdles are high, or where there is a risk of ending up on the losing side of a winner-takes-all standards battle. Coalition members are more than partners; they share directly in the risks and rewards of a new innovation opportunity.

INNOVATION CHALLENGES AND LEADERSHIP IMPERATIVES

Innovation challenge: How can I get traction and maintain progress on a multiyear (marathon) innovation initiative?

Leadership Imperatives

- First, understand whether your innovation is truly a marathon versus a sprint.

- Don't overinvest ahead of learning in new opportunities. Make resources available in a limited and incremental way.

- Understand the actual risk versus the perceived risk—and design experiments accordingly.

- Clearly identify all the assumptions that the success of your innovation depends on—and design experiments to test each of these.

- Realize that success will not be immediate. Learn to experiment, assess, and adapt.

Innovation challenge: How do I pace my innovation investments?

Leadership Imperatives

- Seek to understand the external factors that can either accelerate the time frame for commercializing a new idea or dramatically slow it down. Match the pace of investment to the underlying pace of market development.

- Have patience with marathon opportunities. Take a long view and don't rush premature ideas to market.

- Maximize the ratio of learning over investment by experimenting with new ideas to reduce the uncertainty. Test the fundamental assumptions of the opportunity before committing a large investment.

- Maintain a portfolio of cheap, fast experiments to derisk new opportunities.

PART FIVE

DRIVING INNOVATION TO THE CORE

CHAPTER 10

Dynamically Balancing Supply and Demand

T
O BUILD AND SUSTAIN a robust innovation capability, your company needs to carefully manage both the supply and the demand side of innovation. By *supply* we mean the sheer flow—and the quality—of new ideas entering your innovation pipeline and moving through its various stages. By *demand* we mean the natural, reflexive pull for those ideas within and across the businesses.

When *supply* is low, or more likely, of low quality, one tends to see a kind of *idea inflation*, meaning that opportunities are presented (often unintentionally) with an inflated sense of their value. This is simply because there are few other viable growth opportunities in the portfolio to pursue. The inherent risk here is that an organization invests substantially in what are actually quite mediocre ideas—ones that are unlikely to drive any significant revenue growth.

Conversely, when *demand* is low—when the organization is not naturally and reflexively able to respond to, nurture, and act on potential game-changing opportunities—then innovation withers. What invariably happens is that innovators become cynical and discouraged as they watch their nascent projects go nowhere—which eventually dries up the flow of new ideas entering the pipeline.

Managing both the supply side and the demand side of innovation is a critical balancing act—one that must be mastered if you want to dramatically raise your company's innovation outputs. In this chapter, you will learn specific principles and techniques by which to dynamically manage this supply-demand equation.

DRIVING INNOVATION *SUPPLY*

So far, we have dedicated a lot of ink in this book to maximizing the supply side of innovation—making sure that a surfeit of new ideas and opportunities is being sourced within the organization as well as beyond its borders. In fact, we have outlined a whole set of specific actions that your company can initiate to push up the quantity and quality of ideas entering the pipeline. However, the real key to driving innovation supply is not just focusing on one or two of these actions, as many companies do, but getting all of them to work together *systemically* so that each element functions in concert with all the others in a fully integrated way.

In addition, there are several critical enablers for building a high-performance supply side to the corporate innovation system. They include:

- Broad-based training

- Technology infrastructure

- Coaching and mentoring

- Rewards and recognition

Unless these potential enablers are redesigned to encourage and support innovation—unless they are integrated with one another and set up to enable not just all the activities outlined so far but also *each other*—the supply side will only work in a very piecemeal way. To truly institutionalize innovation—to create the organizational conditions out of which breakthrough ideas can continually emerge—these important enablers must be seen as an indispensable part of the systemic challenge. Let's briefly look at each of them.

Broad-Based Training

An often-heard complaint from senior managers is that most of the ideas they get from their employees are not very good ones—that after democratizing the innovation process, they have to waste valuable management time sorting through a heap of garbage to find a few interesting submissions.

Is this any surprise? What goes wrong with a lot of innovation programs is that ordinary employees are suddenly being asked to submit creative ideas, but they are not being trained to think like radical innovators—to challenge orthodoxies in their company and their industry, to pick up trends that others have ignored, to understand the customer's unvoiced needs, to look at their organization and at the world as a Lego kit of recombinant assets and competencies.

Instead of teaching employees how to stretch their thinking along new lines and develop the kinds of insights that inspire winning ideas, companies seem to hope that those eureka moments will just happen by magic—perhaps while somebody is in the shower or commuting to work.

What they *should* be doing is giving their people a set of tools to extend their capabilities (like the four perceptual lenses we outlined in chapter 3) and training them how to use them to discover new insights and generate radical ideas. Further, they should be teaching employees how to edit or self-screen their own conceptual thinking by assessing an idea against some basic criteria. Potential innovators can be taught how to recognize a big idea—they can be given guides or "rules" that they can apply to, if you will, "interrogate" an embryonic concept; and to frame the basic economic drives of the business opportunity. In short, ordinary people right across the organization can be taught how to become extraordinary innovators.

Is this really possible on a large or even corporate-wide scale? Consider Whirlpool. The company has already trained thousands of its people in the skills and the tools of innovation—employing not just a classroom setting but also broad-based e-learning (as we will go on to describe both in this and the next chapter). Instead of leaving the supply of new, break-the-rules opportunities to chance, Whirlpool has taken practical steps to increase the innovation productivity of its entire workforce, thereby dramatically increasing the likelihood that people will submit a sufficient number of high-quality ideas.

Technology Infrastructure

One of today's most powerful tools for driving innovation supply is information technology. Corporate intranets have already created something close to an information democracy inside organizations—decentralizing a great deal of the knowledge and wisdom that used to be concentrated at the top of the hierarchical pyramid. The next challenge for IT is to create an *innovation democracy*, where the responsibility for generating or nurturing new ideas—and developing new business concepts and strategies—is likewise distributed throughout the organization and beyond its walls.

It is quite typical for corporate Web sites to solicit ideas from employees and customers through a kind of "online suggestion box." This is essentially a good thing to do, but unfortunately, these efforts often fail to produce any significant breakthroughs. The reason they fail is that they are too basic, too passive—they simply sit there waiting for lightning to strike; they don't do very much to create the conditions that produce the lightning in the first place.

For example, they don't invite a rich mixture of different voices to engage in a global conversation around innovation. They don't teach people how to stretch their thinking and ask new kinds of questions. They don't trigger innovation by inspiring people with new insights and perspectives. They don't function like blogs or online forums where somebody starts a thread about a particular idea and then twenty or thirty other people from around the world add their comments and take that idea further so that it can compound and grow. They don't capture the history of an idea so that you can go back and trace its genealogy—so that you can see how it started out, and what was eventually added to it, where people made some critical assumptions, or where they might have missed something. They don't guide would-be innovators on how to develop ideas into business concepts, or how to get traction on an innovation project. In short, these systems don't function as open, corporatewide networks that help to turbocharge innovation.

What is needed today is a forum that actively provokes, guides, and supports innovation—not one that simply requests it. A forum that works like the Internet itself—a pulsing, open-source network where people, ideas, and resources can easily find each other and work together to create new opportunities.

Whirlpool, for example, uses its IT infrastructure—and a software application called Innovation E-Space—as a global operating system for innovation. Open to anyone in the company who has intranet access, Innovation E-Space is designed to make innovation a daily reality at Whirlpool. It offers colleagues all over the world a common forum where they can learn the principles of business innovation, link up with one another to swap ideas and discoveries, keep abreast of current innovation articles, track the progress on innovation activities, and even volunteer to work on each other's projects.

With just a few clicks, Whirlpool employees can start using the four "discovery lenses" we outlined chapter 3 to generate new perspectives and ideas. They can look for inspiration by perusing insights that have already been captured on the system; they can "crash" insights in random ways to spark new thinking; they can submit their own ideas and insights; they can build on existing ideas; they can follow an online tutorial on how to turn ideas into business concepts; they can find innovation coaches and mentors in their region who can help them organize seed funding and prototyping; and they can find people who have the technical skills or experience to advance their ideas. The system has already had hundreds of thousands of hits from Whirlpool's employees worldwide and has become indispensable to the way people share ideas, learn together, and collaborate on innovation projects throughout the company.

Today, there is an abundance of technologies and tools that can help companies create a shared space for connection, conversation, and collaboration. From instant messaging and Web conferencing to online workspaces like Microsoft's SharePoint and IBM/Lotus's Workplace, there are many ways for internal and external people to work together in a virtual environment that crosses time zones and organizational boundaries—almost as if they were situated in the same office and the same company. In fact, if you consider all the technologies we now have at our disposal—groupware, projectware, asynchronous communication, e-mail, intranets, corporate Web sites, blogs, wikis—and you think on the other hand about what drives innovation—connection, conversation, new insights, and so on—the question you have to ask yourself is, Why is it that technology has changed every other process inside companies but it doesn't seem to have made a huge difference to innovation? The answer is that technology per se doesn't solve the problem; it has to be integrated into the fabric of how people work.

Coaching and Mentoring

Technology is clearly only part of the equation. People also need people. Would-be innovators have to know where they can go to get coaching and advice from an impartial mentor—not their boss—who can help them build their idea, qualify it, and get it into a system where it can be formally considered for funding. This is something that another innovation leader, CEMEX, has taken to heart. In every one of the company's cement plants there is a clearly designated *innovation champion*—known to everyone—whose mandate it is to mentor any employee who comes up with an idea and who needs some help in nurturing it.

As we will see in the next chapter, Whirlpool has gone even further by appointing a large number of innovation mentors and consultants throughout the organization, who act as skilled advisers to individual innovators and new project development teams around the world.

Rewards and Recognition

A common misconception exists about increasing the supply of innovation: it's the belief that companies can only make it happen by providing substantial financial rewards to people who come up with successful ideas. This is often wasted motion. For most people, the biggest reward from innovation has nothing to do with money. It has to do with the sheer joy of creating something new, of following an exciting idea that came out of their own head, of working on something that goes beyond the boring confines of their everyday job. It's about having the chance to make a bigger difference in the company than they have ever made before, and about being recognized for their contribution.

Perversely, by offering big financial incentives for successful ideas, a company can actually *decrease* the supply of innovation: it can act as a disincentive to the many people whose ideas don't ultimately pay off. As we have already explained, innovation is a numbers game, and a priori it is very difficult to tell which ideas are going to make it and which ones are not. The message a company should therefore communicate to employees is that "every idea counts." Many financial incentive systems do the reverse: they communicate that any idea that is not ultimately successful is not valuable. This can be very discouraging to those people who go through a lot of thinking and struggling to come up with new business ideas that eventually don't take off.

To return to an analogy we used earlier in the book, it takes a lot of acorns on the ground to produce one oak tree. Every single one of those acorns is valuable to nature's great numbers game, because its chances are based on so many variables: where the fertile ground is, where the sun shines, where the rain falls, and so on. Likewise, it takes a huge number of ideas just to produce one big breakthrough. The person whose idea finally fails should feel just as recognized and rewarded as the person whose idea pays off. What is required, therefore, is an incentive system for innovation where people understand that every idea is needed—that there is value simply in playing the game.

To this end, one very large company has employed a points system that works very much like an airline loyalty program. Individual employees earn points for every idea they submit, and at the end of the year those points can be redeemed against tangible rewards, such as consumer electronics devices or domestic appliances—an MP3 player, perhaps, or a new coffee machine.

Also not to be underestimated is the motivational power of big, inclusive award ceremonies to recognize and celebrate innovation achievements across the company. Since 2001, for example, CEMEX has hosted an annual "Oscars" event called Innovation Day that features awards for the best implemented ideas in a series of categories, such as client services, cost reduction, new products and services, impact on our people, usage and development of technology, and social responsibility. A few hundred projects may be submitted for the awards, from which three finalists in each category are finally selected. Each of these finalists then creates a forty-five- to sixty-second video describing their idea, and puts it on the Web. All employees are invited to view these videos and vote for the final winners. On the day of the ceremony, winners receive a trophy (not money), and the event itself is broadcast to eleven different sites in the company's various Mexican geographies. CEMEX uses this opportunity to communicate the importance of innovation to as many employees as possible, with company presidents and vice presidents delivering speeches that underlie CEMEX's commitment to growth through innovation. By making Innovation Day a big deal, year after year, CEMEX sends a clear message that innovation is a top priority to the company.

DRIVING INNOVATION *DEMAND*

Is your company putting as much effort into driving innovation *demand* as it is into driving innovation supply? Ask yourself: Do the executives who run our company's core business demonstrate genuine interest in radical, new ideas by redeploying adequate resources behind them? Are they held personally responsible for the performance of their unit's innovation pipeline? Do they spend a significant percentage of their time mentoring innovation projects? Failure to drive and manage the demand side of innovation is often where the whole initiative falls flat.

The fundamental challenge here is a *leadership* challenge. It is to make senior executives realize that they themselves are *responsible* for innovation.

Too many companies still view innovation as something that happens at the margins, not in the core business. However, putting innovation on the periphery reinforces the erroneous view that it's not something the business unit executive or the divisional vice president should be worried about—instead, it's the job of the techies over in R&D, or those design freaks in new product development, or those dreamy scientists in the Skunk Works, or one of those starry-eyed business teams in an incubator. In the traditional organization chart, innovation has always been *somebody else's responsibility*. Which means that executives in the core business could just get on with running their day-to-day operations. Most of them have never really felt the need to take personal responsibility for nurturing and mentoring innovation.

In one Strategos survey, which involved fifty large companies (many with revenues in excess of $50 billion), we found that less than half of all managers felt responsible for innovation at all, and of those who did feel responsible, only 17 percent were allocating at least 10 percent of their time to innovation activities.

If you want to drive up innovation demand in your own organization, start by making your senior leaders *responsible* and *accountable* for innovation. Create incentives for them to mentor and nurture the prospective innovators within their ranks.

Jeff Immelt, chairman and CEO of GE, has made it very clear that he expects his divisional presidents to own the innovation agenda in their area of responsibility, and he takes them to task on this when they meet with him every quarter (something Jack Welch never did during his own tenure). Immelt has made his business leaders responsible for submitting at least three "Imagination Breakthrough" proposals per year. These ideas have to take GE into a new line of business, a new geographic area, or a new customer base, and each one must have the potential to generate incremental growth of at least $100 million over the fairly short term. It's a radical departure for GE's executives, who have traditionally been more obsessed with making their numbers than with strategy innovation. But Immelt has changed their compensation packages, tying remuneration to their ability to spur innovation, and as Nicole M. Parent of Credit Suisse First Boston says, "This is a company where managers will do anything to achieve their goals."[1]

Procter & Gamble has taken a similar approach, setting very ambitious performance objectives for its business leaders—objectives that would be impossible to reach by maintaining the status quo or by making incremental improvements. By their very nature, these "stretch targets" create demand. They force new thinking and stimulate a lot of creativity throughout a business division as necessity becomes the mother of invention. They put leaders in a mode where they are desperately looking for a bridge to get from where they are to where they need to be, and this makes new ideas suddenly very welcome, as opposed to unwelcome. Giving management these bold stretch targets is an important component in getting new ideas more positively accepted.

Managing Demand at Emerson Electric

Emerson Electric, the global technology and engineering leader, is known as one of the most reliable earnings machines in the American economy—the company has racked up about five decades of steadily increasing growth. Chuck Knight, who was CEO of Emerson for nearly three of those decades, was respected for the dynamism and discipline he brought to the organization's management processes. Toward the end of his tenure, Knight made an effort to shift the corporate focus from relentless operational efficiency to new growth opportunities and innovation.

What became crystal clear to him was that productivity can be improved in two different ways: either by cutting resources and costs while the top line remains flat, or by keeping resources and costs on a flat line and growing the revenues. This arithmetic may be embarrassingly simple, but it had a profound effect on the company, because the realization was that each of these routes to increased productivity requires very different skills. It takes a certain style of management to cut costs, restructure, reengineer, and downsize, and quite another style of management to create growth through new ideas and initiatives.

Knight wasn't exactly known for his subtlety. Once the innovation imperative had sunk in, he signaled the need for a dramatic change in management thinking by demonstratively ripping up the company's decades-old "planning bible" in front of the organization's one hundred or so top managers. This document contained the very detailed budgeting criteria that had guided Emerson's business unit managers for years. Knight ripped it to shreds with his bare hands and in so many words said, "That was fine, but it's not enough anymore."

At this point, many companies would have put most of their efforts into improving the *supply* side of innovation—that is, identifying a large of number potential growth opportunities for the organization. Emerson certainly worked hard on this, too—very soon its people had generated a few hundred growth initiatives across the thirteen or fourteen business units. But Knight wanted to be sure the company put equal effort into driving the *demand* side. This principally meant raising expectations about the top-line growth rate. He told business unit managers that they themselves were responsible for that growth rate and that he expected them to push it up. He told them he wasn't interested in the natural, underlying growth rate of the markets they were serving—he was going to give them a target, and they were going to have to make up the difference. The message was, "Don't come and tell me life is really hard because your market is only growing by 3 percent per year. I expect more than that, so go find a way to *generate* growth." This put a lot of pressure on the business unit managers to find new ideas and opportunities.

In this context, Knight's great achievement was in dynamically balancing both innovation supply and innovation demand. On the supply side, he organized innovation training and tools for the people in all the business units (as opposed to members of an isolated Skunk Works group). He also made sure those units were making time and space available for the discovery work, and he created some incentives for putting resources into the initiative. This quickly drove up the quantity and the quality of ideas being generated, and ensured that new growth opportunities were linked to the core business of the company.

On the demand side, one of the things Knight did was to build a kind of innovation "war room" at headquarters, right next to his own office. Business units were required to summarize each new growth opportunity they had generated on a separate sheet of paper (which was color-coded per division), and these were hung up on the walls of the war room. A glance at one of those sheets would tell you what a particular opportunity was briefly all about, which division had initiated it, what its risk profile broadly was in terms of certainty or uncertainty, what the scheduled time frame was, how many people were on the project team, and how many resources were going to be put behind it over the next few months. It would also clearly display the name of the business unit leader. These sheets were arranged *vertically* on the walls by the size of the ultimate opportunity (i.e., how much impact it could potentially have on revenue margins) and *horizontally* by where the opportunity was in its development process (i.e., was it still just an idea, or already an experimental prototype, or was it getting close to market?). At any given moment, the war room would have up to two hundred sheets around the walls.

Every time the key divisional leaders came together for the quarterly business review, Knight would pull them aside at some point and take them into the innovation war room. He would interrogate them about every single project in their division: How was the project developing? Had it moved forward in the last few months? Was so-and-so still leading it? Did they have enough resources? Those leaders had to be very careful to have all the answers; otherwise, the war room would quickly become the "woodshed," and they would get quite a thorough dressing down. Also, if their division was color-coded green, for example, they had to make sure that when they walked into that room, there were not just green sheets of paper left on the wall. That would mean that most of their division's innovation projects were still not completed, and again, they would have a problem with Knight.

This was a simple but highly effective device for making sure the key divisional leaders were taking innovation seriously. It communicated that they were being held fully responsible and that they would be regularly drilled about their division's innovation performance. Making it a part of the quarterly business review also meant that innovation was given the same priority as the company's other important performance metrics.

CREATING THE RIGHT PRESSURE POINTS

One of the dilemmas today is that, in most companies, the pressure to innovate is not very real and tangible to managers. What *is* real and tangible—and in many cases enormous—is the pressure to meet the numbers.

Business unit executives have a variety of pressures that hold them accountable for operational performance. They know, for example, that there will be a quarterly or a half-year review. They know the company is monitoring data on a monthly, weekly, daily, or even minute-by-minute basis. They also know that, with all this tracking of sales performance, and margins, and so forth, any variance from expectations will quickly be noted. If they start to go off budget, for example, or they fall slightly behind earnings targets, it won't take very long for something like that to get noticed. On the other hand, senior managers have a lot of levers at their disposal to quite quickly get the numbers back on track. For example, margins can be improved almost instantly by cutting the advertising budget or reducing the head count.

However, in most cases, there is no similar set of pressures on senior executives that holds them directly accountable for the company's *innovation* processes. Inside many organizations, there is a belief that it's very difficult to collect metrics about innovation performance because the process is a lot slower and the payback takes longer. Plus, when it comes to innovation, managers don't necessarily have the levers to quickly change the numbers if they need to. Therefore, their natural bias is to worry a lot more about efficiency, and short-term earnings, and monthly variances from budget than about innovation performance. The challenge for large organizations, therefore, is to create a whole set of things on the demand side that will make leaders as sensitive and responsive to the need to innovate as they are to the need to make the quarterly numbers.

Here are three very important tools for driving innovation demand, all of which concern leadership actions and behaviors:

1. The budgeting process

2. Management compensation

3. Bold growth targets

Let's take a brief look at each of them.

The Budgeting Process

Most big companies invest some portion of their revenue in R&D or new venture funds. This is not a new idea. But instead of pouring all this money into the traditional innovation structures (i.e., R&D, Skunk Works, incubators), why not require the operating units to set aside a certain percentage of their capital or operating budget for projects that meet the test of being radically innovative? Most business unit leaders would quickly respond that they need every penny they can get just to meet their current performance objectives. They might reluctantly be persuaded to give up a small portion of the budget for innovation projects, but only on the understanding that the business unit's performance objectives get relaxed.

The answer from corporate has to be, "No. We expect you to figure out how to do both—we want you to set aside that money for innovation, but we're not going to relax either the performance objectives or the budgeting criteria. You are still going to have to make your numbers." The ability to manage this "dual focus"—both on short-term performance *and* long-term growth—is going to be an increasingly important attribute for senior executives. While it is admittedly a difficult skill to recruit for—and to develop—it is key to making managers accountable for innovation.

Management Compensation

Look at the typical compensation package of a divisional executive. To what extent is the remuneration and reward system tied to innovation performance? Often, it's not linked at all. Management compensation is typically tied to other measures like cost, efficiency, speed, and customer satisfaction—and executives are paid for making progress against those metrics. Therefore, how could we seriously expect business unit leaders to make innovation a priority? One is reminded here of Steven Kerr's classic article, "On the Folly of Rewarding A, While Hoping for B."[2] The title says it all.

What is required is a new set of metrics for evaluating management performance—one that puts innovation at least on a par with other performance objectives. For example, we could ask:

- How many new ideas are currently entering your innovation pipeline?

- How fast are they progressing through it?

- What is the implicit financial value of that pipeline in terms of potential future revenues?

- How many days did you spend last quarter mentoring innovation projects?

- What percentage of your engineering dollars or head count is currently devoted to innovation projects?

These are things that managers can clearly be held accountable for—and *paid* for.

By changing performance metrics and management compensation packages to make them pro-innovation, your company can fuel the fires of innovation deep inside its core business and measurably improve its capacity to invent new business concepts and create new wealth.

Bold Growth Targets

The examples cited earlier in this chapter from GE, Procter & Gamble, and Emerson Electric illustrate the value of setting bold growth targets that stretch senior executives and their organizations. No company outperforms its aspirations. The beliefs of your employees set the upper limit on what's possible. If your expectation for top-line growth is pinned to the industry average, all you will get from your organization is average performance—people will continue to do things the same way, perhaps tweaking a bit here and trimming a bit there. If, on the other hand, you give your divisional executives *unreasonable* growth targets—irrespective of the intrinsic growth rates of the markets they are in—the chances are much higher that they will find innovative ways to dramatically outperform the average. They will be forced to think differently and do things differently.

ASPIRATIONS BEYOND THE NUMBERS

Having said all of the above, we must stress that driving innovation demand is not purely about the numbers. It is also about creating well-articulated and meaningful challenges that speak to employees' hearts as well as their heads. For example, a challenge like "How can we increase our earnings per share by 20 percent?" is certainly not going to inspire as much innovation as the kind of challenge you regularly hear in Apple's Cupertino headquarters: "How can we change the world?"

Warren Bennis, author of *Organizing Genius*, studied some of the greatest project teams in recent history—from Disney's animators to Lockheed's Skunk Works to the Manhattan Project—in an attempt to identify some common characteristics. His conclusion was that, without exception, the teams that really reached epiphanies truly "believed that they would make a dent in the universe." He says that their team members all felt they were enrolled in a deeply meaningful cause—something Bennis describes as "an exciting, insanely significant vision."[3]

Creating an inspiring cause, vision or corporate challenge—whether it involves fundamentally redefining a product category or an industry, or addressing some important unmet customer need, or solving one of today's most pressing global problems such as pollution or poverty—can act as a powerful demand generator for innovation.

Ask yourself: would employees rather be part of a "status quo—let's just meet the budget" sort of company or would they rather work for a firm that inspires them to do bigger things? In our experience, once employees get the feeling that they are part of a vibrant, innovative company that is out to make *history*, and not just profits; once they get hooked on the excitement and energy of innovation, they automatically begin to demand more innovation from themselves and their peers. Thus, the demand for innovation ceases to be the sole province of the CEO or other top level executives. All levels of the organization begin driving innovation.

MEASURING INNOVATION PERFORMANCE

As the old saying goes, "If you can't measure it, you can't manage it." This is especially true for innovation where there is a pressing need to bring focus, clarity, and discipline to a fundamentally creative process.

In our experience, though, very few organizations have an effective system for measuring their overall innovation performance. If you have any doubts about this, ask yourself:

- How many measures do we currently have that focus explicitly on innovation (versus optimization)?

- How many of my colleagues could say as much about our company's innovation performance as they could say about our company's cost efficiency?

- How many people in the organization have personal performance metrics related to innovation?

- Do we regularly measure each operating unit's innovation performance against the rest of the company?

- Do we know how to access and systematically benchmark the innovation performance of other companies in our industry—and in other industries?

Given the importance of innovation as an engine of growth, it always surprises us that many companies still don't measure their innovation performance. For them, the whole innovation process remains something of a black art.

Yet managers tell us that innovation metrics help them and their teams in two ways. First, to make informed decisions based on objective data—especially valuable given the long-term nature and risk associated with certain innovation projects. Second, to help align goals and daily endeavors with the near- and long-term innovation agenda.

But how exactly do you collect precise metrics about innovation performance? For a start, it's not enough to merely adapt existing metrics developed for R&D or new product development. Though somewhat useful, these metrics offer a limited view of a company's innovativeness. They fail to measure the company's overall innovation capability. Another failing is that in emphasizing technology development, they neglect other opportunities like business-model innovation. And their focus on R&D and products makes them less suitable for companies in service industries or outside the high-tech sector.

Likewise, it is not enough to measure just one or two particular aspects of your company's innovation performance. No single metric can convey full meaning in isolation. Just as with the analysis of a company's financials, the analyst must look at several metrics in order to develop a comprehensive view of the company's innovation capability. To effectively manage an innovation pipeline, a company needs to have measures and metrics at every stage—and these must be tied to compensation.

Usually, it is quite easy to establish *output* measures for innovation—for example, the number of new products, services, or businesses a company has launched in the past year, or current cost and pricing advantages that have come from innovation, or the percentage of revenue coming from products or services introduced in the last three years. 3M, for example, aims to have at least 35 percent of its sales at any time coming from products that are less than five years old.

However, it's equally important to measure innovation *inputs*—for example, the percentage of labor hours or the percentage of capital budget currently devoted to innovation projects—as well as innovation *throughputs*—for example, the number of ideas, by division, that are entering the innovation pipeline each quarter, or the ratio of ideas that become experiments and ventures over ideas submitted, or the average time for ideas to advance from submission to prototype to commercial launch, and so on.

A COMPREHENSIVE MATRIX OF METRICS

Whirlpool has detailed metrics for tracking innovation performance at every stage of the pipeline. The company measures not only innovation inputs, throughputs, and outputs across its global organization, but also leadership's involvement in and contribution to innovation, as well as the company's progress in embedding innovation as a companywide capability.

Before taking innovation seriously, Whirlpool struggled with an organization that was in many subtle ways biased *against* innovation. The company understood that merely measuring innovation *output* was not going to do anything to change that. Instead, to achieve the ambitious level of innovation it was aiming for, it realized it had to start measuring the things that affect innovation *input*—for example, the percentage of engineers' time being spent on truly innovative programs or the percentage of the capital budget being invested in innovation activities (e.g., submitting and reviewing ideas for new products and services, and developing ideas through the innovation pipeline).

As a signal of change at that particular point in time, Whirlpool's leadership directed its divisional executives to set aside 15 percent of their capital budget for allocating to innovation projects. They were not given an *additional* 15 percent with which to indulge in "brainstorming" or experimentation. Instead, they were directed to fund innovation from their current operating budget *while still meeting* the same performance objectives as before. The message was clear and framed very simply: Develop and act on business ideas that will:

- Surprise and delight the consumer—consistent with Whirlpool's brand strategies

- Have the potential to wrong-foot competitors

- Offer substantial growth potential

- Be good for and *because of* "us"—based on Whirlpool's competencies and strategic assets

What they were being told was, "No big ideas—no capital."

This directive, which was enforced regardless of historical operating performance, got people's attention very, very quickly. The divisional executives started asking their people, "Are we generating enough new ideas? How many innovation projects do we have in the pipeline? Are they getting enough resources? Have we put the right talent behind them?" What became clear to those leaders was that if they were going to go into the capital budgeting process to fight for more money, they had to develop firsthand knowledge about the innovation projects being run in their division. They realized they couldn't just go in with an "I expect the same amount as I had last year" attitude. They had to earn the money by *demonstrating* innovation. Interestingly, the 15 percent rule was only the beginning. Today, Whirlpool sets aside a full 30 percent of its budget for innovation projects. This has played a critical role in shifting the focus and commitment of top management toward innovation.

Another input measure Whirlpool used was the percentage of *advertising* devoted to truly innovative products. This may sound a little strange, but think about it: in the short run, it's always easier for a division to earn one more buck by advertising its existing products than to try to change customer expectations and behaviors by advertising something new. The default setting in most organizations is "more of the same," which starves new and unproven products of advertising dollars. The argument is usually something like, "We can't put too much money into promoting this new product, because there is no customer base for it yet." But how will a company develop a market for that innovative new product unless it puts the money and energy into finding new customers?

In addition to instituting these input measures, Whirlpool created *throughput* measures to track the number of new ideas being submitted, the number of ongoing experiments and ventures, and the pace at which projects were advancing through the innovation pipeline. Today, any manager of Whirlpool can go online 24/7 and get a comprehensive, real-time window on the company's global innovation activities. Using a dashboard view of the innovation pipeline called I-Pipe (adapted from a Strategos software platform), they can see how many concepts are being produced, which parts of the world they are coming from, how many innovation experiments are currently under way, how many ventures are receiving more serious funding and attention, what the project details are for each of these ventures, how many new businesses are heading for commercialization, and when these businesses will be leaving the pipeline. One of the advantages of I-Pipe comes from "enabling management to focus on areas in need of attention. For example, a dozen innovations that deal with pricing may indicate that there's a problem in that area."[4]

Whirlpool also carefully constructed *leadership* measures to ensure that divisional leaders were held responsible for the innovation performance of their own unit. For example, executives were asked to report on the percentage of time they spent on mentoring innovation teams rather than on day-to-day operations. For annual review meetings between the businesses and the CEO—covering products, operations, and strategy—the presentation templates were changed to make innovation a crucial part of the review.

Then there were metrics to measure Whirlpool's progress at building a deep, corporate-wide innovation *capability*. Executives were asked, for example, what percentage of their employees had received training in the skills and tools of innovation, or what percentage of their employees had innovation as a key performance goal, or how many had been or were currently involved in innovation projects.

Part of Whirlpool's success at innovation embedment came from thinking about metrics in this very comprehensive way. If organizations only use one or two metrics to measure innovation performance, executives can quite easily either game the system or escape it. For example, they might try to ignore innovation by saying, "Well, yes boss, I know you said innovation was really important, but this year we had all these other things to do, and it's just one out of a whole set of other performance metrics, so I'll try to do better next year." Or they might try to game the system by saying, "Okay, we have to hit a certain percentage of revenue from new products. Let's see . . . last year we did yellow Post-it notes, so let's do pink ones this year. That's a new product, right? And next year we'll do green ones." But by building a complex and comprehensive matrix of innovation metrics, Whirlpool gave its executives no place to escape.

The company also linked all of these metrics to compensation. Today, roughly 30 percent of executive compensation at Whirlpool is tied to innovation performance, which makes it the largest single component of the executives' compensation package.

While Whirlpool's disciplined approach to metrics works well for the global appliance giant, it would be a mistake to simply "cut and paste" their system into your organization. Like other elements of organizing for innovation, establishing and managing innovation metrics must be done in the context of your business goals for innovation, your leadership capability and perspective, and your corporate culture. Still, companies that are seriously pursuing innovation as a capability will find the broad frame of "input measures, throughput measures, and output measures" of great use. Table 10-1 describes these as well as additional metrics you may wish to consider:

TABLE 10-1

Innovation metrics

	Input	Throughput	Output
Process	Breadth and depth of "external nodes" in one's open innovation network	Number of new ideas, concepts entering the innovation pipeline Pace at which projects advance from one stage to the next Specific tools available for each step in the innovation process	Number of projects in experiment, prototype, and scale phases of pipeline
People and leadership	Percentage of time spent on truly innovative projects (engineers, marketers, etc.)	Percentage of internal and external individuals contributing to innovation	Innovation performance of one's unit Capability measures (e.g. percentage of employees trained, at what certification level)
Performance and funding	Percentage of budget(s) devoted to innovation (operating budget, marketing, capital, etc.) Clear "Growth gap" measures for each business unit	Holistic view of pipeline to assess/ forecast pipeline quality against targets (e.g., ten projects at experiment stage yield two at scale-up) Size/forecast of the innovation portfolio	Percentage of revenue from new products, services, categories, businesses and/or strategic areas of focus (e.g., a food company's percentage target of innovation revenues from products that are "better for you," or an electronics or automotive firm's percentage target of innovation revenues from products that are "environmental") Total return on innovation investment Patent filings

Source: Strategos analysis.

Concrete Performance Targets

Corporate innovation initiatives come to nothing when the goals are too vague, the supply and demand drivers are not in place, and the performance metrics are undefined or too limited. Successful innovators like P&G, GE, and Whirlpool set explicit performance targets based on some of the innovation metrics we have described, and commit divisional executives to reaching them.

To be clear, however, these and other companies *do not set identical targets and metrics*. Leaders within these and other companies understand that metrics are part of a broader system and that they must reflect the unique culture of the organization as well as the competitive realities of their respective markets.

Still, as you set innovation targets and metrics within your own company, you may want to consider some of the following options:

- Ensure that 2 to 5 percent of all your people's labor hours get devoted to innovation projects that are considered radical.

- Invest 5 percent of your capital budget in your operating unit's innovation pipeline.

- Dedicate 10 percent of your own managerial time to mentoring innovation projects.

- Arrange for at least 20 percent of the people who work for you to receive innovation training.

- Commit to a set of targets for the next twenty-four months: for example, two hundred new ideas submitted, ten experimental innovation projects taken through the pipeline, and two new business ventures ready to be commercialized.

THE "INNOVATION SCORECARD"

What kind of scorecard, if any, does your own organization currently use to measure innovation performance? Mention the word *scorecard* to most businesspeople, and they immediately think of the Balanced Scorecard. However, in most companies, that scorecard is decidedly *unbalanced*—it is weighted heavily toward optimization rather than innovation. This weighting does not reflect a fundamental problem with the Balanced Scorecard framework; instead, it reflects the reality of historical focus within most organizations. Going forward, any organization that aims to build an innovation capability for outperforming its industry will also require a comprehensive set of metrics—an "innovation scorecard"—to ensure that every component of the innovation engine is performing optimally.

Of course, if your company already uses a methodology like the Balanced Scorecard or value-based management, you should reconcile your innovation metrics with that methodology. Whirlpool, for example, includes issues like "new revenue generated from innovation," "health of the innovation pipeline" (projected revenues), and "value extraction," on its Balanced Scorecard—and bonuses are tied to these issues. Even in the absence of such a methodology, you should ensure that your innovation scorecard encourages individual behaviors that aggregate to accomplish companywide goals.

Getting the individual metrics, targets, and incentives right always takes some time and a fair degree of trial and error. For a start, the optimal selection of metrics and the optimal value, or "sweet spot," of any particular metric will vary from company to company. There is no "one size fits all" solution. For example, innovation for an appliance manufacturer like Whirlpool requires different skills, resources, and competencies and is manifest in different ways than, say, innovation for a fashion retailer. The goals or targets of the innovation will vary from industry to industry. However, the generic variables that are measured by the innovation metrics will be quite similar across most industries. Each metric should also be regularly reviewed over time as you accumulate experience in working with and fine-tuning your innovation pipeline.

We believe that as more firms develop an effective scorecard of innovation metrics—as well as a database that validates their relevance—managers, analysts, and investors will eventually be able to assess a company's innovation capability with as much facility as they can currently assess concepts such as market share, leverage, and economic value-added.

FINE-TUNING THE BALANCE

Ultimately, as we pointed out in chapter 4, the goal is to build a high-performance innovation pipeline rather than just some mystical process that will hopefully one day produce something of value.

As such, your pipeline—your engine for wealth creation—should be something you can fine-tune, just as you would adjust and fine-tune a literal car engine. It should be transparent enough to let you constantly monitor innovation supply and innovation demand, and it should allow you to use the right levers to maintain a dynamic balance between the two.

If you notice, for example, that not enough ideas are coming in at the front end of the pipeline, you should be able to use some of the specific levers we have described in this book to push up innovation supply. Conversely, if quite a few ideas seem to be getting stuck in the middle of the pipeline, your company should be able to quickly create the conditions that will help them get through. This might mean relaxing the stage gate criteria a little bit to help projects move more fluidly from one stage of development to another. Or it might mean putting a little more pressure on your business unit executives to free up resources for innovation projects or spend more time mentoring them.

With these measures and mechanisms at their disposal, senior managers should be able to tune up or tune down the system as they need to. For example, they might decide they need to drive up the percentage of radical ideas versus the percentage of incremental ideas entering the pipeline. Or drive up the number of people being trained in the skills and tools of innovation. Or drive up the percentage of discretionary time people are allowed to devote to innovation.

Put simply, it should be easy for management to say things like, "Instead of reserving 10 percent of the capital budget for innovation, this year we will reserve 20 percent," or "Instead of innovation performance representing 5 percent of executive compensation, this year we will make it 30 percent." Each one of these things should be like a slider that can be adjusted up or down according to the situation, as part of a dynamic innovation system.

Again, Whirlpool is a good example. As the company's innovation engine started to fire on all cylinders, CEO Jeff Fettig recognized that so many new ideas were flowing through the pipeline that Whirlpool would be overwhelmed in its capacity to deal with them. The organization was going to face bottlenecks in product engineering because all of these new ideas needed to be worked out in detail, and receive safety approval, and so forth. It was going to hit bottlenecks in manufacturing as Whirlpool introduced more and more variety and disrupted the existing production process. It was going to come up against bottlenecks in sales because the sales force was not yet trained to sell these new kinds of products and product categories. Then Whirlpool had to spend time convincing retailers to devote shelf space to these new things, and in some cases it had to go through the difficult process of entering completely new channels. Thus, there was a need to adjust the flow of ideas to make it more reasonable and remove these bottlenecks.

Once your company gets some experience in working with an effective and transparent innovation pipeline, you will gain some experience in how many ideas you need at the concept stage to generate a sufficient number of interesting experiments, how many projects will make it through these experiments to the prototype stage, and how many will finally make it to the market. You can start to apply probabilities about these ratios and develop an increasingly robust way of looking at the dollar value of the pipeline, using it as the basis for making estimates to the stock market about your company's growth potential.

Thus, when you sit down to do your strategic planning, you can say, "Okay, what is the growth objective we want to set this year for our organization? What percentage of our capital budget do we therefore need to set aside for innovation? What proportion of time do we want key divisional executives to put into innovation this year? How visible should innovation be in the CEO's public conversations inside and outside the firm at this moment? How much strategic variety will we need at the front end of the pipeline, in terms of nascent ideas and first-stage experiments, to deliver the financial impact we are aiming for at the back end?"

INNOVATION CHALLENGES AND LEADERSHIP IMPERATIVES

Innovation challenge: How can we manage the supply side of innovation?

Leadership Imperatives

- Think systematically about driving innovation supply—through broad-based training, technology infrastructure, coaching and mentoring, rewards, and recognition.

- Don't be misled by the notion that companies can only make innovation happen by providing substantial financial rewards to those who come up with promising ideas.

- Don't view innovation as something that only happens at the margins of your organization and not in the core business. The innovation "supply" resides in all parts of your business.

Innovation challenge: How do we sustain a robust demand for innovation?

Leadership Imperatives

- Retool your budget process and management compensation to demand innovation as well as efficiency.

- Set bold growth targets that can only be met through innovation.

- Don't merely create "an online suggestion box" or deploy an idea-management software platform and expect that radically innovative ideas will just "trickle in." Instead, create a forum that actively provokes, guides, and supports innovation rather than simply requesting it.

- Apply a comprehensive set of innovation metrics for tracking innovation performance, including outputs, inputs, and throughputs.

- Don't measure innovation performance by implementing just one or two measures (which can be gamed) or by considering innovation outputs alone (which will help you measure only one part of the overall story).

Innovation challenge: How should we define senior leadership's role in innovation?

Leadership Imperatives

- Leadership needs to pay attention to both the supply side and the demand side of innovation.

- Ensure that the executives running your core business are made responsible for innovation. The temptation is often to delegate innovation accountability to the periphery of the organization.

- Carefully construct *leadership metrics* to ensure that executives are held accountable for innovation performance.

- Set concrete and explicit innovation performance targets, and commit executives to reaching them.

- Avoid confining innovation to the corners of the organization, for example in Skunk Works, incubators, and venture funds.

CHAPTER 11

Building a Systemic Innovation Capability

THROUGHOUT THIS BOOK we've argued that companies really can and must take a more systemic approach to innovation. Indeed, we have outlined the efforts of a very diverse set of companies—such as Whirlpool, CEMEX, W. L. Gore, Google, GE, P&G, and Best Buy—to make innovation a sustainable enterprise capability. What you have probably noticed is that, while all of these companies share a common view about the importance of innovation, each one actually manages innovation in a very different way—and correctly so.

Truth is, there is no single right way to organize an enterprise for innovation. For example, a highly centralized organization would likely not be very successful at applying Google's market-based approach to innovation within its own company. Conversely, Google would likely stall quickly if it adopted—ad hoc—elements of the innovation infrastructure we find at more (relatively speaking) centralized companies like GE, P&G, or Whirlpool.

But whether your organization is highly decentralized or tightly centralized; whether it has vast global reach or is limited to a single geographic region, you will be pleased to know that there is a practical framework you can use as a guide to developing, deploying, and sustaining a systemic innovation capability in the context of your own business. In this chapter, we will describe that framework.

Here's the good news: any enterprise capability has some common components to it—leadership, organizational infrastructures, corporate values, enabling processes, tools, metrics, and skills. And each of these elements of "organization" already exists within any company. So, if you are going to make innovation an intrinsic and systemic competence, your challenge will be to alter these organizational elements accordingly—in ways best suited to your company's culture and ambition. The goal: to deploy a "steady-state" innovation system that is well-matched to your own growth objectives and organization.

In figure 11-1 you will find the four interdependent and mutually reinforcing components that need to come together to institutionalize innovation:

1. *Leadership and organization:* Company leaders and organization aligned around a common vision of innovation—and a shared understanding of the business objective(s) served by innovation

2. *People and skills:* Disciplined approach to building innovation capabilities across the organization

3. *Processes and tools:* Systematic approach and supporting tools to enable idea generation, pipeline and portfolio management

4. *Culture and values:* Collaborative, open culture and incentives that reward challenging the status quo

Let's consider each of these components in turn.

LEADERSHIP AND ORGANIZATION

Building a self-sustaining, "all the time, everywhere" capability for innovation is fundamentally a leadership challenge—it is something that absolutely has to be spearheaded by the CEO. Without the full engagement and commitment of the company's leadership team, the idea of making innovation a core competence doesn't stand a chance.

FIGURE 11-1

Building a systemic innovation capability

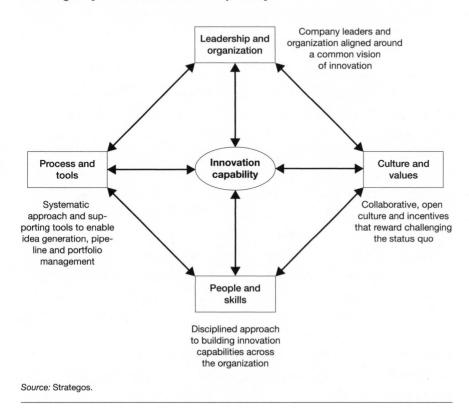

Source: Strategos.

At Procter and Gamble, the mandate for open innovation—70 percent of which should originate outside the organization—came from the man at the top, A. G. Lafley. The mission to drive organic growth at GE by turning a 120-year-old industrial giant into a nimble "imagination company" came directly from CEO Jeff Immelt. The push to turn CEMEX into an innovation powerhouse came from CEO Lorenzo Zambrano. The directive to embed innovation as a core competence at Whirlpool came from former CEO David Whitwam (and his vision of "Innovation from Everyone and Everywhere" has been reinforced and even intensified by the company's current CEO, Jeff Fettig).

But what if you have a CEO who has not yet seen the need to start driving innovation from the top? Our advice would be to take the initiative by launching your own, smaller-scale innovation effort along the lines we have described so far in this book. We have found that the innovation imperative sometimes needs to start percolating somewhere else in an organization, before it eventually gets the CEO's attention.

It's worth remembering that this is how Six Sigma got started at Motorola. It was a midlevel employee who first brought the quality issue to the attention of the senior leadership team, eventually leading Motorola to become one of the quality pioneers in the United States. The fact is, a lot of other large companies had a similar experience during that same period. In many organizations, the awareness for quality began with some mid- or upper-level person—in procurement, or manufacturing, or product design—who started talking about quality, going out and doing study missions, understanding the tools and so forth, and eventually fomenting a revolution.

Similarly today, the issue around innovation embedment may begin to emerge even several levels down from the top, but at some point it escalates and the CEO becomes aware of it and convinced of it. That's when the leadership team begins to catalyze and endorse the whole issue, and to drive it from the top.

When we talk about innovation being driven from the top, it is important to make a distinction. We are not talking here about top-down innovation. We are not talking about centralizing the responsibility for idea generation and strategy development with the people who run the company. In fact, that is the very opposite of what we are arguing in this book. Rather, we are talking about a company's leaders taking principal ownership of the innovation *embedment* process—that is, the process of actively building, sustaining, and managing a corporate-wide innovation capability.

Nancy Snyder, who was made global vice president of innovation at the start of Whirlpool's own massive change effort, describes this process as "a wide range of actions that assimilate, incorporate, internalize, and imbue the entire fabric or lifeblood of an organization with the mind-set and skills of innovation." In her book, *Strategic Innovation* (coauthored with Deborah Duarte), she says that this wide range of actions must be synchronized around a common definition or vision of innovation embedment—a vision that is created and owned by the top team, that is accessible to all levels of the organization, that is both feasible and flexible, that can guide decision making, and that can be clearly and easily communicated.[1] This vision becomes the blueprint for making innovation a core competence.

Innovation Infrastructure

Realizing a company's innovation embedment vision on a large or even global scale requires a tangible organizational infrastructure for innovation.

Whirlpool provides a useful model for such an infrastructure (see figure 11-2). When former CEO David Whitwam announced his vision of "Innovation from Everyone and Everywhere," he simultaneously took on the role of "chief innovation officer" at the company. Former chief operating officer Jeff Fettig (now the CEO) was appointed as the chief architect of innovation embedment. Nancy Snyder describes Fettig's role as "key in making sure that innovation was always top of mind from an operational perspective and didn't become set apart from our 'real business.'"[2]

FIGURE 11-2

Whirlpool's innovation infrastructure

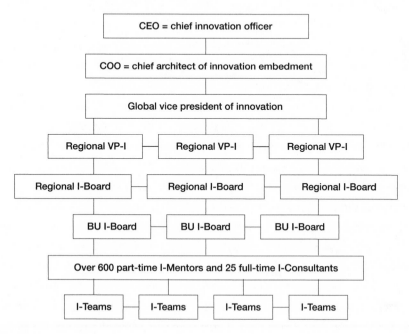

"I" equals innovation.

Source: Nancy Snyder and Deborah Duarte, *Strategic Innovation* (Jossey-Bass/Wiley, 2002).

Snyder herself was appointed global vice president of innovation at corporate headquarters, making her the leading "embedment practitioner" at Whirlpool, with a direct reporting line to the CEO. Once the executive committee had bought into the need for innovation embedment, the next level of leadership—the top twenty-five officers who were running the company's business units (called the chairman's council or leadership council)—was engaged and put in charge of driving and managing innovation embedment and new growth activities.

On a regional level, Whirlpool created new leadership roles called regional vice presidents/general managers of innovation, who would work with the respective regional heads in a visible and senior position. Three managers received this assignment—one for each of the biggest geographical regions: North America, Latin America, and Europe. In all three regions, an innovation board (i-board) comprised of senior leaders was set up to manage and advance the embedment process at the local level. They meet monthly to review progress, set the regional innovation strategy, track ongoing projects, remove barriers, and oversee funding of new ideas, opportunities, and ventures. Three times a year, the CEO reviews the performance of these i-boards in focused innovation reviews. Whirlpool also added a knowledge management resource in each region for democratizing the collection and distribution of innovation-related information.

To generate strategic insights and a large portfolio of new ideas, Whirlpool next created innovation teams—or i-teams—in each geographic region. Membership on the i-teams became a rotational assignment, which in the meantime, has allowed hundreds of people across Whirlpool to take part directly in these activities. Then the company appointed hundreds of part-time innovation mentors along with twenty-five full-time innovation consultants (reporting to the regional vice president/general manager of innovation), who coach and support would-be innovators, helping them push their ideas forward. These are not people who sit twiddling their thumbs, waiting for someone to knock on the door with an idea. Rather, they work closely with the company's divisions to stoke the fires of innovation by actively monitoring and managing the pipeline process.

CEMEX has also succeeded in creating a dedicated infrastructure for innovation. It's headed up by the innovation director, whose dedicated innovation group—with nine full-time employees and millions of dollars in annual budget—commissions innovation platform teams to come up with new ideas around specific innovation themes, or platforms. The teams pitch their ideas to an innovation board, comprised of both internal and external members, that reviews all proposals and makes decisions on seed funding. Promising ideas can receive between a few hundred thousand dollars and several million dollars, and if an idea or project starts to show a lot of potential for the organization, it is quickly transferred back into the operating units.

At CEMEX, innovation is not something that happens in a secluded corner of the organization where nobody can see it. Rather, it has been made a very visible part of the company's everyday activities, with hundreds of trained and dedicated staff—spread through every business and geograph—who serve either as full-time innovation consultants or part-time innovation mentors.

Cross-Boundary Interaction

Building an innovation infrastructure also has to do with enabling innovation *across* business units and functions and geographies rather than merely within them. It is about destroying the structural silos that usually separate people, ideas, and resources, and creating a high level of cross-boundary connection, conversation, and collaboration. It is about exploring "gray space," "white space," and "blue ocean" innovation opportunities that can only be discovered by looking outside traditional business boundaries.[3]

P&G is a good example. The company generates a lot of cross-boundary interaction between people in different business units and fields. R&D facilities have been restructured into twenty-two communities of practice, based on major areas of expertise, which serve as a "virtual" resource pool for anyone from P&G's fifteen business units who is running a project. John W. Leikham, P&G's director of corporate R&D, says of this approach, "We have an incredible ability to cross-fertilize our know-how and to make connections that create real synergies and opportunities to develop new markets in our existing businesses. This 'web of interconnectivity' has been a powerful engine of growth at P&G."[4]

P&G has teams that are set up to innovate within a global business unit (e.g., Fabric & Laundry Care), teams that look for gray-space opportunities that stretch beyond that sector (i.e., outside the existing brand and category operations), and then, at the corporate level, cross-boundary teams that address white-space opportunities that transcend all the various sectors. This third kind of team has been especially useful for breaking down the walls between very strong business units (which have traditionally tended to be quite defensive of their turf), and for building bridges between different kinds of competencies inside the organization in order to create innovative new product solutions. Representatives from all of P&G's business units also meet regularly in a "global-technology council" to address opportunities that transcend boundaries and call for collective know-how.

Once an interesting idea surfaces from one of these groups or from outside the company, P&G has systematic mechanisms for abbreviating the communication channel to top management and for building cross-functional teams around new ideas. These mechanisms get senior management, all the way up to the CEO, interfacing with innovators, removing barriers, shaking loose resources, advancing people's projects, helping them turn nascent ideas into businesses, as well as thinking about which sector to transfer a particular new business to and what kinds of capabilities that sector might need to acquire quickly so that the hand over doesn't lose the company any time.

IBM is another company that is rethinking traditional organizational structures to address new opportunities. Its new venture groups—called Emerging Business Opportunities (EBOs), which we outlined in chapter 9—represent a major shift from the company's old ways of doing things. Instead of sourcing new business opportunities from IBM's scientific researchers, who are usually working on a very lengthy time frame, EBO leaders get most of their ideas from talking to people outside the company—like customers and venture capitalists—and from tapping into IBM's collective expertise. Their job is to bring promising ideas back into IBM's system so that the company can set up teams around these opportunities and try to turn them into new products and businesses.

W. L. Gore has perhaps the most unconventional innovation infrastructure. The company has created a flat, title-free organization where all employees (Gore calls them associates) are linked in a "latticelike" structure instead of a hierarchy. It's a model that relies on direct, person-to-person communication across the organization rather than up and down traditional chains of command. Because there are no fixed reporting lines, anyone at Gore can interact with anyone else. The result is that ideas, technologies, competencies, and people associate in a free-market atmosphere where serendipity—in the form of new and previously unforeseen opportunities for products and businesses—has happened for the company time and again.

Distributing the Responsibility for Innovation

No doubt about it: new organizational structures are a key element in ingraining innovation as a corporate capability. But what the above examples illustrate is that building an infrastructure for innovation involves much more than merely linking R&D with other departments like marketing, industrial design, and customer research. Such restructuring efforts do little to distribute the responsibility for innovation any further than that. They fall far short of embedding innovation as a systemic capability that permeates the entire organization.

To make innovation a pervasive and corporate-wide capability, the responsibility for innovation needs to be broadened beyond these traditional structures and spread throughout a company's businesses and functions. This is exactly what happened to quality in the 1970s and 1980s when it ceased to be the exclusive responsibility of a specific department, and instead, became distributed to every corner of the company.

What is required is a similarly systemic infrastructure for innovation that starts at the corporate level and infiltrates every part of the organization chart. An infrastructure that makes managers accountable at all levels for driving, facilitating, and embedding the innovation process into every nook and cranny of the culture.

Of course, there is no "one size fits all" model for doing this, as the examples above illustrate. Much depends on what works best for your own organization and culture. A critical test of any innovation infrastructure, however, is whether it continues to make innovation the exclusive job of certain individuals and dedicated units, or whether it helps to distribute responsibility for innovation throughout the company.

We would argue that the true innovation champions today are no longer the tinkerers who end up inventing things like Post-it notes, or the design geniuses like Jonathan Ives at Apple. Rather, it is the "architects" who are building infrastructures to embed innovation as a *capability* and to ensure that their companies continue to manage and maintain that capability—people like Nancy Snyder at Whirlpool, or J. Bruce Harreld at IBM, or Larry Huston, formerly at P&G. It is the "process champions" who are setting the spirit of innovation free in companies that are perhaps just as bureaucratic and cost-conscious as yours. People who have faced substantial challenges in their efforts to nurture and coordinate innovation activities throughout their organizations, but who have successfully overcome these challenges. People who have taken on the mighty forces of incrementalism, status quo business thinking, and quarterly results pressure and have actually won.

PEOPLE AND SKILLS

One of the central tenets of this book is that your company should learn how to mobilize and monetize the imagination of every single employee, every single day. Just imagine if you could capture all of the hidden wealth that sits inside your organization in the form of *latent imagination*—all that passion and energy that was never turned on because your company did not have the right processes, mechanisms, and systems for fostering innovation; indeed, because your managerial principles were positively working against that kind of contribution from people.

Increasingly, companies such as Whirlpool, P&G, GE, and IBM are realizing that ordinary employees can actually become extraordinary innovators. Over the years, and with a lot of learning and practice, these companies have enabled broad organizational engagement through mechanisms such as discretionary time allowance, innovation training and tools, an open market for ideas, easy access to incremental seed funding, and structures for mentoring and support. In so doing, they have dramatically raised the innovation potential across their companies—and often beyond their organizations, too.

Decades ago, Toyota showed that quality could be pushed to unprecedented levels by investing in the problem-solving skills of every employee. Likewise, it will be companies that invest in their employees' capacity for creativity that will raise the bar—and eventually take the lead—in today's competitive environment.

In chapter 10, we showed that people can be taught new *skills* for innovation, just as people were trained to significantly improve quality. For example, they can be taught how to discover new strategic insights by challenging industry orthodoxies, by processing what is changing in the world and finding new opportunities in all that change, by leveraging competencies and assets in completely new ways, and by developing a deep understanding about unarticulated customer needs.

Once companies accept that innovation is a skill that can be *taught*, they can begin to seriously tap into and maximize the latent innovation potential throughout their organizations.

As we have previously mentioned, Whirlpool did this by launching a companywide training program aimed at developing and distributing the mind-set and skills of innovation. There are three levels to the program:

1. Every salaried employee, at every level of the company, is required to receive training and certification in at least basic innovation skills. The minimum proficiency level is *innovation ambassador*, somebody who has come to an understanding about the value of innovation, about how the corporate innovation system works at Whirlpool, and about how to use the company's innovation tools and concepts.

2. The next proficiency level is *innovation mentor*, somebody who is trained to *foster* innovation in a leadership role and who acts in this capacity on a part-time basis (the company has hundreds of innovation mentors around the world).

3. The highest, or mastery, level is *innovation consultant*, somebody who becomes a deeply skilled innovation embedment practitioner and who then works full time to help the

organization drive innovation. These i-consultants liaise with the company's divisions to ensure that innovation techniques and best practices are widely adopted and implemented and that nascent ideas are properly supported. They also train new i-consultants and i-mentors, as well as ordinary staff in these divisions, ensuring that innovation training continues to permeate down through the organization, cascading from employee to employee.

Whirlpool's corporate-wide training program was made possible by reallocating existing training resources inside the company, and by making sure that e-learning (via the organization's "Innovation E-Space" IT infrastructure) augmented face-to-face training as a way to spread new skills throughout the company as quickly and cost-efficiently as possible.

A New Role for Human Resources

Building an enterprise capability for innovation repositions the role of human resources. In many organizations, HR has never gone much beyond being a glorified "Personnel" department that busies itself with recruitment and firing, employee compensation and comfort, corporate policies, government regulations, and generic training programs. However, as soon as a company recognizes the strategic and economic value of building a corporate-wide innovation capability, HR automatically moves to center stage.

The new role for human resources must be to help an organization unleash the full potential for innovation and wealth creation that is latent in its human capital. Liisa Välikangas, former director and research director of the Woodside Institute, has spent many years trying to integrate theory and practice around managing innovation as a corporate capability. She says, "HR's role should be to help build this capability company-wide, to design an innovation curriculum, establish an innovation training center, and to support other related internal initiatives. HR professionals can add value by creating a company culture where everyone in the company is responsible for innovation—whether as an innovator, mentor, manager, or a team member."[5]

This is the case at Whirlpool. Dave Binkley, the company's senior vice president of global human resources, says, "All our HR systems—pay, spot awards, the long-term incentive plan, the balanced score card objectives—are hardwired into Whirlpool's innovation strategy."[6] One example is the company's employee performance reviews. Leaders are regularly assessed by their peers, supervisors, and subordinates in 360-degree accountability reviews, which include innovation as one of the main leadership dimensions. Regular employee appraisals help every person in the company understand the link between their own performance (as well as compensation) and the attainment of the company's innovation embedment strategy. In addition, an annual survey asks all employees to rate the company's engagement to its strategy, including issues like "I am involved in innovation" or "My manager supports my involvement."

Companies that want to make innovation a core competence should ensure that HR builds this objective into its recruitment strategy. In 2005, a study conducted by Hay Group and *Fortune* magazine into the ways "Most Admired Companies" develop, implement, and sustain innovation revealed that the most innovative companies tend to employ people who are "high achievers, intellectually curious, and risk takers."[7] They put the emphasis on finding and developing people with the "right stuff."

One of those companies is Procter & Gamble. Knowing that P&G is trying to build and actively reinforce innovation as a corporate-wide capability, Bill Reina, director of global talent supply, has profiled precisely the kind of people P&G is looking for, and has made sure his HR people are trained to sift out the most innovative recruitment candidates. Before applicants even get as far as an interview, they are given a batch of problem-solving tests to help recruiters determine whether or not they can approach challenges in a creative way. When considering what the applicants have done so far in their lives, recruiters are also searching for things that indicate a willingness to embrace and commit to innovation, and to collaborate with others in a results-focused way. Once people get through this screening and hiring process, the goal is to develop their innovation talents in some of the ways we have described above.

Remember, GE became famous for its world-class leadership development. What is to stop your company from becoming famous for developing world-class innovators?

PROCESSES AND TOOLS

It is not enough to train people throughout your organization to think more creatively and to understand the value of innovation. Those people also need practical tools, processes, and mechanisms they can use day by day to turn innovation into a sustainable corporate reality.

As an analogy, think again about quality management. Let's say, for example, that a person is thoroughly trained in Pareto analysis but is not given a tool at the workstation to track quality outcomes by the hour and to look statistically at the distribution of faults. Basically, all of that training will be wasted.

Clearly, the right tools and processes make a big difference to what we can achieve in every aspect of life. Innovation is no exception. Companies often ask themselves why success at innovation continues to elude them; why their efforts to brainstorm seem to yield so little in the way of radical new ideas; why they have such a miserable record at turning promising ideas into commercialized businesses; and why innovation still seems to be "as predictable as a rainbow and as manageable as a butterfly," to quote Robert D. Hof of *Business Week*.[8] One of the answers is this: these companies are asking their people to innovate, but they have not yet equipped them with the tools and the processes that are critical for making innovation happen.

In this book, we have outlined many of the tools and processes that can enable organizations to:

- Continually discover novel strategic insights for stimulating idea generation

- Make innovation everyone's job by engaging ordinary employees in the ideation process

- Systematically innovate across the entire business model to identify new opportunities for growth

- Construct an innovation architecture that brings coherence to a large portfolio of ideas and strategic options

- Rapidly redeploy resources behind promising new ideas

- Manage a pipeline of opportunities from nascent ideas through to market experiments and "close to launch" businesses

- Measure ongoing innovation performance (inputs, outputs, throughputs, leadership engagement, progress at innovation embedment)

- Dynamically balance innovation supply and demand

To a great extent, making innovation a self-sustaining capability is about using tools and processes like these in a systemic and mutually reinforcing way.

Bringing Innovation to Every Workstation

Instead of just encouraging people to come up with new ideas or sending them on a "creativity" seminar, imagine how much more effective their efforts would be if they had a powerful set of tools to stretch their thinking and develop new perspectives (like the discovery lenses we outlined in chapter 3, for example). Further, imagine that every single person in the company had these tools right there at the workstation and that they also had the incentive to use them again and again.

In this respect, most companies still woefully underutilize information technology for driving and enabling "all the time, everywhere" innovation. We know that IT can vastly extend human capabilities. So why is it that very few organizations seem to have thought about IT in the context of a widely distributed capacity for innovation? Sure, they may have systems that network their scientists, engineers, or designers and help them to work creatively together; they may have some kind of knowledge management system for sharing information; but why are they not using IT to bring the skills and the tools of innovation to every workstation? Why don't they use all that incredible processing and communication power to unleash the creativity of every single brain in the company? Why have IT vendors and professionals so far contributed so little to the cause of making innovation an enterprise capability?

What organizations should be doing is creating a compendium of innovation tools, insights, and skills that is open to everybody—just as

Whirlpool, for example, has done with its Innovation E-Space infrastructure (as we described in chapter 10). Rather than merely giving these tools to employees and hoping they might use them, Whirlpool has instituted a leader-led process (like GE's Work-Out) aimed at enabling people to apply things like the four discovery lenses to their own jobs. This sequenced and integrated process, which includes sessions facilitated by the company's innovation consultants and mentors, helps employees to see exactly how they can utilize the innovation tools in their daily work, and thereby helps Whirlpool build a ubiquitous core competence in innovation.

One of the major benefits of IT infrastructures like Whirlpool's Innovation E-Space—or like Shell's companywide GameChanger process for idea submission and seed funding—is that they dissociate ideas from political power. Traditionally, ideas got a free "pass" inside most large organizations if they came from somebody like a divisional vice president, but if an idea came from an ordinary employee, it was usually treated with a lot more skepticism. Open, intranet-based innovation systems tend to change all that by introducing an "innovation democracy."

An analogy we sometimes use is a wonderful old *New Yorker* cartoon of a dog sitting next to a computer keyboard that reads, "On the Internet nobody knows you're a dog." The logic behind Shell's GameChanger system, for example, was to create an intranet-based process for idea submission and review where nobody knows (or cares) whether the idea is coming from a senior executive or an hourly employee.

So far, most of the business software applications around innovation have been rather uninspired—they have never moved much beyond being mundane knowledge management systems, or passive electronic suggestion boxes, or groupware for particular sets of people, or tracking mechanisms for the product development process that follow an idea from stage gate to stage gate.

The reason these systems usually fail to make much of an impact on corporate innovation is that they don't seem to be based on a deep understanding about innovation as a social process. They don't really work to build bridges across the organization in ways that allow ideas, talent, and capital to come together and find each other in an open marketplace.

Metrics and Reward Criteria

As we discussed in chapter 10, innovation embedment also requires a change in metrics and reward criteria. The reality is that, in most companies, whether by fault or design, the measurement systems (like ROCE, RONA, EVA, and ROI)[9] tend to focus people's attention on optimization rather than innovation.

CEOs might preach the need for risk taking and rule breaking, but these are not the metrics they typically use for measuring their managers' performance. Financial rewards and promotions are usually based on that unholy trinity of conventional management: "meet the deadline," "make the budget," and "don't screw up." As we pointed out in chapter 10, organizations that are serious about making innovation a core competence need a new set of metrics to offset this tendency and encourage managers to put as much energy into innovation as they are currently putting into optimization.

The truth is, quality never really took off as a discipline until companies started changing the compensation systems for top management, pegging remuneration to their performance against quality-focused metrics. In our experience, innovation doesn't take off inside an organization either, until managers understand that they are being measured and rewarded based on the health of their innovation pipeline and on whether they close ambitious growth gaps that are tied to the company's innovation platform.

Developing the right set of metrics is a prerequisite for driving the right set of behaviors, as well as for tracking the company's progress on innovation embedment.

CULTURE AND VALUES

Values never come from a "values statement." The fact is, many companies list innovation as a core value in their corporate mission but subconsciously reinforce a culture that inhibits it.

Chris Argyris, an expert on organizational behavior, describes this phenomenon using the terms *theory of action* and *theory-in-use*.[10] What his research basically tells us is that managers may espouse a particular theory of action (e.g., "Our company has to innovate or die"), which they give allegiance to and explicitly communicate to others, but their actual behavior is governed by a subconscious *theory-in-use*, a mental model that is hardwired into their tacit values and assumptions. In other words, these managers are saying one thing but they actually believe something else, without even being aware of this duplicity.

For example, they may say they believe in creativity, risk taking, and rule breaking, but simultaneously enforce standard operating procedures that chastise people for doing things differently. They may say they want an environment where new ideas are welcome from anyone, where nobody gets shot down for making an unconventional suggestion, where people are not afraid of making mistakes, and where there is a high level of trust and support, but when you ask their own employees to candidly describe the corporate culture, it is invariably the reverse of what those managers are preaching. It is a culture where people are discouraged from thinking independently, or from opening their mouths and expressing ideas, or from taking on any unnecessary risks, or from doing anything that might upset the "system"—it is a culture that implicitly tells people, "shut up and don't rock the boat."

Most corporate cultures don't foster innovation; they get in the way of it. When we talk to successful innovators in large companies, we usually hear a familiar story: "I succeeded despite the system." Even more troubling is the fact that most people *expect* innovation to happen that way. They know that the "system" is only doing its job—it is there to enforce conformance, alignment, and continuity, and therefore *of course* it will frustrate the new, the unconventional, and the untested. Nobody is horrified by the idea that innovators have to bend or break organizational rules, that they have to go around a lot of people or go into "stealth" mode to get things done. They accept this as a normal part of organizational life. Yet if somebody said, "We ship world-class products out every day despite the system," or "We delight thousands of customers every month despite the system," we would think their organizations were about to go belly-up.

If would-be innovators can only succeed in an organization *despite* the system—if they have to fight their way heroically through a minefield to push their ideas forward—then by definition, innovation is not a systemic capability in that organization, nor is it a core value that is deeply ingrained in the corporate culture.

Don't Talk About It, Be About It

When companies refer to innovation as a "value," most of them are using the wrong term. If an organization has not yet succeeded in making innovation a truly *tangible* core value for all its employees, the leadership team should be calling innovation an "objective" or a "commitment," not a "value." Innovation may well be something the leaders consider to be an imperative, and that they plan to put considerable effort into, but that does not mean that it has yet become a deep value for the company.

Talking about innovation—using it as a slogan in an advertisement or on a corporate letterhead—does not make it a value. Values are less about what you say and more about who you are. They define the beliefs an organization holds deep down about what is important and right, and they drive the way its people behave on a consistent basis. It is absolutely crucial to make this distinction.

In many ways, we might compare it to building a great brand. Look at BMW. Sure, the company has some clever advertising that tells us BMW is "the ultimate driving machine," but in many ways this advertising is no more creative or insightful than any other car company's. Yet BMW has succeeded in building a brand that customers fall in love with. How? Not just by *talking* about "the ultimate driving machine," but by creating a set of *real product attributes and customer experiences that add up to that statement*. If this were not the case, then "the ultimate driving machine" would just be empty sloganeering. It would mean nothing to people.

Likewise, for innovation to become a genuine value, it has to be deeply internalized and clearly tangible to an organization's employees. It must be something, as Marcus Buckingham might put it, that helps to "change the daily rituals" and "introduce new heroes and language" throughout the organization.[11] It becomes the net sum of a whole variety of messages and behaviors. In fact, in many ways, it is not really something a company can work on directly; it is something that comes from addressing all of these other issues.

That is where there really is something to learn from those companies that seem to be *born* innovators—companies like Virgin, Google and Gore. For innovation to become not just a core competence, but a core value, there has to be a substantial degree of internal consistency between processes, metrics, reward structures, rhetoric, and top management behavior—and it is precisely this synchronicity that one observes in these companies. When a company achieves this type of coherence and maintains it over a period of years, innovation becomes less and less "what people do" and more and more "what people are." It becomes part of an organization's character, part of its essence.

Take Virgin. Two clicks into the company's Web site and there's a big red button that says, "Got a big idea?" Next to that button is a piece of text that reads: "We're big fans of big ideas. Here's everything you need to know about getting your business ideas or suggestions to us." The section sets out some guidelines for submitting proposals, and provides contact details for corporate development teams in every individual Virgin company, in every major geographic region, as well as at headquarters. How many companies in the world would do a thing like that? And, even if they did do it, how many senior managers inside the company would listen to and act on those external ideas?

One of the e-mails Richard Branson received in the last few years was from Gotham Chopra, son of the popular self-help guru Deepak Chopra. It suggested that Virgin get involved in building a new comics and animation company in India, using the subcontinent's rich mythology as an untapped source of content. Chopra said that others had turned his fledging company away because it was too pioneering, based on the logic that "pioneers often get shot in the back." That was all Branson needed to hear. "I'm a pioneer," he said, and within a year, Virgin Comics and Virgin Animation were born.[12] Housed in a creative studio in Bangalore, India, the company already has more than fifty artists and writers. Branson believes it can grow into a multibillion-dollar business, selling not just to India's huge market but exporting titles all over the world.

When you look at most corporate mission statements or value statements, you typically find about eight values, and innovation might be, say, number 4 on the list. At Virgin, out of four or five corporate values, four of them have to do with innovation—things like "Think differently," "Two fingers up at the big boys," "Screw it, let's do it," and "Consumer champion." These are not mere slogans; everyone knows they sum up what Virgin is intrinsically all about. They are the tangible values that drive everything the company does, from the businesses it gets into, to the way it approaches and runs those businesses, right through to the kind of people Virgin hires for its key positions. They have to be people who are energetic, contrarian, and fun; people who are empathetic to customer needs that the "big boys" are not addressing; people who are ready to take a leap into unexplored territory; and people who really want to make a difference in customers' lives.

Basically, any company could make a claim, like Virgin does, that "There's a kind of 'Virgin-ness' in everything we do, from recruiting great people to keeping our promises, or doing business with a cheeky grin." But with Virgin, there is a great deal of congruence between the words and the culture. People both inside and outside the firm intuitively understand what the company is about. That is because they see Virgin's corporate values reflected in *recurring patterns of behavior*.

This explains why ordinary employees at Virgin end up automatically doing things Virgin-style—they find themselves thinking and behaving in ways that are consistent with the corporate values. For example, when the air-conditioning failed on one of Virgin's U.K. trains on a very hot day, a Virgin Trains manager decided to take all the placemats from first class and fold them into fans for the passengers. And when a blind couple flew with Virgin Atlantic on their honeymoon, a customer service representative arranged to send them a congratulations card in Braille.

After a while, this Virgin-style thinking starts to come naturally and spontaneously to people; it becomes almost like a reflex. We like to say that if Virgin sold socks, somebody in the company would suggest that they sell them in packs of three— because one sock always gets lost in the wash!

The point here is that there is more to the spirit of innovation at Virgin than Branson flying around in a hot-air balloon, or doing silly things like wearing a wedding dress at a launch party for one of his businesses. The company has instituted a series of *mechanisms* through which innovation has become a tangible core value. They include:

- Consistent messaging—leaders not only clearly articulate pro-innovation values in many different ways, but provide an everyday model of the kind of behavior they expect from their people

- An open door to the chairman and to the corporate development teams for submitting new ideas

- The company's recruitment strategy and reward structures that encourage risk taking and entrepreneurship

- The company's whole approach to the markets it enters and how it creates value for customers

These are mechanisms that provoke the right attitudes in people, that help to make innovation a widely held and deeply embedded value.

Innovation can only become a true value in a company through collective learning across all its levels, functions, and businesses—usually over considerable time. People need to not just *hear* that ideas are welcome "from everyone and everywhere," or that rule breaking and risk taking are encouraged, or that ideas are allowed to fail without incurring punishment; they need to *experience* these things every day. That is when a corporate value becomes tangible enough to guide patterns of behavior across the entire organizational culture.

MAKING THE CULTURAL TRANSITION

The likelihood is that you work in a company that is not exactly Virgin or Google or W. L. Gore. Maybe your organization has been around for a very long time. Maybe it was founded by a highly innovative individual, but that person is long gone. Maybe your current CEO is someone who understands the innovation imperative, but who is by nature rather bureaucratic, conservative, and careful—not someone who is out there wing walking like Branson. Maybe your organization was once a rule breaker, but over the years has become rusty and dull, and the challenge today is to rebuild that original spirit. How exactly are you going to make the cultural transition?

The only way to do it is by systematically employing the kinds of mechanisms we have outlined in this chapter and throughout this book—the policies, processes, and systems that allow an innovation culture to gradually evolve and then to perpetuate itself. Of course, there are as many potential mechanisms as there are companies, and there is no cookie-cutter recipe for putting them all together. But in our experience, an effective corporatewide innovation system would certainly have to include the things we have described on these pages:

- The visible leadership engagement

- The organizational structures for orchestrating and supporting innovation

- The disciplined approach to building skills and hiring the right people

- The tools and processes for generating novel insights and opportunities

- The mechanisms for redeploying resources and creating an open innovation marketplace

- The ongoing communication and conversation about innovation issues

- The highly inclusive events for input and involvement

- The metrics, management accountabilities, and reward structures

- The regular cultural activities that promote innovation and allow it to thrive

Building a deep innovation capability requires a systemic approach. Not all organizations are up to the task. Yet companies like Whirlpool and CEMEX—both of which were formerly very traditional industrial enterprises—have managed to create such an integrated system of mechanisms for institutionalizing innovation. This explains why they have been able to make the difficult cultural transition where many others have failed. Over time, your company can make the transition, too, if it is prepared to patiently assemble all the components that are critical for making innovation a ubiquitous capability, and if it is prepared to put the necessary drivers in place to sustain that capability. When deployed well, such a corporatewide innovation system can be a major factor in achieving better-than-industry performance.

The reason very few organizations have succeeded at building a deep, ongoing capacity for innovation is that most of them merely dipped their toes into the water, initiated piecemeal activities here and there, and hoped that by throwing some money at these initiatives, they would somehow bear fruit. They never dove into innovation in a serious and systemic way, working hard to embed it as a core competence that permeates the entire organization and that eventually becomes part of their company's DNA. Let's face it: in the vast majority of organizations, the corporate innovation system is still on the drawing board.

For innovation to become a self-sustaining capability, it has to be something that can eventually run on its own inertia, without anyone acting as a babysitter. We made the point earlier that a company's CEO should be the driving force for corporate-wide innovation. But what if he or she decides to join another firm or retire, or suddenly dies, or is diagnosed with an incurable disease? Should people inside that organization (and on Wall Street) start to worry that the company will lose its capacity for innovation?

Ask yourself, Would Toyota suddenly lose its world-class ability to manage quality if it got a new CEO? Would the Four Seasons forget how to take superb care of its guests if somebody else was at the helm of the hotel chain? Core competencies do not come and go with the changing of the guard. They become part of a company's bloodstream.

Thus, the cultural transition must be *permanent*. It cannot rely on a charismatic leader or the willpower of a particular team of people to keep the spirit and the capability alive. When David Whitwam passed the leadership reins of Whirlpool to current CEO Jeff Fettig, the company's enterprise-wide innovation system never even missed a beat. To Whitwam's great credit, innovation had by then become a systemic capability that was not dependent on a single brilliant mind or a small cadre of experts. It had become a robust and pervasive system that was resilient enough to accommodate internal or external disruptions (i.e., leadership loss or succession, changes in economic cycles) and to keep rolling on as a reliable, well-oiled engine of growth. It is precisely this kind of long-term transformation that is the ultimate goal of innovation embedment.

INNOVATION CHALLENGES AND LEADERSHIP IMPERATIVES

Innovation challenge: What steps can we take to begin to make innovation one of our core values?

Leadership Imperatives

- Don't rely only on a charismatic few to drive innovation. Move beyond superficial talk and innovation slogans. Innovation needs to become widely and deeply embedded in the organization and culture.

- Ensure that company leadership takes principal ownership. Don't underestimate the importance of the CEO's role in transforming a company's managerial DNA.

- Take a holistic view of your organization's innovation capability, paying attention to the four independent components of innovation: leadership and organization, people and skills, processes and tools, and culture and values.

- Align processes, metrics, rewards, rhetoric, and leadership behavior around making innovation a core value.

- Make sure that *everyone* understands that innovation is *everyone's* job.

Innovation challenge: What is the role of human resources and talent management in building a self-sustaining innovation capability?

Leadership Imperatives

- Embrace the notion that innovation is a skill that can be taught—not a talent that only some possess.

- Don't simply train employees in innovation theory. Instead, provide a practical set of tools and processes to be used in the day-to-day business.

- Leverage your IT infrastructure to make innovation tools and skills widely available throughout the organization.

- Empower human resources to drive corporate-wide innovation capability development, and make innovation a critical component of your recruitment strategy.

CHAPTER 12

Making Innovation Sustainable

W HEN A COMPANY has been taking the kind of systematic approach to innovation that we have described in this book and is beginning to see the benefits, there typically comes a moment when the organization experiences a tipping point.

Sometimes the exact point of transition is only realized in retrospect—a company might even ask itself, "How did that happen?" But at a certain stage, a critical mass of employees wake up to the fact that innovation is not just a corporate initiative, or a onetime project, or an activity for a particular group of people. They begin to recognize it as something that has to permeate the entire organization—something that requires different mind-sets, values, skills, behaviors, processes, management systems, metrics, rewards, organization structures, IT solutions, and so on, all across the enterprise. They start to grasp the fact that for innovation to really work, and to be *sustainable*, it has to become a systemic and widely distributed capability—it has to be woven into the everyday fabric of the company just like any other organizational capability, such as quality, or supply chain management, or customer service. What becomes obvious is that innovation has to become *a way of life* for the organization.

Unfortunately, most companies never reach this tipping point. They never move innovation beyond being something that is "bolted on" rather than built in. We've all seen those easy-to-implement, bolted-on approaches to innovation—creating an incubator, setting up an innovation "department," or rushing to an off-site "innovation brainstorming" session. Each of these has some merit, of course, but as piecemeal solutions they are simply not enough. The tipping point only comes when such initiatives are executed as part of a larger systemic goal: that of embedding innovation as an enterprise capability in the organization's core DNA.

One could compare it to putting a pair of really expensive Nike sneakers on somebody who is completely unfit. Of how much practical use are those shoes going to be? They might make it easier for that person to walk around without getting sore feet, but by themselves they are not going to make a huge difference to anybody's health. What is really required is a different lifestyle—regular workouts, a more nutritious diet, new values and behaviors, a whole set of things that need to come together to make a person stronger and healthier.

So it is with companies that think they can succeed at innovation by just adding some new activity or organizational function. Unless they are also willing to drive innovation to the core by making deep, fundamental changes to their management processes and patterns of behavior, these initiatives will only take them so far.

A similar misstep happened with quality. Some organizations assumed that merely by bolting on a quality department, or organizing some quality circles, or appointing a few more inspectors, their quality levels would automatically improve. They found instead that individual and disparate "organizing" actions—especially those not focused on real business problems—did very little to build an enterprise capability for quality.

After that initial stumble, it took quite some time for these companies to learn how to make quality something that was "built in" as an intrinsic organizational capability rather than just bolted on as an initiative or a department. They had to work out how to put all the pieces in place—the training, the tools, the space in people's diaries, the shift in authority to allow hourly workers to stop the production line if necessary, and so on. Every one of those things was a difficult struggle against a whole set of organizational and particularly *managerial* orthodoxies.

It was only when large companies began to rethink a lot of their core managerial DNA that they were able to build a deep and sustainable capability for world-class quality. The real challenge today is to go through the same kind of struggle—the same level of organizational change—in order to embed and institutionalize innovation.

Organizations must recognize the practices, policies, and processes inside their organizations that are toxic to innovation—like traditional management processes that systematically favor perpetuation and incrementalism over new thinking and innovation. They need to realize that building a truly innovative company is not a matter of simply asking people to be more innovative; it's a matter of positively changing those things that today diminish or stunt the organization's innovation potential.

IDENTIFYING INNOVATION IMPEDIMENTS

To make the transition from initiative to enterprise capability, your company needs to identify—objectively—the enablers of and impediments to innovation that exist within your organization. In short, you need to take an innovation health check.

Start by asking a simple question: what things in this organization are limiting our capacity for innovation? It might be helpful to think about these impediments across five or six categories. For example:

- Are there things in our values that get in the way?

- Are there things in our everyday cultural behavior that get in the way?

- Are there things in our management processes—strategic planning, capital budgeting, product development, management compensation, leadership training, succession planning—that get in the way?

- Are there things in our organizational structures or our political structures that get in the way?

- Are there skill deficits, where we simply don't know how to do certain things?

Your goal is to identify the things that are hindering new thinking and innovation, the things that are frustrating experimentation, the things that are stopping talent and capital from flowing to the best ideas. Try to understand exactly which things would need to be changed in your company in order to make innovation a sustainable, corporate-wide capability.

This exercise tends to identify broad categories of impediments that are quite similar across most organizations. For example, people typically say things like the following:

- "The criteria we use in our product development stage gate process tend to kill great ideas too early."

- "Allocational rigidities in our budgeting process make it difficult to get resources behind new ideas."

- "Our senior managers don't seem to care about innovation, because the company's metrics systems don't measure them on it, and the compensation systems don't reward them for it."

- "We lack people who have had any significant training in the skills and tools of innovation."

Beyond these familiar patterns, we find that in every organization the impediments to innovation are subtly different, depending on factors like corporate culture, business model, organizational structure, and so forth.

Once all these things have been identified and grouped—and once people have come to some *consensus* about what seem to be the most challenging impediments to innovation inside your company—you and your colleagues can start developing a game plan for solving these things one by one.

"MANAGEMENT PROCESS MAKEOVER"

"Let's be honest," wrote Gary Hamel in his article, "The Why, What, and How of Management Innovation," "a company's management processes can strangle innovation in a hundred mostly unseen ways—and often do." As Hamel notes, there are fundamental inhibitors to innovation within the everyday work of managers—things like setting goals and laying out plans, motivating and aligning effort, coordinating and controlling activities, accumulating and allocating resources, and acquiring and applying knowledge.[1] At a broader level, there are also inhibitors to innovation within key management processes such as strategic planning, capital budgeting, resource planning, and new product development.

If the forces that frustrate and inhibit innovation are deep and systemic—if they are embedded in industrial management principles and processes—then you will need to look deep inside your company's core managerial DNA. You will need to work hard to surface the political and ideological impediments to innovation, uproot and remove those impediments, and invent new, innovation-friendly management processes founded on new management principles—processes that enable and sustain new kinds of behaviors.

In this book, we have already cited several examples of:

- Radically new management processes that have been created to support innovation

- Existing management processes that have been changed in ways that make them more innovation friendly

These include P&G's Connect and Develop process (chapter 4), Royal Dutch/Shell's GameChanger process (chapter 8), and Whirlpool's Innovation E-Space (chapter 10). There is nothing to stop your company from inventing new organizational processes that are every bit as proinnovation as these. Recall, too, that in chapter 10 we detailed some of the management process innovations and, separately, values that contribute to sustained success at Emerson Electric. You can take a page from Emerson's playbook by critically assessing your own key management processes.

For some illustrative examples, let's play "Management Process Makeover" with three key management processes that are commonly innovation averse in most organizations: strategic planning, capital budgeting/resource planning, and new product/process development (see table 12-1). For each, we briefly unpack the traditional processes to identify some of the common innovation killers. Then, for each, we sketch a reengineered process that is much more conducive to innovation.

TABLE 12-1

"Management Process Makeover"

Strategic planning

Traditional process	Reengineered process
• Focused on strategy perpetuation (backward looking), on increasing share of current served markets, and on short-term objectives for revenue and profit growth (which emphasize incremental innovations)	• Focused on strategy renewal (forward-looking), the creation of new businesses, operational models and markets, and long-term strategic objectives (which emphasize radical innovations)
• Too narrowly defined, reducing the company's identity to its existing business model	• More broadly defined, allowing for expansion of the company's identity beyond its current business model
• Too inward looking, whereby the plan and the numbers create a blindness to changing market realities	• More outward-looking, creating a closer link between strategic priorities and external trends and discontinuities (i.e., changes in the competitive, technological, and customer environments)
• Too calendar-driven, locking up capital a year or more in advance and making it almost impossible to redeploy it flexibly behind new, emerging opportunities	• Dissociated from the annual budgetary cycle, making the process more continuous and flexible—more about strategic *evolution* than strategic planning
• Too numbers-based rather than opportunity-based, killing nascent strategies at a premature stage by expecting unreasonable numerical precision	• More opportunity-based rather than numbers-based, allowing nascent strategies some latitude to experiment and explore new space
• Involvement in strategic planning limited to the same small group of senior executives every year, excluding new voices and new thinking	• Open to a rich diversity of new voices from across the entire organization and even beyond it (customers, strategic partners, etc.), reducing the likelihood of strategy perpetuation
• Ineffective communication of the strategy throughout the organization, leading to confusion about the company's goals and no clear connection between individual jobs and corporate strategy	• Effective communication of strategy, as well as ongoing conversation about strategic issues, throughout the organization; clear links between employees' everyday jobs and the achievement of corporate objectives

Capital budgeting and resource allocation

Traditional process	Reengineered process
• Resources allocated every year to the same old things in approximately the same amounts, perpetuating the status quo	• An internal marketplace for capital that works on the basis of resource attraction rather than resource allocation

Traditional process (continued)

- Too calendar-driven, forcing new opportunities to wait for the next budgeting round to have any hope of funding

- Managed by overly conservative executives who are conventionally trained in finance, and who find it extremely difficult to measure the value of new ideas or the disruptive impact of external changes

- Excessive focus on financial metrics when reviewing nascent ideas, asking detailed questions about business case and profitability when an opportunity is still too embryonic for anyone to know the answers

- Only one place to go for capital: up the chain of command

Reengineered process (continued)

- Shorter budgetary cycle, and a pool of internal venture capital set aside for radical innovation (say, 5 or 10 percent of annual capital budget, or a mandatory proportion of each business unit's budget)

- Open, companywide idea submission system with peer review process for evaluating and funding promising opportunities

- Rapid seed funding for innovation experiments, available in small, staged increments

- Portfolio management of new ideas

Product/process development

Traditional process

- Biased toward making incremental improvements to existing products/processes that fit within existing business structures

- Usually delegated exclusively to R&D or a dedicated new product development department and not made the direct responsibility of business unit managers (who are usually only interested when the new product or process is mature enough to impact their business)

- Emphasis on quality management tends to reject radical ideas that deviate from the company's established processes, which are set up for producing "more of the same"

Reengineered process

- Rebalanced to put increased focus on the creation of radically new products/processes

- A management "switching system" directs incremental improvements into existing channels, while radical innovations are developed by cross-functional task forces

- Special corporate teams are assigned to develop new products and processes that transcend existing business structures

So, are you ready to play Management Process Makeover inside your own company? For an exercise, you might think about some of the ways your organization could innovate around typical HR processes like training and development, hiring and promotion, or performance assessment to make them more innovation friendly.

THE ULTIMATE CHALLENGE

Let's imagine that your organization has progressed well on its journey to embed and institutionalize innovation. Over the last two to three years, you have invested significant time and money in building a corporate-wide innovation capability—perhaps in the ways we have outlined in this book—and by now it is already delivering a stream of game-changing ideas and opportunities. All the necessary processes and mechanisms are in place to make this new capability sustainable in the long term. So what exactly is it that is now keeping you awake at night?

Talk to people who are in this situation—innovation process champions like Nancy Snyder at Whirlpool—and they will tell you the answer: it's how to manage the constant tension between this newly built innovation capability and every other activity in the company. It's how to maintain the balance between continuous, break-the-rules innovation on the one hand and penny-pinching efficiency on the other. It's how to honor the notion of challenging orthodoxy, and radical new thinking, and continuous experimentation, yet at the same time honor the demands of short-term operational excellence. Managing this tension is, in many ways, the final and perhaps most subtle challenge of the innovation embedment journey.

In some organizations, the tension is "managed" by sequestering innovation into some obscure corner of the company, like an incubator or a Skunk Works. Other companies long ago segregated innovation to specific departments like R&D, new product development, or corporate venturing. Over the years, this has tended to institutionalize the notion that innovation is not as important as efficiency. In a sense, innovation has become a "second-class citizen" that does not have the same rights, the same visibility, or the same impetus behind it as operational excellence.

Our argument is that this is no longer an option. What is required today is not segregation but "systemic integration." Getting innovation to "stick" requires a sustained, "soup to nuts" approach aimed at systemically building innovation into every management process in the company.

Companies that are successful at sustaining innovation develop processes, leaders, and teams to master the innovation paradox. They learn to balance the forces of efficiency and innovation instead of "institutionalizing" a trade-off between the two. They understand that there is no trade-off; that both ideals—requiring different approaches, skills, and mind-sets—are equally important and have their role.

BALANCING INNOVATION AND EFFICIENCY

How, then, can your company get innovation and efficiency to successfully "cohabit" in your organization? And how can you manage the inherent and ongoing tension between these two forces? We have a two-step answer.

The first step is to make innovation a full citizen. It has to be represented in your company's metrics, incentives, training, and management processes in the same way that these things tend to further efficiency, alignment, and conformance. Innovation must be recognized to be equal in importance to operational excellence.

Step two is to be attentive, day by day, to the process of mutual accommodation. Instead of minimizing the interaction between your company's innovation and efficiency efforts, you should design your organizational systems so that the two ideals are constantly rubbing shoulders every day. The goal is to have them continually interacting and dealing with each other's differences—even *battling* with one another—so that the interests of each side can always be heard, and so that no side ever scores a decisive and permanent victory over the other.

Think of it like a tug-of-war with the heretics and dreamers at one end of the rope, and the accountants and engineers at the other end. One side is fighting to grow the business, to innovate, to change the rules of the game. The other side is fighting to meet the numbers, to deliver world-class quality, and to make sure the product ships on time. One side says it needs more resources to launch a radical new business idea. The other side says the company can't afford it—they would rather put those resources into advertising the current product range or cutting manufacturing costs. At planning and budgeting meetings, the rope moves this way and that way as each side battles for its own priorities and finds itself having to accommodate the other on these kinds of issues.

The challenge for your company is to maintain this constant creative tension every day in a hundred points of conflict across the organization, as the two forces do battle at the margins. Obviously, there will be trade-offs here and there at the micro level, depending on the merits of any particular case. But by staying alert to how these battles are playing out over time and to how the individual trade-offs are being resolved, you can ensure that neither side ultimately "wins" at the macro level by dominating the other.

What this all adds up to is a very difficult balancing act for today's senior executives, particularly in view of powerful external forces that can very easily throw the "creative tension" between innovation and efficiency out of kilter.

Whirlpool knows this only too well. Just when its fledgling innovation system was beginning to show its first serious results, the organization was hit by the largest spike in commodity prices in history. Suddenly, in a single year, CEO Jeff Fettig had to swallow an additional $700 million in materials costs. That's a big number, even for a $13 billion company. To put it in perspective, Whirlpool's earnings per share at the time were typically in the range of $6 to $7. This spike alone added up to about $7 per share. So the tendency was to start thinking, "Okay, this innovation stuff is all really cute, and we know it's important, and we've made a lot of progress, but right now we've got to get costs out of the system like there's no tomorrow, and we need all hands on deck to do that." This obviously created a lot of controversy in the organization.

The trick, as Whirlpool discovered, was to be able to shift some weight to one end of the rope for a year or so—to let the organization concentrate temporarily on cost reduction—without completely losing the tension from the innovation side. Then, when the numbers had straightened themselves out, the company was able to restore the balance by shifting weight back to the innovation side, without giving up its iron grip on operational efficiency.

What Whirlpool learned was that even in the face of intense cost cutting, the momentum and credibility of a company's innovation activities must be kept alive. People need to see that while innovation has been temporarily scaled back, it is definitely not gone. Some tactics for achieving this include:

- Preserving the organization's innovation infrastructure (i.e., vice presidents of innovation, discovery teams, innovation boards, innovation consultants, and mentors)

- Continuing to publicly recognize innovators (i.e., through award ceremonies)

- Making a clear statement of commitment by keeping some of the company's best people focused on future opportunities

- Publicly and explicitly talking about the tension between innovation and efficiency

The fact is that business always goes through upswings and downswings. At times, a company will be cash rich; at other times, it will be cash poor. These changes in circumstances will naturally pull an organization's attention toward one of the two extremes—either toward operational efficiency when there's a pressing need to cut costs, or toward innovation when the business focus is on growth.

Companies need to stay ever attentive to these external forces. They need to keep subtly shifting their weight and adjusting the emphasis this way or that way to keep the organization's center of gravity in the right place. They need to keep asking themselves, Are we striking the right balance inside our company to match what is going on in the external environment? Given our current circumstances, are we veering too far toward one extreme to the detriment of the other? Do we currently have so many people working on innovation that we're letting operations slip out of our hands? Or are we so consumed with cost cutting these days that we've started to neglect the need for creativity and experimentation?

Getting this creative tension right—honoring both innovation and efficiency while not becoming hostage to either one of them—is an enormously subtle challenge. It's the same kind of tension parents have with their children. How do they balance the love they have for their kids with the discipline they need to give them? If it's all love, love, love and no discipline, the children probably will end up spoiled and lazy. If it's all discipline and very little explicit love, the kids will feel as if they're growing up in boot camp. The answer lies in both extremes. Parents need to somehow find the right mix of both love and discipline and give their children what they need at the right moment, in the right way. They can't just set up some kind of rule that says, "Every Thursday afternoon I am going to whack you on the side of the head, as a general principle, because I know you must have done something you shouldn't have done."

There's a lesson in this for companies that are struggling to embrace the paradox between the relentless pursuit of efficiency and the restless search for radical, value-creating innovations. To a large extent, the answer is to never make a once-and-for-all trade-off.

TENSIONS *WITHIN* INNOVATION

Managing the tension between innovation and efficiency is already difficult enough for any organization. But to make matters worse, several more tensions are inherent to innovation itself. Consider the following examples:

- *Unbounded* and *focused:* On the one hand, we want people to feel unbounded in their thinking—to know that they can basically challenge anything and come up with any kind of idea. But on the other hand, we want innovation to be focused. We want to know whether those new ideas fit into some kind of innovation architecture—some sense of who or what the organization is becoming. We want it to reinforce certain themes or opportunity domains. We want it to take the organization, say, more northeast than southwest. We also want people to understand that there's a huge difference between ideas that are just stupid in a crazy way and ideas that are stupid in a smart way. We don't want to waste our time on things that wouldn't pass a sanity test.

- *Radical* and *prudent:* We want people to generate truly radical ideas with the power to upset an industry's balance, but at the same time, we want to be prudent. We don't want to bet the farm by taking huge billion-dollar risks.

- *Committed* and *tentative:* When we spot a big opportunity— some exciting discontinuity that's at the juncture of several deep changes in the world—we want to be enormously committed to that opportunity. But we also want to stay tentative—we want to approach those opportunities carefully and free from hubris.

- *Creative* and *systematic:* Obviously, innovation requires a lot of creativity and freedom, so we want to give people the training, the tools, and the space for inspiration and experimentation. But we also need a pipeline process that is somehow systematic—that turns all of that wild-haired thinking into some real opportunities with traction behind them.

- *Impatient* and *persistent:* We want to be enormously impatient as an organization—how soon can we turn ideas into money? But we also have to be very persistent, because experimentation and learning take time, and sometimes an opportunity is going to be a marathon, not a sprint. We need to develop an impatience to *learn* and to get to the next stage of the development process, not necessarily an impatience to see a return on investment.

To make innovation a sustainable core competence, a company must learn how to carefully manage all of these subtle tensions and how to dynamically fine-tune them. The ability to do so is what prevents, on one hand, the billion-dollar boondoggles that so often give innovation a bad name, while on the other hand ensuring that innovation doesn't become the victim of next quarter's inevitable budget crisis.

Senior executives need to be able to ask themselves, Do we currently have too much "yin" and not enough "yang" in this innovation process? And if so, how do we rebalance that?

Take the notion that innovation should be unbounded, yet also focused. Often, a company will cast the net very, very broadly at first—people can basically send in any idea that comes into their heads, which is perfectly okay. But later, the firm might realize that it doesn't have the competencies, the infrastructure, or the distribution channels to commercialize many of these ideas. Or the economic climate has changed, and the organization is under pressure to focus more on ideas that could quite quickly make an impact on its core business, and less on ideas for spin-offs and peripheral ventures. So management may decide to rein in the criteria for idea submission. As time goes by, the economic barometer inevitably swings back again, or the company notices that it is getting too many incremental ideas as opposed to radical ones, so the net is opened once more. This is quite a natural process.

Companies that have learned to manage these tensions are highly sensitive to small perturbations within their innovation systems. They watch out for the "market signals" and "internal signals" that they are veering off the road on either one side or the other. And they know how to subtly tune their innovation systems, as we described in chapter 10, to keep these tensions in balance.

The ultimate capacity in all of this—the black belt or maestro level of innovation—comes when your company learns how to keep all of these tensions properly managed and tuned, day by day, month by month, year by year. We can tell you from experience that developing that capacity is going to take a lot of hard work, a lot of trial and error, and a lot of patience.

Finally, you cannot master the finer arts of innovation by reading a book. You simply have to get out there and start building your own corporate innovation system, learning and progressing as you make your way from milestone to milestone, and then learning and progressing some more. The innovation embedment journey is not for the armchair tourist.

YOUR OWN INNOVATION JOURNEY

Our aim in writing this book was to give you a basic understanding of what innovation can look like as a systemic, highly distributed, and sustainable capability—as the work of all your people, all the time, and not as the exclusive province of R&D, or new product development, or some isolated incubator. We sincerely hope it has helped you to start thinking about innovation from this new perspective. We also hope the numerous examples we have used, of companies that in many ways may be similar to your own, have convinced you that it really is possible to mobilize and monetize the imagination of employees, customers, and business partners—every day, everywhere.

We have argued through the pages of this book that innovation is not magic. It's not about bolts of lightning. It may certainly require a degree of serendipity, but there are ways to dramatically increase the odds that serendipity will happen. We have shared a lot of the tools, techniques, and processes we have used inside a wide variety of companies to help them approach innovation both systematically and systemically. We have outlined ways to tackle common innovation challenges and conundrums, and to remove the typical roadblocks to innovation that today's organizations have inherited from the industrial age. And we have provided a step-by-step guide—a blueprint—for driving innovation to the core of everything your company does. In short, we have described exactly what it takes for a company to make the transition from boring to breakout, and from insipid to inspired.

Now this book is over, but your own innovation journey may be just beginning. It is certainly not going to be a quick or an easy one. But neither were the learning journeys your organization probably went through to institutionalize things like Total Quality Management, lean manufacturing, Enterprise Resource Planning, or Six Sigma. And the rewards that will come from making innovation a deep core competence will be at least as significant, if not much more so. Any organization that has struggled with these kinds of challenges knows that building an enterprise capability takes lots of time, commitment, and perseverance. It can't be done with a quick fix. *But it can be done.*

While you can't rush the journey, you can rush to start. The pace of innovation in the external environment is already going hypercritical. Procter & Gamble, for example, estimates that the pace of innovation in consumer products alone has doubled in the last ten years. That means that the pace at which you refresh and reinvent your products, services, strategies, and business models must accelerate accordingly.

Truth is, the real innovation imperative is not the race to drive growth; it's the race for *renewal*—the race to change as fast as the environment is changing around you, the race to find new sources of profit before the old ones disappear, the race to reinvent your strategy and your business model before they become obsolete. Organizations that are not positioned to keep up with this race by virtue of their capacity for innovation will have a very, very difficult time.

Simply put, the faster your company builds a sustainable, corporate-wide innovation capability, the better. In fact, this time next year, you may look back and wish you had started your innovation journey today.

INNOVATION CHALLENGES AND LEADERSHIP IMPERATIVES

Innovation challenge: How do I give innovation the best possible chance to succeed?

Leadership Imperatives

- Identify the most fundamental factors in your organization that are getting in the way of innovation—and remove them.

- Try not to let external forces such as market downturns or rising costs get in the way of your innovation progress. Find ways to address the burning issue without losing focus on growth goals.

- Don't expect to become an innovation champion by just reading this book. Put your reading into practice and start "hitting some shots," learning and progressing as you go, and then learning and progressing some more.

Innovation challenge: How do I deal with the tension between innovation and efficiency?

Leadership Imperatives

- Make innovation a "full citizen"—with the same rights, visibility, and impetus behind it as operational excellence.

- Design your organization to keep innovation and efficiency in tension—so that the interests of each side can always be heard, and so that neither side ever scores a permanent victory over the other.

- Don't ignore the warning signs that indicate when the healthy tension between innovation and day-to-day execution is getting out of kilter.

- Recognize and master all of the subtle paradoxes that exist within innovation, such as being unbounded *and* focused, or creative *and* systematic, or impatient *and* persistent—by continuously "tuning" your innovation system to keep these tensions in balance.

NOTES

Chapter 1

1. James P. Andrew, Harold L. Sirkin, Knut Haanæs, and David C. Michael, "Innovation 2007," Boston Consulting Group. The bibliography references additional innovation surveys by other leading consulting firms.

2. Barry Jaruzelski, Kevin Dehoff, and Rakesh Bordia, "Money Isn't Everything," *Strategy and Business*, December 5, 2005.

3. Michael Schrage, "For Innovation Success, Do Not Follow Where the Money Goes," *Financial Times*, November 8, 2005.

4. Geoff Colvin, "Lafley and Immelt: In Search of Billions," *Fortune*, November 27, 2006.

5. "Ben Franklin Forum on Innovation: What Can You Learn from the World's Top Innovators?" Knowledge@Wharton, February 27, 2006.

6. Geoff Colvin, "Lafley and Immelt."

7. Whirlpool Corporation 2006 Annual Report.

8. "Why Whirlpool Is Cleaning Up," *BusinessWeek*, July 30, 2004.

9. Jeffrey E. Garten, "A New Threat to America Inc.," *BusinessWeek*, July 25, 2005.

10. See http://www.doblin.com/TeamIndexFlashFS.htm.

11. Andrew et al., "Innovation 2007."

12. James P. Andrew and Harold L. Sirkin, with John Butman, *Payback: Reaping the Rewards of Innovation* (Boston: Harvard Business School Press, 2007).

Chapter 2

1. Nancy Tennant Snyder and Deborah L. Duarte, *Strategic Innovation: Embedding Innovation as a Core Competency in Your Organization* (San Francisco: John Wiley & Sons, 2003), 16.

2. Ibid., 75.

3. Ibid., 68.

4. Carol Hymowitz, "Diversity in a Global Economy—Ways Some Firms Get It Right," *Wall Street Journal Online*, November 16, 2005.

5. Quoted by Matthew Boyle, "Q&A with Best Buy CEO Brad Anderson," *Fortune*, April 18, 2007.

6. Scott Page, *The Difference: How the Power of Diversity Creates Better Groups, Firms, Schools, and Societies* (Princeton, NJ: Princeton University Press, 2007).

7. Quoted by Ann Pomeroy, "Cooking Up Innovation," *HR Magazine*, November 2004.

8. Bruce Nussbaum, "Get Creative! How to Build Innovative Companies," *BusinessWeek*, August 1, 2005.

9. Page, "The Difference."

10. G. Pascal Zachary, *The Global Me: New Cosmopolitans and the Competitive Edge: Picking Globalism's Winners and Losers*, 1st edition (New York: PublicAffairs, 2000).

11. Andrew Hargadon, *How Breakthroughs Happen: The Surprising Truth About How Companies Innovate* (Boston: Harvard Business School Press, 2003).

12. David Hill, *Getting Heard: The Science and Art of Effective Communication* (Minneapolis, MN: Lakewood Books, 1997).

13. Personal conversations with Gary Hamel.

Chapter 3

1. Gary Hamel and Liisa Välikangas, "The Quest for Resilience," *Harvard Business Review*, September 2003.

2. Victoria Shannon, "Microsoft on Way to Major Ad Player," *International Herald Tribune*, October 7, 2007.

3. Eric S. Raymond, *The Cathedral and the Bazaar: Musings on Linux and Open Source by an Accidental Revolutionary* (Cambridge, MA: O'Reilly and Associates, 1999).

4. John Naisbitt, *Mind Set!: Reset Your Thinking and See the Future* (New York: Collins, 2006).

5. Robert D. Putnam, *Bowling Alone: The Collapse and Revival of American Community* (New York: Simon & Schuster, 2000)

6. Peter Schwartz, *Inevitable Surprises: Thinking Ahead in a Time of Turbulence* (New York: Gotham Books, 2003).

7. Erich Joachimsthaler, *Hidden in Plain Sight: How to Find and Execute Your Company's Next Big Growth Strategy* (Boston: Harvard Business School Press, 2007).

8. Gary Hamel and C. K. Prahalad, "The Core Competence of the Corporation," *Harvard Business Review*, May–June 1990; Gary Hamel and Aimé Heene, eds., *Competence-Based Competition* (New York: Wiley, 1994).

9. Quoted in Alan Deutschman, "How IBM Learned to Love Risk," *Sydney Morning Herald*, March 15, 2005.

10. Quoted in "Building a Global Loyal Following," *Appliance*, April 2003.

Chapter 4

1. Gary Hamel, "The Why, What, and How of Management Innovation," *Harvard Business Review*, February 2006; Gary Hamel, *The Future of Management* (Boston: Harvard Business School Press, 2007).

2. Paul M. Johnson, *Creators: From Chaucer and Dürer to Picasso and Disney* (New York: HarperCollins, 2006).

3. Gary Hamel and Gary Getz, "Funding Growth in an Age of Austerity," *Harvard Business Review,* July 2004.

4. "Big Blue Brainstorm," *BusinessWeek*, August 7, 2006.

5. This quote is taken from businessinnovationfactory.com.

6. Satish Nambisan and Mohanbir Sawhney, "A Buyer's Guide to the Innovation Bazaar," *Harvard Business Review*, June 2007.

7. Eric von Hippel, *Democratizing Innovation* (Cambridge, MA: The MIT Press, 2005).

8. Mohanbir Sawhney, Robert C. Wolcott, and Inigo Arroniz, "The 12 Different Ways for Companies to Innovate," *MIT Sloan Management Review* 47, no. 3 (Spring 2006).

9. Ming Zeng and Peter J. Williamson thoroughly describe the massive disruption leading Chinese companies are creating in *Dragons at Your Door: How Chinese Cost Innovation is Disrupting Global Competition* (Boston: Harvard Business School Press, 2007).

10. In "The 12 Different Ways for Companies to Innovate," Sawhney, Wolcott, and Arroniz suggest twelve different dimensions of innovation that a company should try to include on its "innovation radar."

11. Gary Hamel, "Innovation: The New Route to New Wealth," *Leader to Leader*, Winter 2001.

12. First framed by the late CEO Charlie Bell.

Chapter 5

1. "iTunes Could Be Apple's 'Trojan Horse' in the Home Audio-Video Market," ABI Research, July 27, 2006; Aaron Ruby, "Could Apple Become Games Console King?" *BusinessWeek Online*, September 26, 2006.

2. Ming Zeng and Peter J. Williamson, *Dragons at Your Door: How Chinese Cost Innovation is Disrupting Global Competition* (Boston: Harvard Business School Press, 2007).

3. For a more detailed framework, see Gary Hamel, *Leading the Revolution* (Boston: Harvard Business School Press, 2002), chapter 3.

4. For more information on Southwest's activity systems, see Michael E. Porter, "What is Strategy?" *Harvard Business Review*, November–December 1996.

5. Kevin Freiberg and Jackie Freiberg, *Nuts! Southwest Airlines' Crazy Recipe for Business and Personal Success* (New York: Broadway Books, 1998).

6. Tom Krazit, "Intel Loses Market Share in Own Backyard," CNET News.com, January 18, 2006.

Chapter 7

1. Larry Huston, speech delivered at American Marketing Association, November 3, 2006; and Keith Grime, speech delivered at Analytical Life Sciences Association Conference (ALSA), May 7, 2007.

2. Henry Mintzberg, *The Rise and Fall of Strategic Planning* (New York: Free Press, 1994).

3. Quoted by John A. Byrne in "Strategic Planning," *BusinessWeek*, August 26, 1996.

4. Published in Nokia's 2000 annual report; also, summarized in several articles, including Gary Hamel, "Innovation as a Deep Capability," *Leader to Leader*, Winter, 2003.

5. "Our Values at Work on Being an IBMer," www.ibm.com.

Chapter 8

1. Gary Hamel, "Bringing Silicon Valley Inside," *Harvard Business Review*, September–October 1999.

2. Ibid.

3. See http://www.shell.com/home/content/gamechanger-en/shell_for_the_home/criteria.html).

4. Charles F. Knight with David Dyer, *"Performance Without Compromise: How Emerson Consistently Achieves Winning Results* (Boston: Harvard Business School Press, 2005).

Chapter 9

1. Alan Deutschman, "The Fabric of Creativity," *Fast Company*, December 2004.

2. Gary Hamel, *Leading the Revolution* (Boston: Harvard Business School Press, 2000).

Chapter 10

1. Quoted by Diane Brady, "The Immelt Revolution," *BusinessWeek*, March 28, 2005.

2. Steven Kerr, "On the Folly of Rewarding A, While Hoping for B," *Academy of Management Journal* 18, no. 4 (December 1975): 769–783.

3. Rowan Gibson, *Rethinking the Future; Rethinking Business, Principles, Competition, Control and Complexity, Leadership, Markets and the World* (London: Nicholas Brealey Publishing, 1998).

4. Kathleen Turner, "Innovation Democracy," *Computerworld*, February 16, 2004.

Chapter 11

1. Nancy Tennant Snyder and Deborah L. Duarte, *Strategic Innovation: Embedding Innovation as a Core Competency in Your Organization, Strategic Innovation* (San Francisco: Jossey-Bass, 2003.

2. Ibid.

3. "Blue Ocean" from W. Chan Kim, Renée Mauborgne, *Blue Ocean Strategy* (Boston: Harvard Business School Press, 2005).

4. Quoted in "The Innovative Organization: Lessons Learned from Most Admired Companies," *Hay Insight Selections* 8, April 2005.

5. Interviewed by George Hall in "Leading the Revolution: The Road to Innovation," *American Society for Training & Development,* September 2003.

6. Quoted by Ann Pomeroy in "Cooking up innovation: when it comes to helping employees create new products and services, HR's efforts are a key ingredient," *HR Magazine,* November 2004.

7. Hay Group's Eighth Annual Analysis of Most Admired Companies in *Fortune* magazine ranking, 2005.

8. Robert D. Hof, "Building an Idea Factory," *BusinessWeek*, October 11, 2004.

9. Return on capital employed, return on net assets, economic value added, and return on investment.

10. Chris Argyris, and Donald A. Schön, *Theory in Practice: Increasing Professional Effectiveness* (San Francisco: Jossey-Bass, San Francisco, 1974).

11. Marcus Buckingham and Donald O. Clifton, *Now, Discover Your Strengths* (New York: Free Press, 2001).

12. Gotham Chopra on Virgin Comics, Newsarama.com, 2006.

Chapter 12

1. Gary Hamel, "The Why, What and How of Management Innovation," *Harvard Business Review,* February 2006.

BIBLIOGRAPHY

Barker, Joel Arthur. *Paradigms: The Business of Discovering the Future*. New York: HarperCollins, 1993.

Brown, John Seely. *Seeing Differently: Insights on Innovation*. Boston: Harvard Business School Press, 1997.

Chesbrough, Henry. *Open Innovation: The New Imperative for Creating and Profiting from Technology*. Boston: Harvard Business School Press, 2003.

Chesbrough, Henry. "The Era of Open Innovation." *MIT Sloan Management Review*, Spring 2003.

Christensen, Clayton M. *The Innovator's Dilemma: When New Technologies Cause Great Firms to Fail*. Boston: Harvard Business School Press, 1997.

Drucker, Peter F. *Innovation and Entrepreneurship: Practice and Principles*. New York: Harper & Row, 1985.

Drucker, Peter F. "The Discipline of Innovation." *Harvard Business Review*, 1985.

Gladwell, Malcolm. *The Tipping Point: How Little Things Can Make a Big Difference*. Boston: Back Bay Books, 2002.

Govindarajan, Vijay, and Chris Trimble. "Strategic Innovation and the Science of Learning." *MIT Sloan Management Review*, Winter 2004.

Grove, Andrew S. *Only the Paranoid Survive: How to Exploit the Crisis Points That Challenge Every Company and Career*. New York: Currency Doubleday, 1996.

Hamel, Gary. *Leading the Revolution: How to Thrive in Turbulent Times by Making Innovation a Way of Life*. New York: Plume, 2002.

Hamel, Gary, and Aimé Heene, eds. *Competence-Based Competition*. New York: Wiley, 1994.

Hamel, Gary, and C. K. Prahalad. *Competing for the Future*. Boston: Harvard Business School Press, 1994.

Hamel, Gary, and C. K. Prahalad. "The Core Competence of the Corporation." *Harvard Business Review*, May 1990.

Hamel, Gary, and C. K. Prahalad. "Strategic Intent." *Harvard Business Review*, 1989.

Huston, Larry, and Nabil Sakkab. "Connect and Develop: Inside Procter & Gamble's New Model for Innovation." *Harvard Business Review*, March 2006.

Kim, W. Chan, and Renée Mauborgne. "Blue Ocean Strategy." *Harvard Business Review*, October 2004.

Kim, W. Chan, and Renée Mauborgne. *Blue Ocean Strategy: How to Create Uncontested Market Space and Make Competition Irrelevant*. Boston: Harvard Business School Press, 2004.

Leonard, Dorothy, and Walter Swap. *When Sparks Fly: Igniting Creativity in Groups.* Boston: Harvard Business School Press, 1999.

Leonard-Barton, Dorothy. *Wellsprings of Knowledge: Building and Sustaining the Sources of Innovation.* Boston: Harvard Business School Press, 1995.

Markides, Constantinos C., and Peter J. Williamson. "Related Diversification, Core Competences and Corporate Performance." *Strategic Management Journal* 15 (Summer 1994).

O'Reilly, Charles A. III, and Michael L. Tushman. "The Ambidextrous Organization." *Harvard Business Review*, April 2004.

Prahalad, C. K., and R. A. Bettis. "The Dominant Logic: A New Linkage Between Diversity and Performance." *Strategic Management Journal* (1986).

Prahalad, C. K., and R. A. Bettis. "The Dominant Logic: Retrospective and Extension." *Strategic Management Journal* 16, no. 1 (1995): 5–14.

Raymond, Eric S. *The Cathedral and the Bazaar: Musings on Linux and Open Source by an Accidental Revolutionary.* Cambridge, MA: O'Reilly & Associates, 1999.

Schwartz, Peter. *Inevitable Surprises: Thinking Ahead in a Time of Turbulence.* New York: Gotham Books, 2003.

Schwartz, Peter. *The Art of the Long View: Planning for the Future in an Uncertain World.* New York: Currency Press, 1995.

Selden, Larry, and Ian C. MacMillan. "Manage Customer-Centric Innovation—Systematically." *Harvard Business Review*, April 2006.

Shapiro, Carl, and Hal R. Varian. *Information Rules: A Strategic Guide to the Network Economy.* Boston, MA: Harvard Business School Press, 1999.

Snyder, Nancy Tennant, and Deborah L. Duarte. *Strategic Innovation: Embedding Innovation as a Core Competency in Your Organization.* San Francisco: Jossey-Bass, 2003.

Sturdivant, Frederick D., and Francis J. Gouillart. "Spend a Day in the Life of Your Customers." *Harvard Business Review*, January 1994.

Thomke, Stefan H. "Enlightened Experimentation: The New Imperative for Innovation." *Harvard Business Review*, February 2001.

Thomke, Stefan H. *Experimentation Matters: Unlocking the Potential of New Technologies for Innovation.* Boston: Harvard Business School Press, 2003.

Thomke, Stefan H. "R&D Comes to Services: Bank of America's Pathbreaking Experiments." *Harvard Business Review*, April 2003.

Ulwick, Anthony W. "Turn Customer Input into Innovation." *Harvard Business Review*, January 2002.

Von Hippel, Eric. *Democratizing Innovation.* Cambridge, MA: MIT Press, 2005.

Von Hippel, Eric. *The Sources of Innovation.* New York: Oxford University Press, 1988.

INDEX

accountability by leadership. *See* leadership and organization for innovation
aiming points, 86, 105, 107, 139–140, 157
allocational rigidities, 172, 258
Amazon.com, 53, 70, 185
Anderson, Brad, 31
Andrew, James, 16
Apple
  business model innovations, 109–110
  collaboratory designs, 37
  innovation architecture, 65, 138
  open innovation use, 175
  radical innovation, 129
Arent, Tom, 24
Argyris, Chris, 245
arithmetic, innovation, 95–97, 107, 210
assets. *See* competencies and assets for innovation
award ceremonies, 10, 207

balanced scorecard, 224. *See also* metrics for tracking innovation performance
balancing innovation and efficiency, 263–266
balancing supply and demand. *See* supply-demand equation
Ballmer, Steve, 50
bandwidth for innovation, 22–26, 195
barriers to innovation
  from budgeting process, 162–163
  from company structure, 163–164
  as identified by CEOs, 22–23, 161
  removing, 234, 236

Bennis, Warren, 216
Best Buy, 4, 31, 59, 70, 87, 130, 229
Bezos, Jeff, 36, 53
Binkley, Dave, 241
"blue ocean" opportunities, 235
BMW, 128, 133, 247
bottom-up approach to strategy making, 87, 151–153
Bowling Alone (Putnam), 57
brainstorming, 14, 16, 77, 86, 107, 256
Branson, Richard, 45, 248, 249
breakthrough innovation, 4, 8, 22, 34, 36, 43, 45, 47, 72, 77, 85, 90, 101, 112, 114, 174, 207, 209
Brin, Sergey, 26, 97
Buckingham, Marcus, 247
budgeting for innovation. *See* resource management
business model innovations
  Apple's use of, 109–110
  cost innovations possibilities, 99, 110–111
  described, 99, 111–114
  holistic thinking and, 115–117
  innovation challenges and leadership imperatives, 122
  model analysis, 113f, 117–120
  model stretching using insights, 120–121
  objectives, 114–115
buzzwords, corporate, 4, 11, 12

capability, systemic innovation. *See* systemic innovation capability

CEMEX
  coaching and mentoring to enable
    supply, 206
  growth platforms, 139
  innovation infrastructure, 234–235
  innovation platform teams, 25–26
  innovation system components, 9–11
  rewards program, 207–208
  systemic innovation capability, 9
challenges. *See* innovation challenges
  summaries
Charles Schwab, 47
cluster of opportunities, 141, 143, 145,
  146, 150, 155
CNN, 67
coaching and mentoring in innovation,
  8, 10, 12, 27, 44, 164, 169, 202,
  205, 206, 208, 209, 214, 220, 223,
  225, 227, 233, 234, 235, 238, 239,
  240, 244, 264
collaborations. *See* partnering for
  innovation
Colvin, Geoff, 6
commitment, financial, 95, 181, 183,
  184, 186, 187
commitment, long-term project, 182,
  183
commitment to innovation, 11, 12, 16,
  24, 151, 178, 208, 219, 223, 228,
  230, 247, 265, 269. *See also* culture
  of innovation; institutionalizing
  innovation
community of volunteers, 93–95
compensation, management, 214–215.
  See also rewards and recognition for
  enabling innovation
competencies and assets for innovation
  borrowing competencies and assets,
    68–69, 175
  getting started with discovery work,
    64–65
  identifying core competencies (*see* core
    competence)
  identifying strategic assets, 62, 67–68
  recombining diverse assets, 62–64

reconceiving the company portfolio,
  64–65
competitive advantage through innovation, 4, 5, 21, 99, 100, 112, 119,
  128, 130, 137. *See also* strategic innovation
Connect and Develop (P&G), 6, 33, 91,
  175, 259
connection and conversation to facilitate
  innovation
  collaborations value, 36–37
  company self-critique, 39, 40, 41, 42
  face time and, 41–42
  IT infrastructures and, 40–41
  maximizing connections, 38–40
  networking and, 33, 36, 44, 50, 86,
    89, 91, 205, 222, 243
  partnering for innovation, 68, 105,
    190, 191, 196
consultants, innovation. *See* innovation
  consultants
consultants, management, 59, 96
convergent phase of innovation architecture, 141–142
core competence
  definition, 62
  innovation as, 4, 7–9, 11, 12, 19, 23,
    24, 230–232, 241, 244, 245,
    248, 252, 267, 269
  leveraging, 62, 102, 104, 143
  understanding, 65, 66, 67
corporate innovation system, 11, 16,
  202, 239, 252, 268. *See also* institutionalizing innovation
cost innovations, 99, 110–111
Craigslist, 57
crashing insights, 86, 101, 103, 104
creative collision, 37, 101
creative tension, 263–265
creativity, 14, 23, 26, 30, 35, 40, 45, 46,
  86–89, 91, 172, 209, 239, 246,
  265, 267
critiquing your own company
  connection and conversation to facili-
    tate innovation, 39, 40, 41, 42

diversity maximization, 35
time and space creation for innovation,
    27
cross-boundary interaction, 39, 235–237
culture of innovation. *See also* institu-
    tionalizing innovation
  building a deep innovation culture,
    250–252
  creating an internal market for talent,
    171–172
  employee involvement (*see* employee
    involvement in innovation)
  encouragement and, 40, 177, 202,
    250
  innovation as a core competence,
    4, 7–9, 11, 12, 19, 23, 24,
    230–232, 241, 244, 245, 248,
    252, 267, 269
  innovation as a tangible value (*see*
    value creation)
  innovation as part of everyone's job,
    27, 32, 156, 262, 268, 269
  instilling innovation as a core compe-
    tence, 4, 7–9, 11, 12, 19, 23, 24,
    230–232, 241, 244, 245, 248,
    252, 267, 269
  need for an innovation mindset,
    255–257
  need for a systemic understanding,
    13–16
  passion for innovation, 41, 152, 153,
    154, 169, 238
  systemic integration challenge,
    262–263
  tactics for keeping innovation alive,
    264–265
  theory of action versus theory-in-use,
    245–247
  time and space creation and (*see* time
    and space creation for innovation)
culture transition, 250–252, 255, 269
Customer Centric Cycle (Best Buy), 87
customer experience mapping, 73–75
customer insights, 69, 71–75, 79, 80,
    103, 104, 121, 139, 140

customer needs. *See* needs, addressing
    unmet customer
customer value, creating, 8, 64, 66, 67,
    68, 79, 109, 113, 117, 119, 121,
    168, 250
  addressing unmet customer needs,
    17, 46, 56, 69–76, 77–80, 104,
    121, 249

DARPA Grand Challenge, 175–176
dashboard, innovation, 3, 220
Dell, 47, 50, 70, 128, 129
Dell, Michael, 45
demand element in innovation. *See*
    supply-demand equation
design rules for innovation pipeline. *See*
    innovation pipeline design rules
dialogue, innovation, 90, 148, 154
Difference, The (Page), 32
discovery insights, 78–81, 85, 86, 101,
    105, 107
discovery lenses, 47, 87, 134, 205, 243,
    244. *See also* lenses of innovation
discovery phases of innovation, 42, 46,
    59, 72, 79, 144
discovery process, 45, 76–77, 79, 106
discovery teams, 77–79, 102, 264
discovery work, 64–65, 77, 105, 120,
    152, 153, 211
Disney, 62–63, 75, 76, 89, 188
divergent phase of innovation architec-
    ture, 141–142
diversity maximization
  characteristics of diversity, 28–29
  company self-critique, 35
  homogeneity at the top and, 29–30
  mixing people up and, 34–35
  non-company people use, 33–34
  in teams of problem solvers, 31–33
  underrepresented constituencies,
    30–31
DNA, organizational, 13, 33, 153, 252,
    253, 256, 259
Doak, Bob, 183

Dragons at Your Door (Zeng and Williamson), 110
Duarte, Deborah, 232

eBay, 37, 99, 126, 129, 184, 185
efficiency versus innovation. *See* sustaining innovation
e-learning, 203, 240
embedment, innovation, 7, 8, 13, 17, 23–25, 218, 221, 231–234, 237–239, 241, 243, 245, 250, 252–254, 256, 257, 262, 268
Emerging Business Opportunities (IBM), 195, 236
Emerson Electric, 210–212
employee involvement in innovation, 3, 4, 8–11, 23–27, 29–31, 32, 40, 42–44, 70, 77, 78, 87–90, 106, 151–154, 156–157, 158, 164, 166, 167, 169, 172, 173, 178, 202–205, 207, 211, 217, 220, 238, 239, 241, 242, 244, 262, 268, 269. *See also* connection and conversation to facilitate innovation; culture of innovation
encouragement, culture of, 40, 177, 202, 250
enterprise-wide innovation. *See* culture of innovation; institutionalizing innovation; sustaining innovation
E-space. *See* Innovation E-space
ESPN, 63
evaluating innovative ideas. *See also* innovation process
    criteria for, 125–127
    innovation challenges and leadership imperatives, 134–135
    limits to incrementalism, 127–128
    radical innovation (*see* radical innovation)
Exelon. *See* PECO Energy Corporation
experience innovations, 99
experimentation, 22, 23, 25, 26, 95–97, 126, 137, 138, 164, 166, 168, 176, 188, 189, 192–196, 197, 220, 226. *See also* innovation process
external sources of innovation, 32, 33, 41, 44, 68, 69, 91–93, 169, 176, 222, 248. *See also* partnering for innovation

face time to facilitate innovation, 41–42. *See also* connection and conversation to facilitate innovation
FedEx, 64, 66–67, 70, 129
Fettig, Jeff, 9, 226, 231, 233, 252, 264
financial commitment to innovation, 95, 181, 183, 184, 186, 187. *See also* sustaining innovation
financing innovation. *See* resource management
first- versus second-mover advantage, 185–186, 190
focus on innovation
    bringing focus, 138–140, 266, 267, 270
    ideation process and, 86, 100, 104–107, 157
Ford, Henry, 36
Freiberg, Kevin and Jackie, 113
funding. *See* resource management

GameChanger at Royal Dutch/Shell, 167–171, 174, 244, 259
Gates, Bill, 45
GE, 4, 5–6, 16, 28, 34, 66, 139, 209, 215, 223, 229, 231, 238, 241
Getz, Gary, 105
Gladiator GarageWorks, 24, 114, 116
Global Me, The (Zachary), 35
Google, 7, 26, 49–51, 50, 65, 94, 97, 170, 229, 248, 250
Gore. *See* W. L. Gore
growth from innovation
    driving, 5, 6, 9, 11, 12, 16, 17, 23, 27, 35, 97, 98, 114, 127, 128, 132,

195, 201, 208–211, 217, 231, 235,
    252, 265, 269
  estimating potential, 226
  initiatives, 169, 210
opportunities, 17, 18, 23, 51, 62, 79,
    85–87, 96, 101, 114, 142, 144,
    157, 171, 173, 179, 185, 195, 201,
    210, 211, 214, 242
  platforms, 139, 141, 157
  strategy, 88, 102
  targets, 209, 213, 215, 226, 227, 230,
    245, 270

Haier, 73
Hamel, Gary, 43, 45, 66, 89, 93, 165,
    180, 258
Hargadon, Andrew, 36
Harreld, Bruce, 195
hierarchy, 29, 32, 162–164, 168, 172,
    237
Hill, David, 37
Hof, Robert D., 242
holistic thinking, 115–117, 253
How Breakthroughs Happen (Hargadon),
    36
human resources' role in innovation,
    240–241, 253, 254. See also rewards
    and recognition for enabling inno-
    vation; training in innovation
Huston, Larry, 92

IBM, 4, 34, 44, 66, 70, 90–93,
    151–152, 195, 209, 236, 238
idea evaluation. See evaluating innova-
    tive ideas; radical innovation
ideation projects/process, 22, 42, 86, 90,
    96, 100, 104–107, 115, 139, 156,
    157, 242
  narrow focus for ideation, 100, 105,
    138, 139, 157
IDEO, 33, 34
IKEA, 47, 99, 128
Immelt, Jeff, 5–6, 33, 209, 231

impediments to innovation, 257–258,
    259
imperatives. See innovation imperatives;
    leadership imperatives
incentives to enable innovation, 94, 95,
    207, 209, 211, 224, 230, 231, 241,
    263
incrementalism, 4, 12, 127–128, 133,
    134, 162, 209, 238, 257, 261. See
    also evaluating innovative ideas
increments of capital and time, investing
    small, 169, 176, 261
incubators, 39, 88, 96, 161, 163–165,
    208, 213, 228, 256, 262
industry innovations, 100
information technology
  infrastructure for, 8, 41, 202, 204,
    205, 227, 240, 244, 254
  innovations in, 98
  leveraging the Internet, 90–91
  organizational, 39, 44, 229, 233,
    234–237, 264
  role in market development, 181,
    185, 190–193, 267
  used to enable supply, 205
  using to facilitate innovation,
    243–244
infrastructure
  at CEMEX, 234–235
  corporate (see innovation architecture)
  innovation, 3, 229, 233–238, 264
  IT (see information technology)
  regional, 7, 8, 23, 24, 205, 233, 234,
    248
innovation architecture
  achieving a shared point of view,
    148–150, 150f
  achieving a shared vision, 142,
    148–153, 156–157, 216, 229,
    232
  aiming points and, 86, 105, 107,
    139–140, 157
  as a blueprint for the future, 155–157
  bottom-up approach to strategy
    making, 87, 151–153

innovation architecture (*continued*)
  building ownership of, 158 (*see also*
    culture of innovation)
  creating and testing, 154–155
  described, 140, 150–151
  diversity versus coherence, 137–138
  innovation challenges and leadership
    imperatives, 157–158
  phases of innovation, 140–142
  process of building, 143–146
  screening and sequencing ideas,
    147–148
  uniqueness to your company,
    153–154
  vectors of innovation, 140, 142–143
innovation arithmetic, 95–97, 107,
    210
innovation boards, 10, 24, 25, 233, 234,
    235
innovation challenges summaries
  business model innovations, 122
  evaluating innovative ideas, 134–135
  innovation architecture, 157–158
  innovation pipeline design rules,
    106–107
  institutionalizing innovation,
    253–254
  lenses of innovation, 80–81
  pacing and derisking investments,
    197
  preconditions for innovation, 43–44
  radical innovation, 134–135
  resource management, 177–178
  supply-demand equation, 227–228
  sustaining innovation, 270
innovation consultants, 8, 24, 206,
    233–235, 239, 240, 244, 264
innovation days, 8, 10, 207, 208
innovation democracy, 173, 204, 244
innovation embedment. *See* embedment,
    innovation
Innovation E-space, 8, 172, 205, 240,
    244, 259
innovation events, 8, 41, 42, 90, 176,
    207, 208, 251

innovation imperatives
  business success versus R&D spend-
    ing, 5
  challenge of innovation, 3–4, 16–17
  company example, 5–6
  crisis of credibility in innovation ini-
    tiatives, 15
  innovation system components, 9–11
  instilling innovation as a core
    competence, 7–9
  leadership and (*see* leadership and
    organization for innovation;
    leadership imperatives)
  need for a systemic understanding,
    13–16
  quality movement parallel, 13–14
  rhetoric versus reality of innovation,
    11–13
innovation mentors. *See* coaching and
    mentoring in innovation
innovation mindset need, 255–257
innovation performance, measuring. *See*
    metrics for tracking innovation
    performance
innovation pipeline design rules
  community of volunteers use, 93–95
  fine-tuning the pipeline, 18, 224,
    225, 270
  ideation projects (*see* ideation proj-
    ects/process)
  innovation categories to consider,
    97–100
  innovation challenges and leadership
    imperatives, 106–107
  Internet leveraging, 90–91
  intracompany innovators' support,
    87–90
  noncompany innovators' use, 91–93
  overview, 85–86
  quality movement parallel, 88
  reaching wide enough, 95–97
  reinventing established products,
    103–104
  rethinking established strategy,
    101–103

innovation process
  avoiding a narrow view, 122
  business model support (*see* business model innovations)
  champions of, 10, 173, 206, 238, 262, 270
  corporate culture and (*see* culture of innovation)
  creating conditions for (*see* preconditions for innovation)
  creativity and, 14, 23, 26, 30, 35, 41, 45, 46, 86–89, 91, 172, 209, 239, 246, 265, 267
  embedding into the corporation (*see* institutionalizing innovation)
  evaluating ideas (*see* evaluating innovative ideas)
  facilitating (*see* connection and conversation to facilitate innovation)
  intra-company innovators support (*see also* employee involvement in innovation)
  leadership's responsibilities (*see* leadership imperatives)
  measuring performance (*see* metrics for tracking innovation performance)
  pipeline management (*see* innovation pipeline design rules)
  resource management (*see* resource management)
  sustaining (*see* sustaining innovation)
innovation projects. *See also* radical innovation
  brainstorming, 14, 16, 77, 86, 107, 256
  evaluating ideas (*see* evaluating innovative ideas)
  financing and budgeting for (*see* resource management)
  ideas through diversity (*see* diversity maximization)
  measuring performance (*see* metrics for tracking innovation performance)
  pipeline management (*see* innovation pipeline design rules)

  quality of ideas, improving, 86, 106, 107, 139, 201–204, 211
  quantity of ideas, increasing, 85–100, 101–106
  R&D and, 4, 5, 14, 27, 39, 88, 89, 91, 92, 96, 109, 122, 169, 175, 176, 181, 208, 213, 217, 235, 237, 262
  tapping customer insights, 69, 71–73, 75, 79, 80, 103, 104, 121, 139, 140
  time and space allowance (*see* time and space creation for innovation)
innovation skills. *See* skills, innovation
innovation strategy. *See* strategic innovation
innovation teams. *See* teams, innovation
innovation tools. *See* processes and tools
innovation training. *See* training in innovation
insights into innovation. *See* strategic insights as a basis for innovation
institutionalizing innovation, 231f.
  See also culture of innovation
  building a deep innovation culture, 250–252
  commitment to innovation, 11, 12, 16, 24, 151, 178, 208, 219, 223, 228, 230, 247, 265, 269
  DNA, organizational, 13, 33, 153, 252, 253, 256, 259
  human resources' role, 240–241
  innovation as a tangible value, 247–250
  innovation challenges and leadership imperatives, 253–254
  leadership and organization (*see* leadership and organization for innovation)
  making innovation sustainable (*see* sustaining innovation)
  people and skills, 238–241
  processes and tools, 242–245
  theory of action versus theory-in-use, 245–247

Intel, 115

Internet leveraging, 90–91, 92, 93, 98, 129, 146, 185, 193, 205, 244

intranet use for innovation, 41, 151, 172, 205, 244. *See also* connection and conversation to facilitate innovation; employee involvement in innovation; information technology

I-Pipe, 220

iPod, 37, 65, 98, 100, 109, 110, 129, 138, 175

IT infrastructures. *See* information technology

Jackson, Chris, 144

job, innovation as part of everyone's, 27, 32, 156, 262, 268, 269

Jobs, Steve, 36, 45

Johnson, Paul, 89

Johnson Controls, Inc. (JCI), 34

journey, innovation embedment, 23, 32, 156, 262, 268, 269

Keeley, Larry, 15

KEEN Footwear, 64

Knight, Chuck, 171, 210–212

Kovac, Caroline, 70

Lafley, Alan G., 6, 91, 231

leadership and organization for innovation
cross-boundary interaction, 39, 235–237
distributing responsibility for innovation, 237–238
imperatives summaries (*see* leadership imperatives)
infrastructure creation, 233–235
leader accountability, 7, 25, 27, 44, 212–215, 228, 230–232, 237, 241
shared vision requirement, 142, 148–153, 156–157, 216, 229, 232

leadership imperatives
business model innovations, 122
evaluating innovative ideas, 134–135
innovation architecture, 157–158
innovation pipeline design rules, 106–107
institutionalizing innovation, 253–254
lenses of innovation, 80–81
ownership of the innovation embedment process, 232, 253
pacing and derisking investments, 197
passion for innovation, 41, 151, 153, 154, 169, 238
preconditions for innovation, 43–44
radical innovation, 134–135
resource management, 177–178
supply-demand equation, 227–228
sustaining innovation, 270

learning and innovation
collectively learning, 250, 268, 270
company example of ignoring learning, 189–193
creative collision, 37, 101
e-learning, 203, 240
from experiments, 96, 126, 168, 176, 179, 181, 182, 186, 188–190, 197, 267
during insight discovery phase, 42, 46, 59, 72, 79, 144
journeys to institutionalize other capabilities, 269
maximizing learning over investment, 189–190
providing opportunities (*see* training in innovation)
during strategy development, 153
tensions within innovation, 263–265, 266–268

Leikham, John W., 235

lenses of innovation
analogies from other industries, 72, 75–76

challenging orthodoxies (*see* orthodoxies, challenging)
collective wisdom and, 77–78
criteria for selecting insights, 78–80
customer experience mapping, 73–75
customer insight and, 69–71
direct observation, 72–73
discontinuities, harnessing, 55–56
discontinuities, identifying, 58–61
discovery lenses, 47, 87, 134, 205, 243, 244
innovation challenges and leadership imperatives, 80–81
leveraging competencies and assets (*see* competencies and assets for innovation)
organizing the discovery process, 45, 76–77, 79, 106
overview, 46–47
recognizing the story in unrelated trends, 55–61
levers for balancing supply and demand, 212, 213, 225
Lexus, 129
limits to incrementalism, 127–128
Linux, 49–51, 94
Lockheed, 163, 164. *See also* Skunk Works, Lockheed
Lucas, George, 36

management compensation, 214–215. *See also* rewards and recognition for enabling innovation
management consultants, 59, 96
management innovations, 99
management processes, 12, 14, 16, 22, 89, 99, 166, 172, 173, 210, 256, 257, 258–261, 263
management process makeover, 258–261
marathons, 180, 181–183
Marcy, Hank, 72
marketplace for ideas, 164–170

measuring innovation performance. *See* metrics for tracking innovation performance
mentors, innovation. *See* coaching and mentoring in innovation
metrics for tracking innovation performance
innovation arithmetic, 95–97, 107, 210
innovation metrics, 222t
measuring inputs, 218–222
measuring performance, 212, 216–218, 225, 234
performance targets setting, 223
personal performance, 12, 215, 217, 221, 223
reward criteria and, 245
Microsoft, 49, 183
Mintzberg, Henry, 142
mission statements, 149–151, 245, 248
model, business. *See* business model innovations
monetary rewards, 87, 206, 207
monitoring for progress, 212, 225, 234. *See also* metrics for tracking innovation performance
motivational tools
culture of encouragement, 40, 177, 202, 250
rewards and recognition (*see* rewards and recognition for enabling innovation)
Motorola, 144, 154, 232
Muller, Amy, 91
mutual accommodation between innovation and efficiency, 263
Myers, Dave, 26
MyPage, 172
MySpace, 172, 180

Naisbitt, John, 55
narrow focus for ideation, 100, 105, 138, 139, 157
narrow view of innovation, 122

NASA, 174
needs, addressing unmet customer, 17, 46, 56, 69–76, 77–80, 104, 121, 249
Nespresso (Nestlé), 99, 180, 181–183
Netflix, 130–131, 180
networking, social, 57
networking to foster innovation, 33, 36, 44, 50, 86, 89, 91, 205, 222, 243
networks' impact on market development, 184, 185
Nokia, 59, 140, 144–146, 147, 154, 156

observation to facilitate innovation
  expanding your perspective (*see* lenses of innovation)
  monitoring customers (*see* customer insights)
  use of direct observation, 72–73
Omidyar, Pierre, 37
open innovation, 6, 33, 68, 91, 92, 175, 222, 231, 251
open market for ideas, 38, 39–40, 238
open market spaces search, 107
operating system for innovation, global, 40, 205
operating systems, computer, 49, 94, 138, 175
operational efficiency/excellence, 22, 87, 210, 212, 262–265, 270
operational innovations, 98
operational perspective of innovation, 233, 260
organizational culture. *See* culture of innovation
organizational players in innovation infrastructure, 233
organizational values. *See* culture of innovation; value creation
organization charts and innovation, 39, 233
Organizing Genius (Bennis), 216
orthodoxies, challenging
  challenging the leader, 49–51

company examples, 47–48
  doing the opposite, 51
  getting started, 51–52
  identifying orthodoxies, 52–55
  orthodoxies described, 47, 48–49
outputs measurement. *See* metrics for tracking innovation performance
outside, using competencies and assets from, 69, 175. *See also* competencies and assets for innovation
outside innovators, 6, 29, 33–35, 37–38, 40–41, 44, 89, 91–94, 167, 175, 177, 178, 231, 236. *See also* partnering for innovation
outside the core, opportunities, 115, 131, 181, 235, 236
outside your industry, analogies from, 72, 75
ownership of innovation architecture, 158
ownership of the innovation embedment process, 232, 253

pacing and derisking investments
  actual versus perceived risk, 186–188
  cautions about untested assumptions, 191–192
  company example of ignoring learning, 189–193
  experiment, assess, adapt, 193–194
  first- versus second-mover advantage, 185–186, 190
  innovation challenges and leadership imperatives, 197
  maximizing learning over investment, 189–190
  new opportunities assessment, 180–181
  portfolio management, 194–196
  sharing risk, 196
  understanding immediate opportunities (sprints), 184–185
  understanding long-term opportunities (marathons), 181–183

Page, Larry, 26, 97
Page, Scott, 32, 35
Palmisano, Sam, 90, 151–152
paradoxes, innovation, 138, 262, 266, 267, 270
partnering for innovation, 36–37, 68, 90–92, 105, 190, 191, 196
passion for innovation, 41, 151, 153, 154, 169, 238
Payback (Andrew and Sirkin), 16
PayPal, 129, 184–185
PECO Energy Corporation, 101–103
peer panel review of ideas, 95, 168, 261
peer-to-peer Web-based marketplace, 37, 109, 184
perceptual lenses. *See* lenses of innovation
personal performance metrics, 12, 215, 217, 221, 223
perspectives, facilitating innovation
  developing fresh, 41, 43, 46, 77, 79, 85, 205, 243
  examining business model from new, 117
  generating companywide, 144
  importance of different, 28, 30, 32, 34, 38, 42, 43, 46, 77, 85, 204
pharmacogenomics, 130
pipeline for innovation. *See* innovation pipeline design rules
platforms
  growth, 139, 141, 157
  teams at CEMEX, 25–26
Player, Gary, 38
portfolio, company
  of competencies and assets, 46, 64–65
  of customer problems, 139
  of experimental projects, 97, 137, 166, 170, 171, 178, 194–196, 197
  of insights, 78
  management, 230, 231, 261
  shaping innovation, 142, 144, 148, 242
  of strategic options/growth opportunities, 17, 96, 106, 127, 134,

137, 139–140, 156, 179, 201–222, 234
power locus shift, 170
Prahalad, C. K., 66, 180
preconditions for innovation
  connection and conversation (*see* connection and conversation to facilitate innovation)
  diversity maximization (*see* diversity maximization)
  innovation challenges and leadership imperatives, 43–44
  time and space creation (*see* time and space creation for innovation)
processes and tools
  brainstorming, 14, 16, 77, 86, 107, 256
  corporate infrastructure support (*see* innovation architecture)
  customer inputs (*see* customer insights)
  description and examples, 242–245
  for enabling innovation, 13, 14, 16, 90, 91, 213, 230, 238, 242, 243, 248, 250, 251, 253, 259, 262
  intracompany innovators' support (*see* employee involvement in innovation)
  IT and (*see* information technology)
  management (*see* management processes)
  for managing and multiplying resources, 161, 166, 172
  motivational (*see* motivational tools)
  people and skills, 238–241
  recalibrating existing, 14, 40, 89, 173, 253, 256, 259, 261, 263
  time and space creation (*see* time and space creation for innovation)
  training in innovation (*see* training in innovation)
process innovation, 98, 99, 119
Procter & Gamble, 6
  collaboration with external partners, 91–92

Procter & Gamble (*continued*)
  cross-boundary interaction, 235–236
  customer problems analysis, 139–140
  demand drivers, 209
  human resources' role, 241
  innovation motto, 194
  noncompany people's use, 33
  open innovation program, 175
  use of direct observation, 72–73
product innovations, 98
projects, innovation. *See* innovation
    projects
prototyping, 165, 168, 194, 211, 226
Putnam, Robert, 57

quality movement, 13–15, 16, 22,
    88–90, 232, 237, 239, 242,
    245–257, 269
quality of ideas, improving, 86, 106,
    107, 139, 201–204, 211. *See also*
    innovation projects
quantity of ideas, increasing, 85–100,
    101–106. *See also* innovation projects

R&D and innovation, 4, 5, 14, 27, 39,
    88, 89, 91, 92, 96, 109, 122, 169,
    175, 181, 208, 213, 217, 235, 237,
    262
radical innovation. *See also* innovation
    projects
  definition and examples, 128–131
  innovation challenges and leadership
    imperatives, 134–135
  potential impact evaluation, 132–134
  radical versus risky, 131–132
Raymond, Eric, 51
reallocation of resources. *See* resource
    management
recognition. *See* rewards and recognition
    for enabling innovation
recruitment for innovation, 33, 241, 254
regional innovation infrastructure, 7, 8,
    23, 24, 205, 233, 234, 248

Reina, Bill, 241
renewal, strategic, 16, 98, 260, 269
research and development. *See* R&D and
    innovation
resource management. *See also* supply-
    demand equation
  allocating discretionary budgets,
    166–167
  assessing ideas as a portfolio of proj-
    ects, 170–171
  barriers as identified by CEOs, 22–23,
    161
  barriers from budgeting process,
    162–163
  barriers from company structure,
    163–164
  correlation between innovation re-
    sources and competitive out-
    comes, 174
  creating an internal market for talent,
    171–172
  hybrid organization elements,
    172–173
  innovation challenges and leadership
    imperatives, 177–178
  marketplace for ideas, 164–170
  metrics and reward criteria, 245
  productivity drivers, 173–176
  removing barriers to innovation, 234,
    236
  Silicon Valley model, 165–166
revenue from innovation, 4–6, 9, 37, 63,
    97, 126–128, 132, 166, 181, 195–
    196, 201, 211, 218, 221, 222, 224
revenue potential, 3, 9, 214, 224
rewards and recognition for enabling
    innovation, 206–208, 214–215,
    245
  award ceremonies, 10, 207
  incentives and, 94, 95, 207, 209, 211,
    224, 230, 231, 241, 263
  monetary, 87, 206, 207
risk, actual versus perceived, 186–188.
    See also pacing and derisking
    investments

rotational assignments, 234
Royal Dutch/Shell, 105, 167–171, 176

Saffo, Paul, 183
Sawhney, Mohanbir, 93
scaling up, 190–192, 195, 196
Schwartz, Peter, 57
scorecard, balanced, 223–224. *See also*
    metrics for tracking innovation
    performance
serendipity and innovation, 38–42, 95,
    237, 268
service innovations, 98
shared vision, 142, 148–153, 156–157,
    216, 229, 232
Shell. *See* Royal Dutch/Shell
Silicon Valley model, 35, 38, 97, 162,
    165–167
Sirkin, Harold, 16
Six Sigma, 11, 27, 99, 232, 269
skills, innovation, 8, 9, 16, 24, 27, 44,
    88–89, 203, 221, 225, 230, 232,
    238–240, 243, 251, 253, 258
Skunk Works, 39, 88, 96, 161,
    163–164, 208, 211, 213, 228,
    262
    Lockheed, 163–164, 216
Snyder, Nancy, 23, 24, 232, 233–234
social networking, 57
Southwest Airlines, 47–48, 112–114
space for innovation. *See* bandwidth for
    innovation; time and space creation
    for innovation
sprints, 180, 184–185
Starbucks, 70, 131–132, 182
Star Wars, 36
Steelcase, 34
strategic innovation
    bottom-up approach to, 87, 151–153
    competencies and assets (*see* competen-
        cies and assets for innovation)
    competitive advantage through inno-
        vation, 4, 5, 21, 99, 100, 112,
        119, 128, 130, 137

corporate infrastructure design (*see*
    innovation architecture)
discovering novel insights (*see* cus-
    tomer insights; lenses of innova-
    tion; strategic insights as a basis
    for innovation)
financial commitment (*see* resource
    management; sustaining inno-
    vation)
growth and (*see* growth from inno-
    vation)
growth strategy adoption, 88, 102
identifying strategic assets, 62, 67–68
managing risk (*see* pacing and derisk-
    ing investments)
renewal, strategic, 16, 98, 260, 269
rethinking established strategy,
    101–103
theory of action versus theory-in-use,
    245–247
Strategic Innovation (Snyder), 232
strategic insights as a basis for inno-
    vation
    business model stretching, 120–121
    crashing insights, 86, 101, 103, 104
    criteria for selecting, 78–80
    from customers (*see* customer insights)
    discovering novel strategic insights
        (*see* lenses of innovation)
    reinventing established products,
        103–104
    rethinking established strategy,
        101–103
strategic renewal, 16, 98, 260, 269
Strategos, 209, 220
supply-demand equation. *See also*
    resource management
    budgeting process as a demand driver,
        213–214
    coaching and mentoring in inno-
        vation, 206
    demand drivers as a leadership
        challenge, 208–209
    demand drivers at Emerson Electric,
        210–212

supply-demand equation (*continued*)
  growth targets as demand driver, 215
  high aspirations and, 215–216
  incentives to enable supply (*see* incentives to enable innovation)
  innovation challenges and leadership imperatives, 227–228
  innovation metrics, 222t
  management compensation and, 214–215
  measuring innovation inputs, 218–222
  measuring innovation performance, 212, 216–218, 225, 234
  performance targets setting, 223–224, 228
  pipeline management, 225–226
  rewards and recognition for innovation, 206–208
  scorecard use, 223–224
  technology infrastructure leveraging, 204–206
  training in innovation, 203–204
sustaining innovation. *See also* institutionalizing innovation
  balancing innovation and efficiency, 263–266
  financial commitment to innovation, 95, 181, 183, 184, 186, 187
  impediments identification, 257–258, 259
  innovation challenges and leadership imperatives, 270
  mutual accommodation between innovation and efficiency, 263
  need for an innovation mindset, 255–257 (*see also* commitment to innovation; culture of innovation)
  systemic integration challenge, 262–263
  tactics for keeping innovation alive, 264–265
  tensions within innovation, 266–268
  traditional versus reengineered management processes, 258–261

training provisions (*see* training in innovation)
Sutton, Robert, 33
systemic innovation capability, 4–7, 9, 11, 13, 15, 16, 17–19, 27, 39, 43, 46, 201, 217, 218, 221, 229, 230–232, 237, 238, 240, 241, 247, 251, 252, 255–258, 269. *See also* institutionalizing innovation; lenses of innovation; supply-demand equation

talent, 23, 33, 40, 41, 155, 157, 161, 163, 164–167, 171–173, 177–178, 219, 241, 244, 253, 254, 258
Target, 116–117
targets, bold growth, 209, 213, 215, 226, 227, 230, 245, 270
targets for innovation, 223–224, 228
teams, innovation. *See also* employee involvement in innovation
  discovery teams, 77–79, 102, 264
  diversity and (*see* diversity maximization)
  diversity in teams at Whirlpool, 32–33
  innovation teams creation at Whirlpool, 23–25
  platform teams at CEMEX, 25–26
  time and space creation, 23–24, 25–26
technology use. *See* information technology
tension, creative, 263–265
tensions within innovation, 266–268
Tesco, 192
theory of action versus theory-in-use, 245–247
360-degree accountability reviews, 241
3M, 26
throughput measures, 220–222
time and space creation for innovation. *See also* bandwidth for innovation
  company self-critique, 27

dedicated team creation, 23–24, 25–26
described, 22–23
discretionary time scheduling, 26, 211
innovation days, 8, 10, 207, 208
made into company policy, 24–25
tools for innovation. *See* processes and tools
Toyota, 239
tracking innovation performance. *See* metrics for tracking innovation performance
training in innovation
coaching and mentoring (*see* coaching and mentoring in innovation)
human resources' role, 240–241, 253, 254
people and skills, 238–241
as a supply enabler, 203–204
trends, recognizing the story in unrelated, 55–61
Turner, Ted, 36
tutorial for innovation, 205

University of Phoenix, 114, 115
University of Queensland, 174

Välikangas, Liisa, 240
value creation. *See also* culture of innovation; innovation imperatives; institutionalizing innovation
as a core competence, 65–68, 163
for the customer, 8, 53, 62–64
in diversity, 34
financial value in innovation, 3, 23
innovation as a tangible value, 7, 14, 15, 16, 33, 214, 226, 239, 242, 247–250, 253, 254, 257, 266
new opportunities assessment, 100–111, 168, 170, 175
pacing and derisking investments, 179, 185, 188, 191, 201

through the business model, 112–119, 121
through collaboration, 90–91
through serendipity, 38–42
through strategic decisions, 80, 86
value extraction, 112, 224. *See also* innovation pipeline design rules; lenses of innovation
values in the company. *See* culture of innovation
vectors of innovation, 140, 142–143
venture capital model, 34, 96, 126, 162, 170, 190, 236, 261
Virgin, 196, 248–249
visibility of innovation, 10, 151, 226, 234–235, 251, 262, 270
vision for innovation, shared, 142, 148–153, 156–157, 216, 229, 231–233
Vodafone, 146
volunteering for innovation projects, 172, 205. *See also* employee involvement in innovation
von Hippel, Eric, 94

Wal-Mart, 116–117
Webvan, 189–193
Weird Ideas That Work (Sutton), 33
Whirlpool
balancing innovation and efficiency, 264–265
business model innovations, 114, 116
capability measures, 221
coaching and mentoring to enable supply, 206
diversity in teams, 32–33
human resources' role, 241
innovation as a core competence, 7–9
innovation infrastructure, 233–235
innovation teams creation, 23–25
input measures, 218–220
leadership measures, 220–221
pipeline management, 226

Whirlpool (*continued*)
  reinventing established products,
      103–104
  systemic innovation capability, 7, 32
  technology infrastructure use, 205
  throughput measures, 220
  training in innovation, 203–204
  training program, 239–240
  use of talent pool, 172
Whitwam, Dave, 7, 231, 233, 252

Williamson, Peter, 110
W. L. Gore, 26, 183, 236–237

Xerox PARC, 163, 164

Zachary, Greg, 35
Zambrano, Lorenzo, 9–11, 231
Zeng, Ming, 110

ABOUT THE AUTHORS

Peter Skarzynski is CEO and a founder of Strategos (www.strategos.com), the international strategy and innovation firm. For over twenty-five years, Peter has worked with executives across industries to help them set direction, act on new growth opportunities, and build and deploy an innovation capability. He is particularly passionate about helping clients energize and mobilize their organizations as they pursue key strategic initiatives. His writings have appeared in *Chief Executive, Management Review*, the Peter F. Drucker Foundation, the *San Jose Mercury News*, and the *Wall Street Journal*. Peter resides in the Chicago area with his wife and six children. He can be reached at pskarzyn@strategos.com.

Rowan Gibson is a global business strategist, a bestselling author, and an expert on radical innovation (www.rowangibson.com). His last book *Rethinking The Future* (Nicholas Brealey Publishing) is an international bestseller, published in over twenty languages.

Over the last two decades, Rowan's international clients have included some of the world's largest and most successful organizations. He teaches them how to seize new growth opportunities, create new markets, and even transform industries by recalibrating their whole organizational system around the paradigm of innovation. Rowan is a popular speaker across Europe, the United States, and Asia, and his books, articles, interviews, and columns have been widely read around the globe. He is married with two children and is currently based near Düsseldorf in Germany. He can be reached at rg@rowangibson.com.